Lockheed
Aircraft
Cutaways

Lockheed
Aircraft
Cutaways

The History of Lockheed Martin

Mike Badrocke & Bill Gunston

Contents

First published in Great Britain
in 1998 by Osprey Publishing Ltd,
81 Fulham Road, London SW3 6RB

© *Cutaway artwork* Mike Badrocke
© *Cutaway artwork* Mike Badrocke/ Air
International pp 87, 125

© *Main Text:* Bill Gunston

Captions provided by Dennis Baldry
Editor: Shaun Barrington
Picture research: Tony Holmes
Design Manager: Mike Moule
Design: Ted McCausland
Page layout: Malcolm Smythe
Index: Janet Dudley

ISBN 1 85532 775 9

Printed in China

*For a catalogue of all books published
by Osprey Aviation please write to:*

**The Marketing Department
Osprey Publishing Ltd, 1st Floor
Michelin House, 81 Fulham Road
London SW3 6RB**

The author, illustrator and publishers
would like to thank the Lockheed Martin
Corporation for their help in producing
this book through the provision of
photographs. Other archive photographs
reproduced with the kind permission of
Aerospace Publishing and Michael
O'Leary, unless otherwise stated.
With thanks also to John Ailes, David G.
Berryman and John Hall.

Please note: in order to make the best
possible use of the gatefold pages in this
volume, the entries for the Vega and
Air Express (pp 17 and 18) are not in
chronological order. The Vega marks
the official creation of the Lockheed
Aircraft Company in December 1926
and therefore, of course, predates the
Model 4 Explorer.

Front of jacket, below left: **RAF C-130,
St Mawgan, September 1967.
(Photo David G. Berryman)**

Half title page: **Alan Loughhead
(centre) with Arthur Goebel and
Harry Tucker's Vega, "Yankee
Doodle."**

Title page: **C-5A Galaxy "Empire
State," of the 105th Airlift Group,
137th Airlift Squadron, delivers an
SR-71 at Stewart Air National Guard
Base, New York. Now that's what
you call a company PR event ...**

Opposite: **"Rosie the Riveter", one
of the 35,000 female employees
clocking on at Lockheed at the
wartime peak of production in 1943.**

The story began early in this century with Victor Loughead (pronounced Lockheed) and his two younger half-brothers Allan and Malcolm. Victor was a qualified engineer in Illinois, with impressive credentials, and in 1909 he wrote a book, *Vehicles of the Air,* followed a year later by *Aeroplane Designing for Amateurs.* In the same year, 1910, Allan moved from California to Chicago to work for James Plew on the Montgomery glider and a Curtiss pusher. In December of that year two of Plew's pilots failed to get the Curtiss airborne. Allan Loughead tweaked the engine and, having never previously tried to fly an aeroplane, took off and made a number of increasingly confident circuits followed by a safe landing.

Jack Northrop points the way forward for Allan Loughead (right) and Gerard Vultee. What they are considering are the clean lines of the prototype Vega.

Returning to San Francisco, Allan persuaded Malcolm to join him in designing and building a flying machine. Called the Model G to cloak the fact it was their first effort, this three-seat seaplane, powered by an 80hp Curtiss V-8, was a thoroughly sensible creation. On 15 June 1913 the brothers launched it from the foot of Laguna Street and Allan made the first flight. Later that day he took his brother as passenger.

At the Panama-Pacific Exposition in 1915 the Model G carried over 600 passengers and earned $4,000. The brothers were in business, changing their name to Lockheed in 1918. On 28 March 1918 Allan flew the first of a planned production run of big F-1 flying boats. Part of the design task was assigned to a young mechanic, John K. Northrop. Though the prototype once carried 12 passengers, the end of the war meant cancellation of orders. What to do? Northrop devised a method of making an almost perfectly streamlined half-fuselage by forming glued sheets of veneer over a concrete mould; the two halves were then joined. The result was the extremely pretty S-1 single-seat sporting biplane, but in the post-war glut of cheap aircraft there were no takers.

In 1926 Northrop, then working for Douglas, schemed a streamlined cabin monoplane using the moulded-veneer method. Allan managed to obtain funding to set up the Lockheed Aircraft Company in December 1926, in a small workshop on the corner of Sycamore and Romaine in Hollywood. Northrop joined them, and the result was the Vega, the first type featured in this book. This proved a great success, and in March 1928 Lockheed moved into much bigger premises on Mission Avenue in nearby Burbank. Despite considerable success, in April 1929 the major stockholder decided to take a large profit and sold the firm to a holding company called Detroit Aircraft. He got it right, because three months later the market crashed and in the Depression nobody had money to buy aircraft. Detroit Aircraft went into receivership on 27 October 1931, the Lockheed subsidiary finally giving up the following April

Out of the blue came one Robert E. Gross, a 35-year-old Harvard graduate who by sheer dynamic effort had prospered as an investment banker. On 6 June 1932, accompanied by aircraft salesman Carl B.Squier and aircraft designer Lloyd C.Stearman, he walked into the LA District Court. Judge Hollzer asked "Do you have the $10,000 deposit on the purchase price of $40,000 ?" Gross did. The judge said "Since no other persons have come forward, I approve the sale of Lockheed". He then looked over his glasses at Gross and added "I hope you know what you are doing".

Stearman was elected president, Richard Von Hake chief engineer and Hall L. Hibbard assistant chief engineer. They studied a 10-seat stretched Orion made of metal, but Gross persuaded them to go for twin engines. The result was the Model 10 Electra. Having no wind tunnel, they sent a model to the University of Michigan. Here Clarence L. 'Kelly' Johnson pointed out potential stability problems and suggested using twin fins. Soon afterwards he joined the company, but it almost went broke right at the start when one wheel failed to extend on the precious Electra prototype, in which was locked up nearly all the infant firm's capital. Gross dictated to visitor Jimmy Doolittle TRY LANDING AT UNION, GOOD LUCK, which Doolittle wrote in chalk on his Orion. The whole workforce rushed to Union, which had a firefighting crew and longer runway. Marshall Headle made a textbook landing there, and the rest of the story could be written

Lockheed moved up into bigger and much more powerful aircraft, always concentrating on having the fastest in the sky. Back in 1930 Detroit Aircraft had developed the Altair into the XP-900 two-seat fighter, tested by the Army as the YP-24, but Lockheed's designers had made their name entirely with quite modest aircraft sold in the main to private individuals. In

Two key engineers for the fledgling company, Hall Hibbard, (left) and (below) Clarence Johnson.

1936, however, Gross allowed the Hibbard/Johnson team to have a stab at meeting the Army's requirement for a high-speed bomber (XPB-2), later recast as an escort fighter (XFM-2). By sheer technical merit, the Lockheed 11 almost won, being numerically placed a close second behind the Bell XFM-1. Lockheed's submission put the struggling company "on the map" so far as the Army was concerned, and in early 1937 it was one of the six firms invited to submit proposals for a twin-engined high-altitude interceptor with unprecedented performance. Johnson came up with an extraordinary configuration which won the competition. Lockheed received a contract on 23 June 1937 for a prototype of the Model 22, with Army designation XP-38. This was an utterly different aeroplane from anything Lockheed had attempted previously, and the exceedingly complicated engineering design took 18 months. Eventually it would lead to more than 10,000 aircraft named Lightning, almost all of them made by Lockheed.

Just five weeks after Lockheed received the XP-38 contract, Marshall Headle took off in the prototype Model 14. Though of impressively advanced design, and the fastest airliner in the world, it was less economic than the DC-3, which in any case had already been adopted by all the largest US carriers. Then, out of the blue

The parasol-winged Air Express, produced for Western Air Express. A Vega special with an open cockpit, but still with wooden fuselage; see page 19.

in April 1938, Gross heard that Great Britain had sent a "purchasing commission", which had arrived with $25 million to spend on military aircraft to speed their belated and frantic rearmament programme As a private venture the company had already begun constructing a wooden mockup of the proposed B14, a military version of the airliner. This was urgently finished, and Gross invited the British team to Burbank. The United Kingdom eventually placed an order for 200 aircraft, with more to come. At the time this was the largest order ever placed with the US aircraft industry. Gross later said "There has probably been no single thing in American aviation which has stirred up so much enthusiasm … For a small company we put on quite an effort."

Thus, it was the little island across the Atlantic that catapulted Lockheed into the big time. The huge contract was won mainly by Lockheed's obvious enthusiasm, but there was also a fair element of luck. Company Secretary Cyril Chappellet recalled that "We had an order from Japan for 20 Model 14s. There was nothing else in sight but the end of the line. If we hadn't had this business our factory would have been empty, and the British would hardly have dared to place an order. So we owe the Japanese a vote of thanks for having placed us in a position to plunge into large-scale production and an expansion program that has never stopped since". The author recalls a wartime Hollywood epic in which a character says "She works at Lockheed". This name obviously came first to the mind of the screenwriter, as being that of a huge planemaker. Female employees, each dubbed "Rosie the riveter", accounted for over 35,000 of the 94,380 who clocked on at Lockheed at the wartime peak in June 1943 – a bit different from the 332 of late 1934. A proportion of these worked at a subsidiary called Vega, which had originally been formed in 1937 as the AiRover Co. Lockheed started it to reduce overheads in such work as fitting the Unitwin engine into an Altair, but it went on to make four Vega 35 trainers of North American Aviation design, and then occupied a giant new plant at Union Air Terminal where it made the Ventura and Harpoon. Soon it was also making 2,750 B-17 Fortresses and the prototype XP2V Neptune, and in November 1943 Vega was absorbed into the parent firm.

Between 1 July 1940 and 31 August 1945, Lockheed delivered 19,077 aircraft, almost all of them large and complex, making it (on simple numerical grounds) No 5 US planemaker. After the War, however, the future looked bleak, and the firm began record-

F-104s under construction. As for so many companies, it was military orders which transformed Lockheed from a specialist, niche manufacturer into a giant.

ing losses on its trading. The bright spots were the P-80 and its offshoots the F-94 and, especially, the T-33; and the Constellation and P2V Neptune also sold steadily. On the other hand, nothing came of various lightplanes, or the Saturn local-service transport, the gigantic Constitution, the XF-90 fighter or the vertical-takeoff XFV-1

As it did for its rivals, salvation arrived in the form of the Berlin Airlift and Cold War, followed by war in Korea. In late 1950 the Air Force asked Lockheed to reopen the vast wartime plant at Marietta, Georgia, where Bell had built B-29s. Lockheed sent 151 people from Burbank, and by the end of 1951 they had been joined by more than 10,000 local hires. After refurbishing B-29s this plant built 394 Boeing B-47 jet bombers. The airlift led to the development at Burbank of an impressive turboprop airlifter, the C-130 Hercules. This was transferred to the new Georgia Division, and has remained in production at Marietta ever since, with prospects of continuing until 70 years after its first flight. Korea resulted in design of the F-104 Starfighter. This was an example of a design team being over-influenced by the front-line fighter pilots. They

cried out for speed and altitude at the expense of almost everything else. The result was a fighter that was useful mainly for making the headlines and setting records. It is to Lockheed's credit that, by using every sales pitch in the book, it managed to sell this not-very-useful aircraft all over the world, most of them being intended to fly at low level using the newly invented inertial guidance and either drop a nuclear weapon or else photograph the damage. Right at the end of the programme Italy developed a version which could do quite a fair job as an interceptor, which was its original design mission. As a USAF fighter, the F-104 was designed under 'Kelly' Johnson at a special secure establishment. This began in 1943 in a "packing-case and canvas lean-to next to the wind tunnel". Here Johnson gathered Bill Ralston, Don Palmer and a handful of other handpicked engineers. Their remit was to design advanced aircraft -- in later years utterly unlike anything else -- faster than anyone else, for lower cost and in absolute secrecy. This establishment, with its many unique methods, both internal and with the customer, gradually became the stuff of legend. It was eventually given an official title,

The unmissable profile of the F-117. This full-scale mock-up was constructed in 1979. The "black" program was not just top secret, it was "SAR", Special Access Required.

initially ADP (Advanced Development Projects) and then the Lockheed Advanced Development Co, but from almost its inception it was better known as "The Skonk Works" after the whisky still in the Li'l Abner comic strip. This became The Skunk Works, with a skunk-like carpet in the foyer. It moved to Palmdale, but its best-known products – the U-2/TR-1, A-12/YF-12A/SR-71 and F-117 – were tested at remote sites such as Groom Lake. In 1995 it was officially retitled the Lockheed Martin Skunk Works, but is increasingly threatened by shortsighted Washington bureaucracy.

In 1953 Lockheed formed a Missile Systems Division, and today missiles and space form a major part of its portfolio, as do electronics, shipbuilding and, above all, communications and information. Areas of activity which eventually proved rather unfruitful included VTOL aircraft and helicopters, nuclear engineering, rocket propulsion, SSTs and business jets. The turboprop Electra led to the Navy Orion which in 1998 was still an active programme whose reputation might well lead to the company being selected to create a successor. The even bigger L-1011 TriStar eventually came to a dead end, but today's mighty Lockheed is discussing ways of returning to the field of commercial jets.

In September 1977 the fact that aircraft had ceased to be the chief product was reflected in the company being renamed Lockheed Corporation. In March 1993 Lockheed completed the purchase of the vast General Dynamics plant at Fort Worth, Texas, bringing with it the F-16 programme. On 30 August 1994 the merger with Martin Marietta was announced, and the name was changed to Lockheed Martin Corporation. The author found this name-change surprising, and was even more astonished when a company centred in sunny California chose to move its head office to Bethesda, Maryland, and its aircraft production to the Georgia plant. Here the biggest programme is the F-22 Raptor. Could Lockheed win the potentially huge JSF programme as well?

In early 1996 Lockheed Martin purchased Loral Corporation's defence electronics and systems integration business for $9.1 billion. In early 1998, an $11.6 billion transaction was being planned which added Northrop Grumman, though there were some questions in Congress. This would put Lockheed Martin's employment well beyond the 200,000 level, much higher even than in 1943, and its annual income will soon nudge $40 billion. CEO Peter Teets says no further major acquisitions are planned. There are not many significant folk left to buy!

MODEL 4 EXPLORER

FOUR DOWN . . .

In 1928 the Japanese offered a prize for the first non-stop flight between the USA and Japan. The result, funded by Tacoma businessmen, was the first flight of NR856H *City of Tacoma* on 18 June 1929. Designated Model 4 Explorer, it was based on the fuselage of the Vega (p 17) and Air Express but fitted with a low-mounted wing of increased span and an enlarged tail.

The first *City of Tacoma* tests its 450hp Wasp shortly after completion at Los Angeles. The pilot's forward view came second to fuselage fuel.

A simple fixed landing gear was fitted, and the engine was a 450hp Wasp in a long cowling. The single-seat cockpit was well aft, behind tankage for no less than 751gal (902 US gal, 3,414 litres) of petrol.

Taking off for the record flight on 28 July 1929 pilot Harold Bromley was blinded by fuel spewing from the filler cap, and in the resulting crash N856H was damaged beyond repair. The engine and some other parts were salvaged and built into the second *City of Tacoma*, flown on 18 September 1929. Gerard Vultee then had a horn-balanced rudder fitted, and this caused such severe flutter that this aircraft

Harold Bromley before the crash in 1929. "The sun was strong that day." But it was fuel that (temporarily) blinded him.

also crashed, though with only minor injury to the pilot Herb Fahy. Undaunted, Lockheed built a third Explorer, with a

redesigned vertical tail, the Model 7 NR100W. This was destroyed taking off from Muroc on 24 May 1930. Lockheed built yet a fourth aircraft, NR101W. On 9/10 November 1930 this did make the first non-stop flight from New York to the Canal Zone, but it too was damaged beyond repair 11 days later. The parts were built into the Orion-Explorer, described later. This too had a tragic history.

DATA FOR NR856H:	
Span	48ft 6in (14.78m)
Length	27ft 6in (8.38m)
Wing area	313 sq ft (29.08m²)
Weight empty	3,075lb (1,395kg)
Maximum takeoff weight	9,008lb (4,086kg)
Maximum speed	165mph (266km/h)
Cruising speed	128mph (206km/h)
Range (est)	5,500 miles (8,851km)

BUILT TO ORDER

In 1929 Charles Lindbergh asked whether Lockheed could, for the price of a standard Vega, sell him a special aircraft tailored to his survey flights for PanAm. The result was the Model 8 Sirius, flown on 30 November 1929. It closely resembled the unhappy Explorer, and was likewise powered by a fully cowled 450hp Wasp, but it had a smaller wing (close to Air Express size), much reduced fuel capacity (346.5gal, 416 US gal, 1,575 litres) and tandem cockpits, which at the suggestion of Mrs Lindbergh, were later fitted with sliding canopies.

Lindbergh was finally satisfied, and the couple left on 20 April 1930, setting a new one-stop record to New York of 14h 45min 32sec. This aircraft subsequently made survey flights throughout the world, on most of which it was fitted with a pair of Edo floats and Wright Cyclone engines, initially of 575hp and later of 710hp. In July 1931 Lindbergh and his wife made a survey of a northern Pacific route to Japan via

Alaska, Siberia and the Kuriles, but the route was politically impossible to establish. Like the Vega *Winnie Mae*, the first Sirius rests in the National Air and Space Museum.

Subsequently Lockheed delivered 12 more Wasp-engined Model 8 aircraft, plus one made by Detroit Aircraft. They had various equipment and accommodation, for use as private machines, company executive or demonstrator aircraft or even as armed military aircraft. Most had tandem open or enclosed cockpits, and one (Model 8C) added a two-seat cabin.

Jack Northrop gives Lindbergh a handshake before a test flight in the initial Wasp-powered Sirius. This aircraft was built to Charles and Anne Morrow Lindbergh's personal specification, painted black-red and named Tingmissartoq – Eskimo for 'the one who flies like a big bird'. The handsome spats were soon replaced by floats and, ultimately, retractable gear to Lindbergh's design.

DATA FOR LINDBERGH'S AIRCRAFT IN ITS ORIGINAL FORM AS A WASP-ENGINED LANDPLANE:	
Span	42ft 9.5in (13.04m)
Length	27ft 1in (8.25m)
Wing area	294.1 sq ft (27.32m²)
Weight empty	4,289lb (1,945.5kg)
Maximum takeoff weight	7,099lb (3,220kg)
Maximum speed	185mph (298km/h)
Cruising speed	150mph (241km/h)
Range	975 miles (1,569km)

ALTAIR

A NEAT IDEA

When Lindbergh was discussing the Sirius he asked Lockheed to design an alternative wing with retractable landing gear.

The result was one of the first neat inward-retracting schemes ever designed. This wing was mated to the fuselage of a company-owned Model 8A Sirius and flown in September 1930. It later became the Y1C-25 of the Army Air Corps. It was followed by ten further Altairs, four of which had originally been built as a Sirius. Three were Detroit-built DL-2As with a light-alloy stressed-skin fuselage.

The most famous was *Lady Southern Cross*, in which Sir Charles Kingsford Smith (one of the four-man crew who first crossed the Pacific, Oakland to Brisbane in 1928 in a three-engined Fokker F.VII) and navigator P. G. (later Sir Gordon) Taylor made the first flight from Australia to the USA. Two Altairs (one the Gold Eagle and the other the Navy XRO-1) had a 645hp Cyclone engine, while another was the testbed for the Menasco Unitwin double engine.

Megastar: Lady Southern Cross was capable of 217mph (350km/h); the landing gears were hand-cranked.

The Y1C-25 for the US Army Air Corps was a hot ship in 1930.

DATA FOR DL-2A:	
Span	**42ft 9in (13.03m)**
Length	**28ft 4in (8.636m)**
Wing area	**293.2 sq ft (27.234m²)**
Weight empty	**3,235lb (1,467kg)**
Maximum takeoff weight	**4,895lb (2,220kg)**
Maximum speed	**207mph (333km/h)**
Cruising speed	**175mph (282km/h)**
Range	**580 miles (933km)**

REAL NUMBERS

The Model 9 Orion not only enabled Lockheed to break out of the rut it had got into, with rather special aircraft built in small numbers, but it also had a salutary impact on all the world's planemakers.

Like the Vega, (see p 17) it was designed as a passenger carrier, and it essentially mated the fuselage of the Vega, with the cockpit ahead of the cabin, to the tail, wing and retractable landing gear of the Altair. It was made in useful numbers, and would have found even more sales had it not been for the Depression and the bankruptcy of Detroit Aircraft.

The first Orion was powered by a 410hp Wasp which drove a hydraulic pump to retract the landing gear (on the Altair the pilot had had to work a hand-crank). It had an open cockpit, and the passenger cabin had three seats along each side. Freelance pilot Marshall Headle, who had tested several Lockheed aircraft, made the first flight in March 1931. This aircraft was followed by a further 34, one originally built as a metal-fuselage Altair DL-2A.

The Orion 9D was an improved version with a longer fuselage and larger tailplane. The seventh Orion 9D was the first Lockheed aircraft to be fitted with flaps. These were of the plain type, driven hydraulically.

25 Orions served on scheduled routes in the USA. Two sold to Swissair caused such a stir in Europe that Lufthansa ordered the Heinkel He 70 to try to compete. Several Orions were powered by Wright Cyclone engines, and a French example had a Hispano-Suiza radial. 13 went to Republican forces in Spain, where they were equipped with machine guns and bomb racks.

Orions enabled Varney Speed Lanes to operate an 86 minute schedule between San Francisco and Los Angeles.

DATA FOR ORIGINAL MODEL 9:	
Span	42ft 9.25in (13.037m)
Length	27ft 8in (8.433m)
Wing area	294.1 sq ft (27.32m2)
Weight empty	3,420lb (1,551kg)
Maximum takeoff weight	5,200lb (2,359kg)
Maximum speed	220mph (354km/h)
Cruising speed	175mph (282km/h)
Range	750 miles (1,207km)

MODEL 9 ORION

MODEL 10 ELECTRA

STARTING AGAIN

In summer 1932 Robert Gross determined that the reborn Lockheed should start afresh with the very latest type of aircraft. His goal was a fast commercial transport, if possible larger than the previous designs and probably of all-metal construction. As outlined in the Introduction, Gross eventually decided the new aircraft should be twin-engined.

The first Model 10 Electra was tested by Marshall Headle at Mines Field, Los Angeles, from 23 February 1934.

The airframe was almost wholly light alloy, and designers Hibbard and Von Hake managed to make the deep main spar cross the fuselage at the bulkhead between the cockpit and the ten-seat cabin, so passengers did not have to step over it.

The 450hp Wasp Junior engines were fully cowled and drove Hamilton Standard two-pitch propellers. The main landing gears had neat single legs with fork ends, retracting backwards electrically. The wings were fitted with electrically driven split flaps, a new

feature for Lockheed.

The tail had twin fins and rudders slightly further apart than the engines. Baggage could be loaded into the nose, and sometimes also into the rear fuselage. Today the only feature that might earmark the Model 10 as a design from over

60 years ago was the reverse slope of the windscreens.

Smaller and Faster

The precious prototype, X233Y, survived its one-wheel landing (see Introduction) and soon found customers. Despite the fact that it carried four

Amelia Earhart poses with her ill-fated Model 10E Electra. Twelve extra fuel tanks were distributed in the wings and cabin, which held 1,000 gal (1,200 US gal), giving a range of up to 4,500 miles (7,200 km).

fewer passengers than a DC-2, the Electra had smaller engines and was faster. It was followed by 148 production aircraft. From the fifth off the line conventional windscreens were fitted, and earlier aircraft were modified.

More than 100 were fairly standard Model 10A ten-passenger transports, powered by R-985 Wasp Junior engines.

The Electra was a smash hit and put Lockheed into the black. G-AEPN was delivered to British Airways.

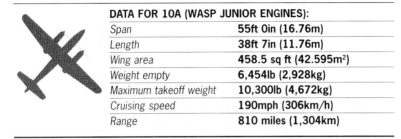

DATA FOR 10A (WASP JUNIOR ENGINES):	
Span	55ft 0in (16.76m)
Length	38ft 7in (11.76m)
Wing area	458.5 sq ft (42.595m²)
Weight empty	6,454lb (2,928kg)
Maximum takeoff weight	10,300lb (4,672kg)
Cruising speed	190mph (306km/h)
Range	810 miles (1,304km)

The 18 Model 10Bs, including the Coast Guard XR3O-1, were powered by 440hp Wright R-975 Whirlwinds. The most powerful were the 15 Model 10Es, with 600hp R-1340 Wasp engines. A completely redesigned research aircraft was the Army's XC-35, with 550hp turbosupercharged Wasp engines and a circular-section fuselage with very small windows able to be pressurized to 10lb/sq in (0.7kg/cm²). This aircraft could cruise at over 280mph (451km/h) at over 20,000ft (9,072m). A few Electras made notable long distance flights.

International Success
Electras were exported to airlines in ten countries. No fewer than 31 were registered in Europe. One that appeared on front pages was G-AEPR of British Airways, which conveyed British Prime Minister Neville Chamberlain to Munich on his first meeting with Hitler.

SMALLER BUT NOT CHEAPER

MODEL 12 ELECTRA JUNIOR

In 1935 the Bureau of Air Commerce invited manufacturers to compete for a requirement for a twin-engined transport even smaller than the Electra. Lockheed could also see that such an aircraft might appeal better than the Electra to corporate or even private customers, because it would be likely to fly faster and further on the same engines. The Bureau demanded that the prototype should fly before 30 June 1936 (the end of the fiscal year), and Lockheed just managed it, Headle making the first flight on 27 June.

Compared with the Model 10, the 12, named Electra Junior, had the same cockpit, fuselage cross-section, 450hp R-985 Wasp Junior engine installations and systems, but a slightly longer nose, smaller wing, shorter central fuselage, reduced horizontal-tail chord and slightly smaller vertical tails. A detail change was that the main landing gears had a straight shock strut attached to the inner end of the axle, though the wheel did not turn

to lie flat in the nacelle (which was lengthened) but remained upright as it retracted.

Military Salvation
As a basic passenger transport it normally had three seats on each side of the aisle instead of five, but very few Electra Juniors were sold to airlines, mainly because of uncompetitive seat-mile costs. Despite this, total production came close to that of the earlier aircraft, at 130.

Most were sold to military or paramilitary customers. The US Army designation was C-40 and the Navy designation JO; the largest single customer was the Dutch East Indies with 36. Of these, 17 were Model 212 air force crew trainers with a

dorsal turret, a fixed gun and external racks for eight 100lb (45kg) bombs. Two, for the Argentine air force, were Model 12B aircraft powered by 440hp R-975 Whirlwind engines. Three ostensibly standard 12As supposedly belonging to British Airways had exciting "cloak and dagger" careers as Sidney Cotton's special photo-reconnaissance aircraft. These made numerous brilliantly suc-

On a 1937 delivery flight from Amsterdam to Jodhpur, India, a Model 12 averaged 210mph (337km/h), despite four fuel stops.

cessful missions over sensitive parts of Germany even after the outbreak of World War 2 (leading to the formation of the RAF's official Photo Reconnaissance Unit).

DATA FOR STANDARD MODEL 12A:	
Span	**49ft 6in (15.09m)**
Length	**36ft 4in (11.074m)**
Wing area	**352 sq ft (32,7m²)**
Weight empty	**5,765lb (2,615kg)**
Maximum takeoff weight	**8,400lb (3,810kg)**
Cruising speed	**213mph (343km/h)**
Range (standard tankage)	**800 miles (1,287km)**

RECORD BREAKER

As outlined in the introduction, in December 1926 Allan Loughead formed a new company called Lockheed, and at once hired Northrop to help create the streamlined aircraft they had been discussing. Northrop suggested that their future aircraft should be named after stars, and proposed that the first should be called the Vega.

The objective was to combine the monocoque fuselage of the preceding S-1 biplane with a clean cantilever wing in order to a achieve a purity of aerodynamic form scarcely seen since the Deperdussin racers of before World War 1. The principal passenger aircraft in use in the US in the late 1920s were Fokker F.VIIs and Ford Trimotors, with room for eight to fifteen passengers. The feeling was that something smaller and faster would find a market. A major task was to construct a significantly larger concrete die for each half fuselage, so that the finished structure could accommodate a cockpit immediately ahead of the main spar and a four-seat cabin under the wing. The circular section was continued to the front where it terminated in a flat fireproof bulkhead immediately behind a radial engine. A large area on top was cut away for the cockpit and wing. The cockpit was boldly enclosed by a frame holding transparent panels, in 1927 an unusual feature. On each side of the cabin were four cutouts for windows, one on the left being large enough for a door. The completed fuselage was then skinned in doped fabric.

No Struts
The wing was totally new, having a wooden structure with an

The brilliant Model 1 Vega transport outpaced contemporary fighters. At the 1928 National Air Races in Cleveland, Vegas swept the board.

DATA FOR VEGA:	
Span	41ft 0in (12.50m)
Length (5C landplane)	27ft 8in (8.43m)
Wing area	275 sq ft (25.55m²)
Weight empty (1)	1,650lb (748kg)
(5C landplane)	2,565lb (1,163.5kg)
Maximum takeoff weight (1)	2,900lb (1,315kg),
(5C)	4,880lb (2,214kg)
Maximum speed (1)	135mph (217km/h)
(5C landplane)	185mph (298km/h),
but Ruth Nichols set a	210.685mph
women's record at	(339.055km/h)
Cruising speed	118-160mph
	(190-257.5km/h)
Range variable up to	2,600 miles (4,184km)

MODEL 1 VEGA

aerofoil profile deep enough (Clark Y-18 at the root) to need no bracing struts. There was one main spar of multi-ply spruce, and auxiliary spars and ribs built up from struce strips and ply. The wing was then covered in ply veneer and doped fabric, the ailerons having fabric only.

It was then located on top of the fuselage cutout and bolted to particularly strong frames. Legend has it that serious consideration was given to adding "cosmetic" struts merely to reassure customers that the aircraft would be safe. The tail was all-wood, and the main landing gear could hardly have been neater, with a main strut on each side pin-jointed to the main-spar bulkhead and braced by simple V-struts. On the nose was attached a Wright Whirlwind J5 nine-cylinder radial rated at 220hp, with direct aft-facing exhaust pipes. It drove a 9ft 6in (2.9m) Standard two-blade steel propeller and was fed from a pair of wing tanks housing 80 gal (96 US gal, 364 litres).

Independence Day
The completed fuselage and wing were towed behind separate cars to a field at Inglewood, where the Vega was assembled. It was painted orange, and had a large red star on the fin, with registration 2788.

Eddie Bellande, a celebrated pilot of the day, made the first flight on (appropriately) the 4th of July 1927. After exploring handling for an hour he gave his considered verdict: "You'll sell this ship like hot cakes."

On 20/21 May 1932, Earhart's first Vega took her non-stop across the Atlantic (from Harbour Grace, Newfoundland, to a meadow near Londonderry in Northern Ireland), in 15h 8min. Three months after becoming the first woman to fly the Atlantic, Earhart set the first female non-stop record across America, flying from Los Angeles to New York in 19h 5min. Crowds flocked to see record-breaking pilots, though Earhart was understandably miffed to be nicknamed 'Lady Lindy' due to a supposed resemblance to Lindbergh.

The first Vega was sold to newspaper magnate George Hearst Jr, who entered it in the Dole Race to Hawaii. Later, Alan Lockheed admitted that the sale price of $12,500 represented a loss: "But the prestige of selling the Vega to Hearst was tremendous." Tragically the Vega, equipped with greatly augmented tankage, disappeared over the ocean in that event, but by that time the aircraft's appearance and performance was bringing a growing queue of customers.

From No 3 onwards all had a larger and more rounded vertical tail. Lockheed built 28 Vegas of various sub-types with the Whirlwind J5 engine, some fitted with a ring cowl and/or with skis or floats. Subsequent aircraft had either the 300hp Whirlwind J6 or, in the main later batches, the 420hp or 450hp Pratt & Whitney Wasp, usually inside a long-chord cowling. Most of the later landplanes had spatted wheels, and all had strengthened structure to take account of a considerable increase in gross weight.

Winnie Mae
The second Vega, X3903, made remarkable flights over the North Pole and later over Antarctica ("the greatest feat of all aviation" according to the *New York Times*) in the hands of Capt (later Sir) Hubert Wilkins and Ben Eielson. Another made the first non-stop crossing of the USA in 18h 58min, and Vegas made more than 40 other record flights. Amelia Earhart used six Vegas in making many of these flights. Certainly the most

the two

flights made

Vega 5B

Wiley Post and

days 15h

by Post flying

43min). Other

solo

56min 36sec)

ard engine,

9,928ft,

e for a basic

0. Many Vegas

s were put into

executive air-

peration, the

being Braniff.

egas. It actual-

e with Interna-

17 Septem-

ther Lockheed

and a further

ced by Detroit

by others.

pressed in

World War 2, and at least five survive today.

Model 3 Air Express

When the Vega appeared Western Air Express was using Douglas M-2 biplanes to carry the mail, cruising at 100mph (161km/h). Attracted by the more modern Vega, it got Lockheed to produce a special mail-carrying version. To meet the request of the pilots, Northrop moved the pilot to the rear, in an open cockpit. In turn this required raising the wing above the fuselage (it was also made slightly larger), and the cabin was equipped for 100 cu ft (2.83m³) of mail or four passengers. The engine was the 410hp Wasp, but Lockheed built six further aircraft with 420hp Wasp or 525hp Hornet engines with long-chord NACA cowlings. (See page 7.)

DATA FOR AIR EXPRESS:

Span	42ft 6in (12.95m)
Length	27ft 6in (8.38m)
Wing area	288 sq ft (26.75m²)
Weight empty (Wasp)	2,533lb (1,149kg)
Maximum loaded	4,375lb (1,985kg)
Maximum speed (cowled Wasp)	176mph (283km/h)
Cruising speed	151mph (243km/h)
Range	750 miles (1,207 km

Lockheed Vega 5C

1 Starboard navigation light, above and below
2 Aileron horn balance
3 Starboard aileron
4 Smooth finish fabric covering glued to all skin panels
5 Plywood wing skin panelling
6 Aileron hinge control
7 Aileron cable pulleys
8 Wing rib structure
9 Trailing edge ribs
10 Starboard fuel tank, total capacity of both tanks 96-US gal (80-Imp gal, 364-lit)
11 Fuel filler caps
12 Wing lifting fittings
13 Sliding cockpit roof hatch
14 Fuel contents sight glass
15 Fuel cock
16 Windscreen panels
17 Light alloy engine cowling panels, split along centreline
18 Engine oil tank, capacity 10-US gal (8.3-Imp gal, 38-lit)
19 Pratt & Whitney Wasp SC1, 9-cylinder radial engine
20 Engine gearcase
21 Two-bladed fixed pitch metal propeller, 9-ft diameter
22 Cooling air intake
23 Starboard mainwheel fairing
24 Cowling baffle plate
25 Exhaust collector ring
26 Engine bay fireproof bulkhead

27 Rudder pedal box
28 Engine bearer struts
29 Exhaust silencer
30 Cockpit floor
31 Pull-out cockpit steps
32 Control column
33 Instrument panel
34 Hand portable fire extinguisher
35 Pilot's seat
36 Tailplane trim control
37 Underfloor mail compartment
38 Battery
39 Main undercarriage leg strut fixing
40 Front spar attachment main frame
41 Cockpit bulkhead
42 Pilot's seat backrest, integral with cockpit door
43 Wing spar attachment joint
44 Aileron cable pulley
45 Passenger seating, six-places
46 Main spar box section structure, spruce booms and plywood webs
47 Port fuel tank
48 Cabin window panels
49 Rear spar attachment fuselage main frame
50 Passenger seat in folded position for access
51 Box section rear spar
52 Cabin entry door
53 Wing root/fuselage fairing
54 Rear two-place bench seat
55 Luggage rack

56 Cabin rear bulkhead
57 Fuselage skin fabric covering
58 Starboard tailplane
59 Fin rib and spar structure
60 Rudder hinge post
61 Plywood skinned rudder
62 Rudder and elevator hinge controls
63 Trimming tailplane pivot mounting
64 Light alloy tailcone
65 Tail navigation light
66 Port elevator
67 Tailplane plywood skin panelling
68 Port tailplane rib and spar structure
69 Trimming tailplane sealing fairing with leather rubbing strips
70 Cable operated tailplane incidence screw jack
71 Skid elastic cord shock absorber
72 Tailskid
73 Tailplane control cables
74 Laminated 3-mm ply fuselage skin panelling, built as two half shells
75 Fuselage skin shell support sub frames and longerons
76 Port aileron
77 Aileron hinge control link

78 Aileron rib structure, plywood covered
79 Port aileron horn balance
80 Wing tip spruce edge member
81 Port navigation light, above and below
82 Open girder spruce wing ribs
83 Skin support stringers
84 Retractable landing light
85 Pitot head
86 Leading edge nose ribs
87 Port aileron control cables
88 Alternative leading edge fixed landing light
89 Main undercarriage rear V-strut
90 Shock absorber leg strut
91 Front V-strut
92 Boarding step
93 Wheel spat fairing
94 Wheel hub brake
95 Port 30 x 5-in mainwheel, 27 x 11-in alternative
96 Tyre inflation valve access

Mike Badrocke

FROM AIRLINER TO MARITIME PATROLLER

In 1936 Lockheed at last began to climb out of the doldrums and make serious money. This enabled it to take the biggest decision so far and build the prototype of a larger and much more powerful transport, with the same seating capacity (up to seven seats on each side of the central aisle) as the DC-2, but with much higher cruising speed.

Gross had first thought about such an aircraft in late 1935, and took a deliberate decision not to try to sign up a major carrier; he told the author "They were pretty much committed to Douglas, we believed we could sell to smaller airlines".

Built for Speed

The resulting Model 14 Super Electra overstretched the tiny engineering staff, and Marshall Headle was unable to begin testing the prototype, X17382, until 29 July 1937. From the start it looked like being a success, and it was certainly the

most advanced civil aircraft of its day. Of entirely stressed-skin construction, the airframe was notable for the highly loaded wing, with a huge and powerful Fowler flap running out on five rails on each side, a row of fixed slots ahead of the ailerons, and an interior sealed to form integral fuel tanks. Partly to avoid having too steep a floor angle on the ground, the wing was placed almost in the mid position. Unlike the rival Douglases, the fuselage had no parallel constant-section portion at all, but had a deep curvaceous form designed for speed. The capacious underfloor space was hardly used, baggage being put in the nose. The tail followed

Hibbard's predilection for twin fins and rudders.

The prototype was powered by twin 875hp Pratt & Whitney Hornet engines driving variable-pitch propellers. Later fully-feathering propellers were made standard. Customers also had the choice of engines in the 900-1,200hp class, either the Wright R-1820 Cyclone or the Pratt & Whitney R-1830 Twin Wasp. Like the model 12, each main landing gear had a single strut, inboard of the wheel, with hydraulic retraction back into the nacelle. Compared with the similarly powered DC-3 the Model 14 burned fuel at the same rate but was much faster, so it went further for each pound of fuel;

it carried only 14 passengers however (only 11 if a galley and stewardess was provided) compared with about 21. Moreover, the Douglas had a head start, and had already been adopted by the major US airlines. Gradually, the higher speed of the Lockheed brought customers, and two special flights brought exceptional publicity. In July 1938 NX18973 was flown by Howard Hughes and crew round the world in four days.

> **Without the British there would have been far fewer, if any, military Model 14s for the USAAF. An also-ran behind the DC-3 paid off.**

On 15 September 1938 G-AFGN of British Airways took Prime Minister Chamberlain to meet Hitler at Munich, bringing back a piece of paper promising "peace in our time".

Military Salvation 2

Sadly, various serious faults, including tail flutter, caused a loss of confidence, and in fact (partly because pilots were not used to such advanced aircraft) many had only short lives. Only 112 Model 14s were sold, though 120 more were made under licence in Japan. The chief European customers were KLM of the Netherlands and

LOT of Poland, most of whose fleets escaped to the UK in 1939-40. But what transformed the programme, and catapulted Lockheed into the big time, was the fact that the British Air Purchasing Commission picked a military version of the Model 14 as its first massive US purchase for the RAF.

By early 1938 it was evident to Gross that the Model 14 would always be an also-ran behind the DC-3, and in April of that year he sanctioned the construction of a bomber version, with the unused space under the wing turned into a bomb bay and with gun turrets

in the nose and above the fuselage. At this point Gross learned of the British team's arrival, and in five frantic days and nights the mockup was ready for their inspection. The British were impressed by Lockheed's enthusiasm, by the quoted price and by the prior British familiarity with the Model 14. They asked for many changes, notably for the nose turret to be replaced by a glazed navigator station. On 23 June 1938 the British signed a contract for 200 Model 414s, plus as many more (to a maximum of 250) as could be delivered by December 1939, for a contract price of $25 million. This was at that time the biggest contract ever signed by an American aircraft manufacturer. Called Hudson Mk I, the 414 had 1,100hp Cyclone G102A engines, a bomb load of 750lb (340kg) and a crew of five. At first the completed aircraft were protected by a Cocoon and delivered by sea, the first arriving on 15 February 1939. Lockheed delivered the 250 ahead of time, and eventually supplied 1,338 under direct British contract and 1,302 under Lend-lease contracts.

Applications in all
All Hudsons had th
frame, the Mk I hav
0.303in Browning g
in the nose and two
bulky Boulton Paul
The Mk II had Ham
Hydromatic propell
III had 1,200hp G2
Cyclones and extra
from side windows
tral hatch, the Mk I
tralia had 1,200hp
and so did the RAF
numbers were built
and A-29 for the US
other Allied air forc
calling the AT-28 th
VI.
The AT-18 (300 deli
a USAAF crew train
having a Martin tu
twin 0.5in guns, an
two U-boats sunk b
aircraft were claime
PBO-1 version.
The total of all mili
14 derivatives was 2
pleted in May 1943
majority were opera
coastal Command,
they had a distingu
in almost every wai
among other things
first air/sea-rescue a
drop lifeboats to do
crew.

DATA FOR MODEL 14:		
Span		65ft 6in (19.96m)
Length		44ft 4in (13.51m)
Wing area		551 sq ft (51.19m2)
Weight empty	14W	10,750lb (4,876kg)
	Hudson I	11,630lb (5,275kg)
	Hudson VI	12,929lb (5,865kg)
Maximum takeoff weight		
	14W and Hudson I	17,500lb (7,938kg)
	Mk VI	18,500lb (8,392kg)
Maximum speed	(I)	246mph (396km/h)
	(VI)	284mph (457km/h)
Cruising speed	(14W)	231mph (372km/h)
Range with full payload	(14W)	2,125 miles (3,420km)
	(I)	1,960 miles (3,154km)
	(VI)	2,160 miles (3,476km)

RELAUNCH
MODEL 18 LODESTAR, VENTURA, B-34, PV-1 AND PV-2 HARPOON

By 1939 it was clear that, though the expanding factory was overloaded by the British Hudson order, the Model 14 was basically uneconomic, and its bad press had made it unsaleable in the United States.

Indeed, Northwest had returned its fleet. Accordingly Gross decided to increase its seating capacity and attempt a fresh launch under a new name. The fourth Northwest aircraft was given an extra section of fuselage enabling two more rows of seats to be accomodated, for a maximum of 18. It retained its 875hp P&W R-1690 Hornet engines. On 21 September 1939 Marshall Headle took this aircraft, re-registered as NX17385, on its second "first flight" as the prototype Model 18 Lodestar.

Wing wake turbulence was cured by extending the wing trailing edge slightly behind the flaps and raising the tailplane above the rear fuselage. The Model 18 was still uneconomic compared with a DC-3, except when fitted with bench seats for 26 passengers, but from the start it sold steadily to US and foreign airlines, and also to corporate customers. As well as the Hornet (18-07) the engines were various Cyclones and (18-08) Twin Wasps, as in the case of the Model 14. In 1940 the US Navy began ordering R5O versions for VIP, passenger or paratroop use. After Pearl Harbor civil aircraft were impressed into the Navy, and as the C-56/57/58/59/60 into the Army Air Force.

Many impressed Lodestars were transferred to the RAF and, especially, to BOAC which used 38 throughout its Empire

Peeling away from the camera ship, this preserved PV-2 Harpoon is a member of the Confederate Air Force. PV-2s remained operational with the Portuguese Navy until the 1970s.

network until 1949. The USAAF adopted the Cyclone-engined C-60A as a standard paratroop transport and glider tug, and repeat orders brought the Model 18 total up to 625.

In Japan Kawasaki built 121 very similar aircraft designated Ki-56. After 1945 many Model 18s were rebuilt as high-speed executive aircraft. In Sept 1939 the British Air Ministry began

DATA FOR MODEL 18 VARIANTS:

Span	(except PV-2)	**65ft 6in (19.96m)**
	(PV-2)	**75ft 0in (22.86m)**
Length	(18)	**49ft 10in (15.19m)**
	(Ventura, B-34)	**51ft 5in (15.67m)**
	(PV-2)	**52ft 1in (15.87m)**
Wing area	(except PV-2)	**551 sq ft (51.19m²)**
	(PV-2)	**686 sq ft (63.73m²)**
Weight empty	(18-07)	**11,250lb (5,103kg)**
	(C-60A)	**12,500lb (5,670kg)**
	(Ventura I)	**17,233lb (7,817kg)**
	(PV-1)	**20,197lb (9,161kg)**
	(PV-2)	**21,028lb (9,538kg)**
Maximum takeoff weight	(18-07)	**19,200lb (8,709kg)**
	(C-60)	**21,000lb (4,630kg)**
	(Ventura I)	**26,000lb (11,794kg)**
	(PV-1)	**34,000lb (15,422kg)**
	(PV-2)	**36,000lb (16,330kg)**
Maximum speed	(Ventura I)	**312mph (502 km/h)**
	(PV-1)	**322mph (518km/h)**
	(PV-2)	**282mph (454km/h)**
Cruising speed	(18-07)	**197mph (317km/h)**
	(18-08)	**248mph (399km/h)**
	(Ventura I)	**272mph (438km/h)**
	(PV-1, PV-2)	**171mph (275km/h)**
Range with maximum load		
	(18, typical)	**1,090 miles (1,754km)**
	(Ventura I)	**925 miles (1,489km)**
	(PV-1)	**1,360 miles (2,189km)**
	(PV-2)	**1,790 miles (2,881km)**

discussing military versions as a Hudson successor and replacement for the Blenheim. The resulting Model 37 was built at the new Vega plant and thus became the Lockheed-Vega Ventura. Slightly longer than the Lodestar, recognition features included a dorsal turret further forward than on the short-body Hudson and a kink under the rear fuselage for an improved gun installation. The RAF received 394 Ventura I and II bombers, powered by Pratt & Whitney R-2800 Double Wasp engines respectively rated at 1,850 and 2,000 hp, with a bomb load of 2,500lb (1,134kg) and armament of two fixed 0.5in guns in the nose and up to eight 0.303in for defence. Fuel capacity was slightly reduced, to 471gal (565 US gal, 2,139 litres). Vega followed with 387 Ventura V aircraft used by all Commonwealth air forces, of which the South African AF was the exception in retaining Venturas in service until 1968.

Production was brought up to 1,600 by AAF orders for the B-34 Lexington and Navy orders for the PV-1. Most B-34s served as navigation trainers, though some had radar and

served in the reconnaissance role. Nearly all B-34s and PV-1s had twin 0.5in guns in the dorsal turret. The PV-1s, which replaced the B-34 on the assembly lines in July 1942, had radar, much greater fuel capacity (and, like the Ventura V, provision for drop tanks), a modified weapon bay able to accommodate a 3,000lb (1,361kg) load, and wing racks for eight rockets. The AAF also ordered 550 aircraft powered by the 1,700hp Wright R-2600 Double Cyclone as the O-56 armed observation platform, but only 18 were delivered with the designation B-37.

Final Variant
In 1943 Vega redesigned the PV-1 into the PV-2 Harpoon. The obvious changes were the extended outer wings and enlarged vertical tails, and another dramatic increase in internal fuel to 1,551gal (1,863 US gal, 7,052 litres) with integral tanks almost tip to tip. The bomb bay could accommodate 4,000lb (1,814kg), and standard armament was eight 0.5in and eight rockets. The PV-2 first flew on 3 December 1943, and 535 were delivered in various versions.

AN AWKWARD SIZE

In the mid-1930s the Menasco engine company began testing its Unitwin, comprising two 260hp C6S-4 six-cylinder engines mounted close side-by-side driving a common gear-box for a single propeller.

A freewheel enabled either engine to continue the drive with the other stopped. The objective was twin-engine reliability and safety in an aircraft which could be flown by any pilot (without needing a multi-engine rating). Lockheed's Hall L. Hibbard agreed that the new subsidiary, AiRover Co, should test the Unitwin in an Altair testbed. In December 1937 this began flying, with good results.

Prophetic Beginning

Accordingly, Mac Short, president of Vega (AiRover renamed), instructed a team under Jack Wassall to design an attractive small "feederline" transport around this double engine. The resulting Starliner had a mixed-construction airframe with a typical Lockheed tapered wing with split flaps, a side-door cabin for a pilot and five passengers, and nosewheel landing gears which protruded

slightly when retracted. The first flight, on 22 April 1939, ended abruptly when the Hamilton propeller suddenly returned to fine pitch. The aircraft was then fitted with a twin-fin tail, but was again slightly damaged when the nosewheel jammed in the up position.

No Room

Perhaps shortsightedly, in 1940 the project was abandoned. The Starliner was too small to appeal to airlines, and too large for most private customers. The last nail in its coffin was the desperate need for more plant capacity for military aircraft.

The Vega Starliner was destined to remain at Burbank, but its name was revived for the ultimate version of the Constellation.

DATA IN FINAL FORM FOR VEGA STARLINER:	
Span	45ft 0in (13.7m)
Length	32ft 5in (9.88m)
Wing area	250 sq ft (23.2m2)
Weight empty	4,590lb (2,082kg)
Maximum takeoff weight	6,250lb (2,835kg)
Maximum speed	210mph (338km/h)
Cruising speed	155mph (249km/h)
Range	700 miles (1,126km)

P-38 LIGHTNING

FORK-TAILED DEVIL

Utterly unlike any other Lockheed aircraft, and also visually and technically unlike any other warplane, the P-38 was nevertheless a great success. It was in fact the only American fighter (almost the only US combat aircraft) to remain in production throughout World War 2.

In February 1937 the Army Air Corps issued a specification for a pursuit and bomber escort able to fly for one hour at 360mph (579km/h). 'Kelly' Johnson quickly decided the job called for two Allison V-1710 liquid-cooled engines, and studied every possible way in which these could be installed. Eventually he settled for mounting them on the front of two booms carrying the twin-finned tail, the pilot and guns being in a short nacelle on the centreline. This radical configuration lent itself to the use of a nosewheel-type landing gear. In the course of the following year the growing engineering staff decided to use a relatively thin "laminar" wing profile, with powerful Fowler flaps. The engines were

made to drive handed (turning in opposite directions) propellers, with their exhaust piped inside the booms to escape through General Electric turbosuperchargers in the top of each boom above the trailing edge. Each engine was cooled by a pair of radiators in the tail booms and intercoolers in the wing leading edges. Estimated performance included a scarcely believable speed of 400mph, and Lockheed's Model 22 received an order for a prototype, the XP-38 (37-457).

RAF Rejection
The Air Corps assigned Lt Ben Kelsey as project officer. He

began taxi tests in December 1938, when the XP-38 skidded into a ditch. On 11 February 1939 Kelsey and the new fighter hit the headlines by crossing the US (refuelling at Amarillo and Dayton) in 7hr 2min, unfortunately undershooting at New York's Mitchel Field and being destroyed. An order for 13 YP-38s followed. These had 1,150hp V-1710-27/-29 engines with spur gears which raised the propeller thrust lines, cooled by enlarged boom-mounted radiators. In the nose were a 37mm gun with 15 rounds, two 0.5in and two 0.30in. In April 1940 the Anglo-French Purchasing Committee placed an order for 667

The P-38J entered production in August 1943 and was built at the rate of 15 a day by Lockheed and Convair.

P-38s, with neither turbos nor handed propellers. The RAF tested three and rejected the rest, which were completed as various USAAF versions, but the order was a huge spur to the programme.

First Kill
Following 29 P-38s with one 37mm and four 0.5in guns came 36 P-38Ds and then 210 P-38Es, the first to adopt the RAF name Lightning, with the

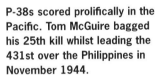

P-38s scored prolifically in the Pacific. Tom McGuire bagged his 25th kill whilst leading the 431st over the Philippines in November 1944.

Gs, followed by the H with 1,425hp V-1710-89/-91 engines.

Top US Aces
The P-38J was visibly different, with the intercooler inlet between the oil cooler intakes in a deep jowl under each engine. The final block, the P-38J-25, introduced hydraulically boosted ailerons and electrically driven dive flaps under the outer wings to prevent high-Mach problems. The most numerous version of all was the last, the P-38L. Powered by -111/-113 engines giving no less than 1,475hp up to 30,000ft (9,144m), these could carry up to 4,000lb (1,814kg)

of bombs or rockets, and many had a nose with either bombing radar or a glazed compartment for a bombardier. Together with an initial block of 113 made by Convair at Nashville, these brought total production to 10,037. A handful were modified as P-38M two-seat night fighters, and substantial numbers were built or modified as F-5 photo-reconnaissance aircraft in 13 versions. Some P-38s operated on skis, while others flew special ECM missions or served as urgent ambulances carrying two litter cases in external pods.

Though the P-38 was never quite able to dogfight with,

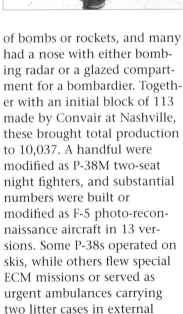

The great Dick Bong (seated) relaxes with other victorious P-38 pilots of the 9th FS after a multi-kill mission to Balikapan on 10 October 1944.

say, an Fw 190 or A6M, these complicated and luxurious aircraft performed superbly on every war front including "shuttle" round trips to the USSR. The P-38 was the sole mount of the two top-scoring US pilots, Majors Richard I.Bong and Thomas B.McGuire Jr, and perhaps the greatest interception mission ever flown was the destruction of Admiral Isoroku Yamamoto's aircraft after an outward trip of

big gun replaced by a 20mm with 150 rounds. The first combat-ready version was the P-38F, powered by 1,325hp V-1710-49/-53 engines, with pylons under the inner wings for drop tanks or 1,000lb (454kg) bombs. On 14 August 1942 an F based in Iceland shot down an Fw 200C to score the first US victory against the Luftwaffe. Various improvements were introduced in successive blocks of Fs and

P-38J/L Lightning
 1 Starboard navigation light
 2 Starboard aileron
 3 Aileron mass balance weights
 4 Starboard leading edge fuel tank, total internal capacity 341 – Imp gal (410 US gal, 1552-lit)
 5 Zero-length rocket installation (early P-38L)
 6 Fuel filler cap
 7 Aileron cable quadrant and hydraulic booster
 8 Trim tab
 9 Fixed tab
10 Starboard outboard Fowler-type flap segment
11 Flap guide rail and operating cables
12 Wing panel corrugated inner skin stiffener
13 Intensifier intake, cabin and gun heating
14 Engine exhaust duct to supercharger turbine
15 Starboard leading edge reserve tank
16 Starboard main undercarriage retraction jack
17 Engine bearer struts
18 Exhaust manifold cooling air scoop
19 Detachable cowling panels
20 Coolant header tank
21 Curtiss-Electric constant sped right hand tractor propeller
22 Propeller spinner
23 Intercooler/oil cooler air intakes

24 Gun compartment access doors, port and starboard
25 Machine gun muzzles
26 Cannon muzzle
27 Gun camera installation (P–38J)
28 Nose cone structure
29 Four 50-calibre (0.5-in, 12.7-mm) machine guns
30 Ammunition feed chutes
31 Cartridge case ejector chute
32 Ammunition magazines, 500–rpg
33 VHF antenna
34 Aft retracting nosewheel
35 Torque scissor links
36 Shimmy dampers and reservoir
37 Retraction/drag strut
38 Nosewheel door
39 Cartridge case ejectors
40 Nosewheel leg pivot mounting
41 Hydraulic retraction jack
42 Cannon ammunition magazine, 150-rounds
43 Cannon feed chute
44 AN-M2 'C' 20-mm cannon
45 Armoured bulkhead
46 Nose compartment sidewall structure
47 Rocket launcher attachment fittings (P-38J)
48 Underfloor nosewheel bay
49 Cockpit floor level
50 Rudder pedals

51 Control column, offset to starboard
52 Instrument panel
53 Instrument panel shroud
54 Armoured windscreen panel
55 Lynn-3 reflector sight
56 Rear view mirror
57 Rearward hingeing canopy upper segment
58 Headrest
59 Pilot's head armour
60 Roll-down side window panel
61 Pilot's armoured seat
62 Control column handwheel
63 Engine throttle and propeller control levers
64 Wing root fillet
65 Leading edge engine control runs
66 Port leading edge reserve tank
67 Chordwise tank bay stiffeners and inner skin panel
68 Ventral signal lights
69 Port inboard main fuel tank
70 Fuel filler caps
71 Radio equipment bay
72 Tank bay skin panel and spanwise corrugated inner stiffener
73 Flap drive motor and screw jack
74 Boarding step, extended
75 Step operating latch/grab handle
76 Starboard inboard Fowler-type flap segment

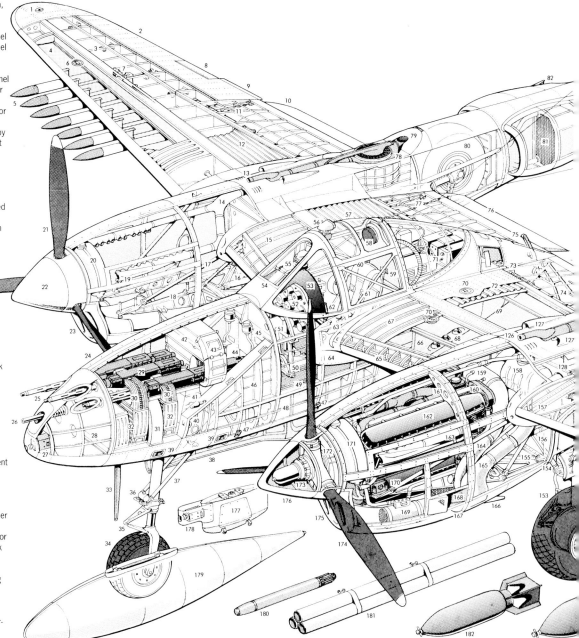

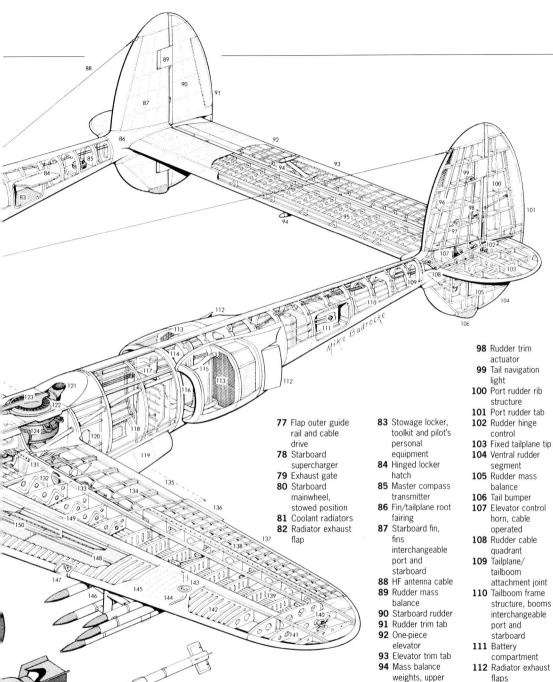

116 Radiator fixed intake
117 Vertical flare launcher
118 Port main undercarriage wheel bay
119 Mainwheel door
120 Wheel bay and supercharger housing sidewall structure
121 Supercharger exhaust gate
122 Exhaust driven turbine
123 Turbine and bearing cooling duct
124 Port intensifier intake
125 Engine exhaust duct to turbine drive
126 Port intensifier intake
127 Supercharger cooling air intakes
128 Outer wing panel main spar joint
129 Corrugated skin stiffener butt joints
130 Mainwheel leg bay mounted supercharger intake air filter
131 Rear spar joint
132 Supercharger ram air intake
133 Flap push-pull control rod and operating cable drive
134 Flap shroud ribs
135 Port outboard Fowler-type flap
136 Aileron fixed tab
137 Port aileron
138 Aileron rib structure
139 Outer wing panel rib structure
140 Port navigation light
141 Wing tip structure

98 Rudder trim actuator
99 Tail navigation light
100 Port rudder rib structure
101 Port rudder tab
102 Rudder hinge control
103 Fixed tailplane tip
104 Ventral rudder segment
105 Rudder mass balance
106 Tail bumper
107 Elevator control horn, cable operated
108 Rudder cable quadrant
109 Tailplane/ tailboom attachment joint
110 Tailboom frame structure, booms interchangeable port and starboard
111 Battery compartment
112 Radiator exhaust flaps
113 Port engine coolant radiators, inner and outer
114 Oxygen bottle
115 Coolant pipes

77 Flap outer guide rail and cable drive
78 Starboard supercharger
79 Exhaust gate
80 Starboard mainwheel, stowed position
81 Coolant radiators
82 Radiator exhaust flap
83 Stowage locker, toolkit and pilot's personal equipment
84 Hinged locker hatch
85 Master compass transmitter
86 Fin/tailplane root fairing
87 Starboard fin, fins interchangeable port and starboard
88 HF antenna cable
89 Rudder mass balance
90 Starboard rudder
91 Rudder trim tab
92 One-piece elevator
93 Elevator trim tab
94 Mass balance weights, upper and lower
95 Tailpane rib structure
96 Port fin structure
97 Elevator operating cable

142 Leading edge tank bay inner corrugated skin stiffener
143 Tank filler cap
144 Ventral pitot head
145 Leading edge skin panel
146 Five-round cluster-type 'Christmas-tree' rocket launcher (late model P-38L)
147 Landing light (P-38L)
148 Port leading edge fuel tank
149 Main spar booms and capping strip
150 Ventral dive flap, electrically operated
151 Main undercarriage leg pivot mounting
152 Mainwheel leg strut
153 Port mainwheel, aft retracting
154 Retraction/drag strut
155 Engine bearer cast sub-frame
156 Engine bay firewall
157 Upper engine bearer support structure
158 Engine oil tank
159 Carburettor intake duct
160 Air cooled magneto housings
161 Cowling support structure
162 Allison V-1710-89/91 (P-38J) or V-1710-111/113 (P-38L) V-twelve engine
163 Port exhaust manifold
164 Intercooler exit duct to carburettor

165 Inercooler inlet duct
166 Cooling air exhaust flap
167 Ventral intercooler radiator
168 Oil cooler exhaust
169 Outboard oil cooler, twin coolers inboard and outboard
170 Forward engine mounting
171 Coolant header tank
172 Armoured spinner backplate
173 Propeller hub pitch change mechanism
174 Port Curtiss-Electric constant-speed propeller, left hand tractor
175 Oil cooler and intercooler air intakes
176 Port propeller spinner
177 Port wing pylon, mounted beneath inner wing panel
178 Gin camera installation (P-38L)
179 125 Imp gal (150-US gal, 568-lit) external tank
180 4.5-in (11.5-cm) M8 rocket projectile
181 M10 triple-tube 'Bazooka' rocket launcher, fuselage side mounted on P-38J
182 500-lb (227-Kg) HE bomb
183 1000-lb (454-Kg) HE bomb
184 4.5-in (11,5-cm) rocket

P-38 LIGHTNING

Milo Burcham displays the 5,000th P-38 built at Burbank. This special red Lightning emerged in July 1944 and was retained by Lockheed with the registration N138X.

DATA FOR P-38L:		
Span		52ft 0in (15.85m)
Length		37ft 10in (11.53m)
Wing area		328 sq ft (30.47m2)
Weight empty	(D)	11,780lb (5,343kg)
	(L)	12,800lb (5,806kg)
Maximum takeoff weight	(D)	15,416lb (6,993kg)
	(L)	21,600lb (9,798kg)
Maximum speed	(D)	390mph (628km/h)
	(L)	414mph (666km/h)
		in each case at 25,000ft
		(7,620m)
Service ceiling	(D)	39,000ft (11,887m),
	(L)	44,000ft (13,411m)
Range with drop tanks	(D)	975 miles (1,569km)
	(L)	2,600 miles (4,184km)

DATA FOR XP–49:	
Dimensions as P-38 except	
Length increased to	40ft 1in (12.22m)
Weight empty	15,464lb (7,014.5kg)
maximum takeoff weight	22,000lb (9,979kg)
Maximum speed	406mph (653km/h)
Range	680 miles (1,094km)

550 miles (885km) from Guadalcanal to Shortland Island, the Japanese leader's known destination. After the war Lightnings served with France and Italy.

XP-49

In March 1939 the Army Air Corps called for proposals for fighters upgraded with more powerful engines. One result was a series of studies on P-38 derivatives designated XP-49 powered by the Pratt & Whitney X-1800 or Wright R-2160 engines. By March 1940 these were seen as too powerful, and replaced by the Continental IV-1430, rated at 1,540hp. These inverted-vee engines were well matched to the basic airframe, but progress was slowed by other programmes being given higher priority.

When the single prototype (40-3055) was flown on 14 November 1942 it differed in many respects from a P-38, with a pressurized cockpit, modified engine installations and cooling systems, stronger landing gears and planned armament of two 20mm and four 0.5in.

It was later fitted with XIV-1430-13/-15 engines rated at 1,600hp at 25,000ft (7,620m) and larger vertical tails. The XP-49 was judged inferior to late-model P-38s, and was scrapped in 1946.

PROMETHEUS BOUND

In April 1940 Lockheed was asked to produce, at no cost to the War Department, a prototype of an advanced version of the P-38. This project was to suffer interminable changes in the basic requirement, engine, armament and mission, but was from the start intended to have engines in the 1,600-2,000hp class and, from May 1940, two seats with at least one turret.

By 1942 a second prototype was added, the mission being a long-range attack aircraft (possibly with a navigator/bombardier in the nose), or bomber destroyer, or escort fighter, or radar-equipped night fighter.

This vacillation was compounded by low priority, and it is no surprise that only one XP-58 was built, and that it did not fly until 6 June 1944 – by chance, D-Day – by which time there was no chance of production.

It was finally powered by two Allison V-3420-11/-13 engines each made up of two P-38 engines driving a single four-blade propeller, the rating with turbo-supercharger being

3,000hp at 28,000ft (8,534m). Forward-firing armament (never fitted) would have been four 37mm or one 75mm and two 0.5in, while a gunner in the tail of the nacelle would have controlled dorsal and ventral turrets each with two 0.5in. Bomb load could have been 4,000lb (1,814kg). But it was all "would have been." The XP-58 was delivered to Wright Field on 22 October 1944, becoming an instructional airframe.

About one-third larger than the P-38, the Chain Lightning promised devastating armament, flashing performance and long-range. Despite 6,000hp, it failed to find a role to justify production after mid 1944.

DATA FOR XP-58:	
Span	70ft 0in (21.34m)
Length	49ft 5.5in (15.075m)
Wing area	600 sq ft (55.74m²)
Weight empty	31,624lb (14,345kg)
Maximum takeoff weight	43,000lb (19,505kg)
Maximum speed	436mph (702km/h)
	at 25,000ft (7,620m)
Range (internal fuel)	1,250 miles (2,012km)

CONSTELLATION

STATE OF THE ART LUXURY

In 1937 Bob Gross let Hibbard start scheming a transport with four engines in the 1,200hp class, the Excalibur (see Introduction). This grew in weight and capacity until in June 1939 it was about to be signed for by PanAm. Then Lockheed heard that Howard Hughes, owner of TWA, and Jack Frye, whom Hughes had moved up to be president of the airline, were looking for someone to build an even bigger and better transport, able to convey passengers in luxury non-stop between the East and West Coasts at 300mph. Partly because nobody else would take the task on, Lockheed accepted it.

The Model 49, later called Constellation, was probably the biggest design and development effort aviation had seen up to that time. It was made doubly difficult (and in some ways better) because Hughes studied almost every rivet; after all, he was paying the bills. In early 1940 Hughes signed for nine, at an unprece-

dented $425,000 each, soon increasing the buy to 40. PanAm quickly followed with another 40. After Pearl Harbor manufacture of commercial aircraft was halted, but in 1942 the USAAF told Lockheed to keep building the TWA aircraft as C-69s, and then ordered 313 to be built as military aircraft.

Boeing's Eddie Allen was hired to head the test crew for the C-69's first flight, at Lockheed Air Terminal, on 9 January 1943. Amazingly, it made five more flights before nightfall, finally landing at Lake Muroc. Though a C-69, and

painted olive-drab with military insignia, it was registered NX25600, and was certainly the most advanced civil aircraft in the world. The wing was almost a bigger version of the P-38's, with enormous Fowler flaps but no slots. On it were the nacelles for four 2,200hp Wright R-3350-35 Duplex Cyclone engines driving 15ft (4.57m) Hamilton three-blade propellers. The fuselage was of the circular section dictated by pressurization, but in side view it was unique, having a curvaceous fish-like profile. This looked beautiful,

Qantas Empire Airways (the carrier adopted its current name in August 1967), was an obvious customer for the Model 749.

but offered no actual advantage and made both design and manufacture more difficult. The Excalibur would probably have had a bluff nose like the Boeing 307 or 377, but the "Connie" had a conventional form with a tip (which later housed radar) and a row of nine shallow windows round the cockpit. To reduce pressurization stress all other

The first USAF airborne early warning Constellations entered service in October 1953 and were designated RC-121C. All Warning Stars featured a heightfinding radar above the fuselage, Azimuth surveillance radar below.

windows were circular. All units of the landing gear had twin wheels, and the tail followed the Excalibur in having triple fins and rudders. All flight controls were hydraulically boosted.

At the end of the war contracts were cancelled with only 15 C-69s completed. Lockheed elected to buy back government tooling and continue with commercial versions, seating from 50 to 80 passengers. Lockheed offered Double Wasp or Centaurus engines, but the customers all stuck with different sub-types of R-3350 Duplex Cyclone, despite severe and protracted problems with the engines, propellers and electrical system. Following 73 Model 049s, Lockheed made 14 Model 649s with engines uprated to 2,500hp and provision for a Speedpak cargo pannier attached under the fuselage (later available on other versions). Next came 119

Model 749s with outer-wing tanks and stronger structure, priced at about $1 million.

By 1950 it was clear that the forthcoming R-3350 Turbo-Compound engine would make possible a heavier aircraft with a stretched fuselage. To produce the L-1049 Super Constellation Lockheed converted

the original prototype to have extra plugs ahead of and behind the wing, incidentally switching to square passenger windows. The longer body increased seating to about 100 passengers and made this graceful aircraft look even better. The stretched aircraft flew on 13 October 1950, and was followed by 24 rather sluggish interim 1049s with the original engines, followed by 49 1049Cs with 3,250hp Turbo-Compound engines, four 1049Ds for cargo, eighteen 1049E passenger aircraft, 104 "Super-G" 1049Gs with

3,400hp engines and tip tanks, and 53 long-range 1049H Supers convertible to passengers (up to 104) or cargo (36,000lb, 16,330kg).

Unexpectedly, Lockheed were fortunate to sell a remarkable 47 sub-types to the USAF and Navy. These included the PO-1/WV-1/WV-2 and RC-121D Warning Stars, which were the first AWACS-type platforms. Other unusual variants included 30 former Navy EC-121K and P aircraft converted into USAF "Igloo White" relay stations in the Vietnam war. Several of the Navy and Air

DATA FOR CONSTELLATION:				
Span	(basic)	**123ft (37.49m)**	1049G	**137,500lb (62,370kg)**
	(with tip tanks)	**126ft 2in (38.46m)**	1649	**160,000lb (72,576kg)**
	1649	**150ft (45.72m)**	Cruising speed (049)	**275mph (443km/h)**
Length	049-749	**95ft 2in (29.01m)**	(749)	**327mph (526km/h)**
	1049	**113ft 7in (34.62m)**	(1049)	**255mph (410km/h)**
	(with radar, typical, also 1649)	**116ft 2in (35.41m)**	(1649)	**290mph (467km/h)**
Wing area	049-749	**1,650 sq ft (153.29m2)**	Range with maximum payload	
	1049	**1,654 sq ft (153.657m²)**	(049)	**2,290 miles (3,685km)**
	1649	**1,850 sq ft (171.865m²)**	with	**18,400lb (8,346kg)**
Weight empty	049	**55,345lb (25,104kg)**	(749)	**1,760 miles (2,832km)**
	749	**58,970lb (26,749kg)**	with	**16,300lb (7,394kg)**
	(1049)	**69,210lb (31,394kg)**	(1049)	**2,880 miles (4,635km)**
	(1649)	**91,645lb (41,570kg)**	with	**18,800lb (8,528kg)**
Maximum takeoff	049	**86,250lb (39,123kg)**	(1049G)	**4,140 miles (6,663km)**
	749	**107,000lb (48,535kg)**	with	**18,300lb (8,301kg)**
			(1649)	**4,940 miles (7,950km)**
			with	**19,500lb (8,845kg)**.

Force aircraft cruised at over 400mph (644km/h) on the power of 6,000ehp Pratt & Whitney T34 turboprops, while the fourth Navy R7V-2 was powered by Allison 501 turboprops to help development of the Electra.

These military aircraft played a major role in increasing total production to one prototype, 233 Constellations and 578 Supers.

The very last version was the L-1649 Starliner. This was developed from 1954 to enable TWA to meet the non-stop Atlantic capability of the DC-7C. The 3,400hp Turbo-Compounds were geared down to drive 16ft 10in (5.13m) propellers mounted further from the fuselage on a totally new wing of increased span, with huge machined skins, a thinner profile and straight taper to square tips. The fuselage was slightly stretched, and increased fuel capacity raised takeoff weight to 160,000lb (72,576kg).

Lockheed lost money selling only 44 of this super-graceful version, which entered transatlantic service on 1 June 1957, only a short time before Britannias, Comets and 707s.

L-1049C SUPER CONSTELLATION
1 Nose cone
2 Landing and taxying lamps
3 Front pressure bulkhead
4 Hydraulic brake accumulator
5 Radio mast
6 Nosewheel leg door
7 Steering jacks
8 Twin nosewheels
9 Nosewheel leg strut
10 Retraction linkages
11 Pitot tube mast
12 Rudder pedals
13 Instrument panel
14 Instrument panel shroud
15 Windscreen wipers
16 Windscreen panels
17 Copilot's seat
18 Control column
19 Pilot's seat
20 Flight deck floor level
21 Radio operator's station
22 Flight engineer's station
23 Starboard crew door
24 VOR aerial
25 Engineer's instrument panel
26 Radio racks
27 Cockpit bulkhead
28 Navigator's chart table
29 Underfloor battery bay
30 Nosewheel doors
31 Forward entry door
32 Cabin bulkhead
33 Crew rest area
34 Radio aerial mast
35 Overhead luggage racks
36 Starboard emergency exit window
37 Forward cabin seating

38 Forward underfloor freight hold, total freight hold volume 728 cu ft (20.61 m³)
39 Radio altimeter
40 Ventral freight door
41 Port emergency exit windows
42 Ventral ADF sense aerial
43 Toilet compartments, port and starboard
44 Wardrobes
45 Main cabin four abreast seating
46 Cabin wall trim panels
47 Starboard inner engine nacelle
48 Starboard wing integral fuel tank, total fuel capacity 6.550 US gal (247601)
49 Supercharger oil cooler
50 Starboard outer engine nacelle
51 Detachable engine cowling panels
52 Spinner
53 Hamilton Standard three-bladed propeller
54 Leading edge de-icing boots
55 Fuel system piping

56 Outer wing panel joint rib
57 Outboard integral fuel tank
58 Starboard navigation light
59 Static dischargers
60 Starboard aileron
61 Aileron balance weights
62 Fuel venting system piping

63 Aileron control hydraulic booster
64 Aileron tab
65 Fuel jettison pipe
66 Starboard Fowler-type flap
67 Flap guide rails
68 Starboard air conditioning plant
69 Fuselage centre section construction
70 Wing/fuselage attachment main frames
71 Centre section bag-type fuel tanks
72 Central flap control motor

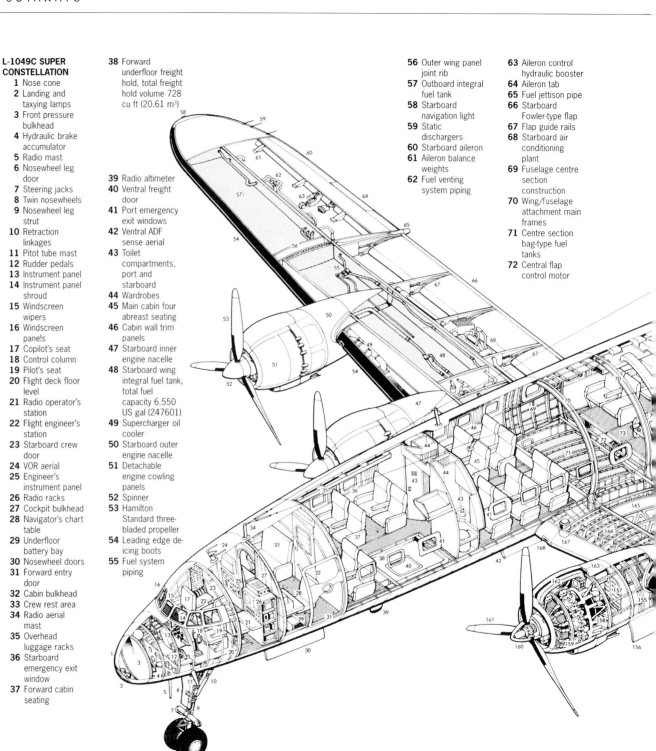

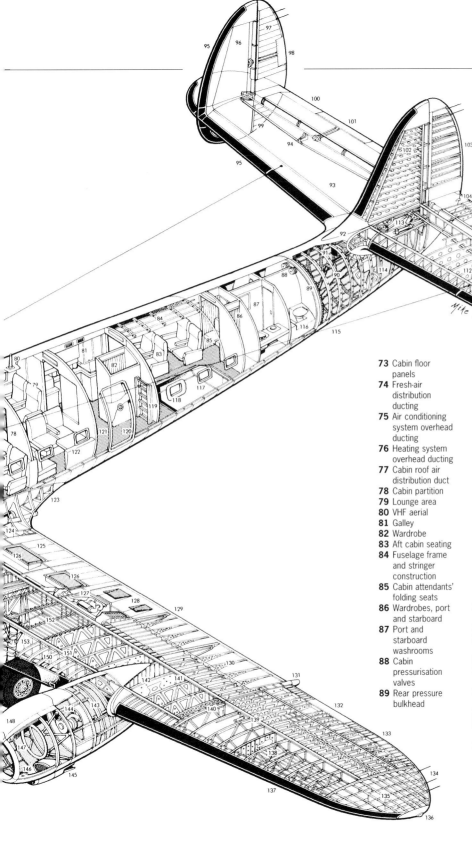

Mike Badrocke

73 Cabin floor panels
74 Fresh-air distribution ducting
75 Air conditioning system overhead ducting
76 Heating system overhead ducting
77 Cabin roof air distribution duct
78 Cabin partition
79 Lounge area
80 VHF aerial
81 Galley
82 Wardrobe
83 Aft cabin seating
84 Fuselage frame and stringer construction
85 Cabin attendants' folding seats
86 Wardrobes, port and starboard
87 Port and starboard washrooms
88 Cabin pressurisation valves
89 Rear pressure bulkhead

90 Tailcone construction
91 Elevator mass balance weight
92 Fin/tailplane fillets
93 Starboard tailplane
94 Rudder control rods
95 Leading edge de-icing boots
96 Starboard fin
97 Fabric covered rudder
98 Rudder trim tab
99 Lower rudder segment
100 Starboard elevator
101 Elevator trim tab
102 Centre fin construction
103 Centre rudder
104 Tail navigation light
105 Port elevator construction
106 Elevator tab
107 Port fin construction
108 Static dischargers

109 Port rudder construction
110 Tailplane tip fairing
111 Leading edge de-icing boots
112 Tailplane construction
113 Rudder and elevator hydraulic boosters
114 Tailplane attachment frame
115 HF aerial cable
116 Aft toilet compartments, port and starboard
117 Rear underfloor freight hold
118 Rear cabin emergency exit window
119 Ladder stowage
120 Passenger entry door
121 Entry lobby
122 Folding table
123 Wing root fillet construction
124 Cabin heater unit

125 Port flap shroud panels
126 Life raft stowage bays
127 Port air conditioning plant
128 Heat exchanger air exhaust ducts
129 Port Fowler-type flap
130 Flap shroud ribs
131 Fuel jettison pipe
132 Aileron tab
133 Port aileron construction
134 Static dischargers
135 Wing tip construction
136 Port navigation light
137 Leading edge de-icing boots
138 Port outboard fuel tank bay
139 Outer wing panel main spar
140 Outer wing panel joint rib
141 Rear spar
142 Wing rib construction
143 Engine nacelle construction
144 Air conditioning

system turbine
145 Oil cooler air duct
146 Oil cooler
147 Engine mounting ring
148 Carburettor intake duct fairing
149 Twin mainwheels
150 Leading edge nose ribs
151 Front spar
152 Wing stringer construction
153 Main undercarriage leg strut
154 Retraction linkage
155 Main undercarriage wheel well
156 Mainwheel doors
157 Engine firewall
158 Exhaust collector ring
159 Wright R-3350-DA1 Turbo-compound, 18-cylinder two-row radial engine
160 Propeller hub pitch change mechanism

MODEL 33 LITTLE DIPPER

STANDARD ISSUE?

In 1944 John Thorp, working in Mac Short's Special Projects Group, began in his own time designing a simple light aircraft which he thought might be used by "aerial cavalry", each trooper flying one. Perhaps surprisingly, his idea was backed by Bob Gross.

In April 1944 Bob Gross agreed to make the idea a company project, and the civil-registered NX18935 flew in late August 1944. Powered by a 50hp engine specially built by Aircooled Motors, using two cylinders from that company's standard Franklin engines, it had an all-metal airframe with a constant-profile wing fitted with flaps, simple fixed tricycle landing gear and a cockpit which after the first few flights was fitted with a canopy hinged on the port (left) side. It was a delight to fly, but unfortunately (perhaps without trying too hard) Lockheed failed to find either a military or a civilian market.

The Little Dipper was sold for scrap in January 1947, but it did lead to the Model 34 Big Dipper.

DATA FOR LITTLE DIPPER:	
Span	25ft 0in (7.62m)
Length	17ft 6in (5.334m)
Wing area	104 sq ft (9.66m2)
Weight empty	425lb (193kg)
Maximum takeoff weight	725lb (329kg)
Maximum speed	100mph (161km/h)
Range	210 miles (338km)

Today the neat Little Dipper would not look out of place at Oshkosh, but after World War 2 thousands of qualified pilots had the pick of surplus light aircraft with better range and payload. The military dismissed it.

FROM LITTLE ACORNS ...

John Thorp's Little Dipper sparked off company interest in a slightly larger aircraft, and, under chief project engineer Bob Reedy, Thorp designed the Model 34 with two seats side-by-side in the nose, with a door on each side.

The constant-profile low wing was fitted with flaps which were hinged well below the wing on brackets. Other features included fixed tricycle landing gear, a "slab" all-moving tailplane and a two-blade propeller behind the tail driven by a flexible shaft from a 100hp Continental C100-12 engine above the wing, with fan-assisted cooling from inlets under the wing and exits in the top of the fuselage. Prentice Cleaves made the first flight in secret at Palmdale on 10 December 1945. The only problem was a vicious stall at the wing root. A modification was devised, but this had not been fitted when, taking off from a short uphill runway at Burbank, a wing-root stall destroyed the aircraft on 6 February 1946. Lockheed decided to abandon the saturated lightplane market.

DATA FOR BIG DIPPER:	
Span	31ft 0in (9.449m)
Length	22ft 2in (6.756m)
Wing area	160 sq ft (14.86m2)
Weight empty	935lb (424kg)
Maximum takeoff weight	1,450lb (658kg)
Cruising speed	119mph (191.5km/h)
Range	390 miles (628km)

A Model 049 Constellation looms behind the short-lived Big Dipper. Its unfortunate crash promptly ended Lockheed's interest in light aviation. With better luck, the Model 34 might have rattled Cessna and Piper.

MODEL 34 BIG DIPPER

F–80 SHOOTING STAR

MODEL F–80 SHOOTING STAR

While the amazingly advanced L-133 fighter and its L-1000 turbojet came to nothing, 'Kelly' Johnson studied more practical jet fighters as soon as he learned of British jet engines. On 16-19 June 1943, at a conference at Wright Field, he agreed to design a fighter to be powered by the British Halford (de Havilland) H.1 Goblin engine. He undertook to have it flying in 180 days.

Assisted by Don Palmer and Bill Ralston, a special team built the L-140 in a secret shed that formed the genesis of the Skunk Works. Painted dark green and designated XP-80, it was completed in 143 days. Ignoring the warning of a British engineer that the inlet ducts were too flimsy, ground running at Muroc began on 10 November 1943. On 17 November both air ducts collapsed, wrecking the H.1's compressor. De Havilland took the engine out of the second prototype Vampire and sent it to Lockheed. With new inlet ducts of thicker material the XP-80 began its flight-test pro-

gramme on 8 January 1944. Milo Burcham turned the test into a cracking low-level demonstration.

The prototype was nick-named *Lulu Belle*; the official name was announced as Shooting Star. Features included a laminar-profile wing with a remarkably sharp fixed leading edge, electrically driven split flaps and hydraulically boosted ailerons. The fuselage had a deep but narrow nose

housing six 0.5in guns. The cockpit above the leading edge had a sliding bubble canopy, while low on each side were the curiously profiled engine inlets. The complete rear fuselage could be removed to expose the engine.

After the fifth flight the wings and tail surfaces were all given rounded tips. These were repeated on subsequent aircraft, which were slightly larger, had engine inlets further aft

F-80s fought hard in Korea. On 8 November 1950 Lt. Russel J. Brown of the 51st Interception Wing became the first jet fighter pilot to shoot down another.

feeding a General Electric I-40 engine of 4,000-lb (1,814-kg) thrust, and had many other updates including a pressurized cockpit. The second of two XP-80A aircraft had a second seat for a flight-test observer. Next came 13 Service-test YP-80As; four of these carried out tactical trials in Italy during the final weeks of the War, and one was fitted by Rolls-Royce with a 5,000-lb (2,268-kg) Nene engine. All 13 had ammunition increased from 200 to 300 rounds per gun, internal fuel tankage was increased from 237 to 404gal (1,077 to 1,837 litres) and provision was made for a 137-gal (623-litre) drop tank under each wingtip. Loaded weight was increased by over 50 per cent, necessitating new main landing gears. In December 1944 Lockheed received an order for 500 P-80As, each priced at $75,913, followed by a second batch of 500 priced at $55,913. Two similar contracts were placed with North American Aviation, with combined output to reach 30 per day.

High Losses

With the War's end, procurement was slashed, but less than for most other aircraft. Eventually Lockheed delivered 563 P-80A fighters, which, after June 1948 were redesignated as F-80As. Their unit price was about $95,000. Most received a water/alcohol injection system to boost thrust on takeoff, and in 1947-48 all survivors were fitted with zero-length launchers for ten 5-in rockets. During construction 38 were equipped as unarmed F-14A (later redesignated RF-80A) photo-reconnaissance aircraft, leaving 525 as fighters, and 114 were built as such. In 1951 a further 70 F-80As were modified into upgraded photo aircraft designated RF-80C. Mainly because of engine immaturity the accident rate of the P-80A was the highest in the Army

The Shooting Star looked startling in 1944 and completely outclassed the somewhat pedestrian British Meteor. Drop tanks were introduced on the YP-80A.

Air Force, 36 being lost between March and September 1946 alone.

The Burbank factory next produced 240 F-80Bs, powered by an Allison J33-A-21 engine (effectively an I-40 made under licence), rated at 5,200 lb (2,359 kg) with water/alcohol injection. The main modification was a slightly thinner wing with thicker skins, but other changes included a primitive ejection seat, faster-firing M3 guns, provision for rocket bottles to assist takeoff, improved cockpit cooling and a canopy defrost/demist system. Production of the Shooting Star was completed by the delivery between October 1948 and June 1950 of 799 F-80C aircraft. Of these, 50 were TO-1 (later called TV-1) advanced trainers for the Navy and Marine Corps.

The basic aircraft could hardly be distinguished from earlier versions, but retroactive modifications cleared the C model to carry either the 192-gal (873-litre) Fletcher tank centred on each wingtip or the even larger 221-gal (1,005-litre) Misawa underslung tip tank. Two additional underwing hardpoints were added to enable various loads of ordnance to be carried apart from rockets, such as two 1,000-lb (454-kg) bombs, or fragmentation bombs, or napalm. More than 50 F-80s were the subject of experimental modifications involving aerodynamics, systems, armament and propulsion. For example, one tested a rapid-fire rocket gun, while two others were fitted with Marquardt ramjet engines on the wingtips.

Korean Contribution
By chance, the last F-80 was delivered just as the Korean war started. In that conflict the F-80 (almost all the C model) and RF-80A played a major role. In 98,515 sorties they dropped 37,137 tons (45,193 short tons) of bombs and launched over 81,000 rockets. On the other hand, 277 (virtually half the F-80C production) were lost, including 14 in air combat and 113 to ground fire. On 16 June 1947 a specially modified aircraft designated P-80R was flown by Col Al Boyd to a World Speed Record of 623.78mph (1,003.811km/h). After the war many F-80s served in the Navy, Marine Corps, Air National Guard and with six air forces in Latin America. One F-80C (48-356) was lengthened and converted into the TP-80C with two cockpits with dual control. This led to one of Lockheed's greatest successes, the T-33 trainer.

Ejection seats were still a novelty on the Shooting Star, but saved many lives if the J33 flamed out. These F-80Cs are equipped with Misawa tip tanks. There was a huge contribution in Korea, and a huge price to pay.

DATA FOR F-80C:	
Span	38ft 9in (11.81m)
Length	34ft 5in (10.49m)
Wing area	237.6 sq ft (22.07m²)
Weight empty	9,420lb (3,819kg)
Normal loaded weight	12,200lb (5,534kg)
Maximum takeoff weight	16,856lb (7,646kg)
Maximum speed at sea level	594mph (956km/h)
Cruising speed	439mph (706.5km/h)
Initial climb	6,870ft (2,094m)/min
Service ceiling	46,800ft (14,265m)
Combat radius with bombs (hi-lo-hi)	100 miles (161km)
Range	825 miles (1,328km)

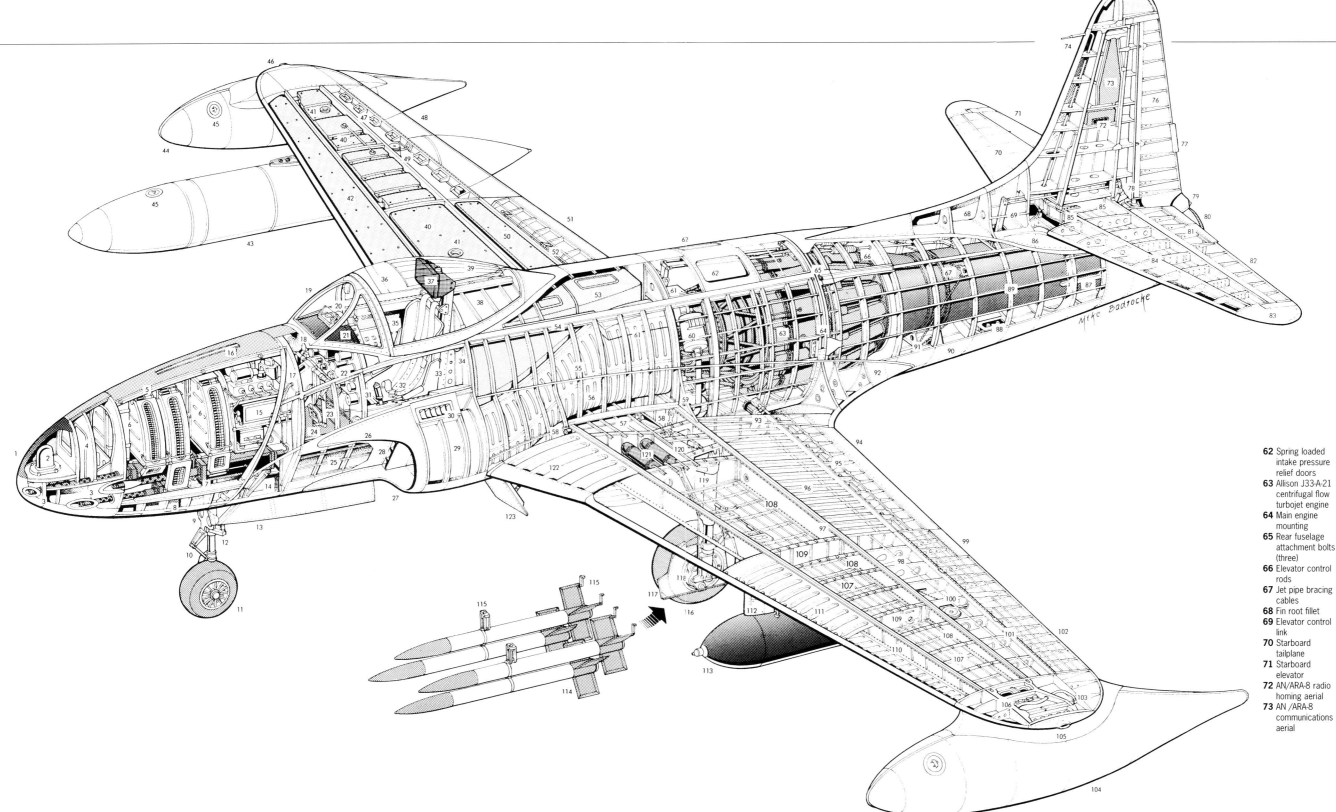

33 Pilot's ejection seat
34 Cockpit rear bulkhead
35 Starboard side console panel
36 Sliding cockpit canopy cover
37 Ejection seat headrest
38 Canopy aft decking
39 D/F sense antenna
40 Starboard wing fuel tanks
41 Fuel filler caps
42 Leading edge tank
43 Fletcher-type tip-tank, capacity 200 US gal (757 l)
44 Tip tank, capacity 165 US gal (6251)
45 Tip tank filler cap
46 Starboard navigation light
47 Aileron balance weights
48 Starboard aileron
49 Aileron hinge control
50 Trailing edge fuel tank
51 Starboard split trailing edge flap
52 Flap control links
53 Fuselage fuel tank total internal capacity 657 US gal (2 4871)
54 Fuselage main longeron
55 Centre fuselage frames
56 Intake trunking
57 Main undercarriage wheel well
58 Wing spar attachment joints
59 Pneumatic reservoir
60 Hydraulic accumulator
61 Port and starboard water injection tanks

62 Spring loaded intake pressure relief doors
63 Allison J33-A-21 centrifugal flow turbojet engine
64 Main engine mounting
65 Rear fuselage attachment bolts (three)
66 Elevator control rods
67 Jet pipe bracing cables
68 Fin root fillet
69 Elevator control link
70 Starboard tailplane
71 Starboard elevator
72 AN/ARA-8 radio homing aerial
73 AN /ARA-8 communications aerial

74 Pitot tube
75 AN/ARC-3 radio "pick-axe" antenna
76 Rudder construction
77 Fixed tab
78 Elevator and rudder hinge controls
79 Tail navigation light
80 Jet pipe nozzle
81 Elevator tabs
82 Port elevator construction
83 Elevator mass balance
84 Tailplane construction
85 Fin/tailplane attachment joints
86 Tailplane fillet fairing
87 Jet pipe mounting rail
88 Gyrosyn radio compass flux valve
89 Rear fuselage frame and stringer construction
90 Fuselage skin plating
91 Jet pipe support frame
92 Trailing edge wing root fillet
93 Flap drive motor
94 Port split trailing edge flap
95 Flap shroud ribs
96 Trailing edge fuel tank bay
97 Rear spar
98 Trailing edge ribs
99 Port aileron tab
100 Aileron hinge control
101 Upper skin panel aileron hinge line
102 Aileron construction
103 Wing tip fairing

104 Tip tank
105 Port navigation light
106 Tip tank mounting and jettison control
107 Detachable lower wing skin/ fuel tank bay panels
108 Port wing fuel tank bays
109 Inter tank bay ribs
110 Front spar
111 Corrugated leading edge inner skin
112 Port stores pylon
113 1,000lb (454kg) HE bomb
114 5-in HVAR ground attack rockets (10 rockets maximum load)
115 HVAR rocket mountings
116 Port mainwheel
117 Mainwheel doors
118 Wheel brake pad
119 Main undercarriage leg strut
120 Retraction jack
121 Oxygen tanks
122 Wing root leading edge extension
123 Port ventral airbrake

IN FOR THE LONG HAUL

On Saturday 6 December 1941, the day before Pearl Harbor, Mac Short (who also features in several other chapters of the Lockheed story) issued an internal work order for a Navy patrol bomber to follow the PV.

Vega's chief engineer, John B. Wassall, had already done two months of project studies, using twin R-2800 or R-3350 engines to create an aircraft with considerably greater range and endurance despite having a heavier weapon load and slower landing speed. Unfortunately, Vega was already over-committed, and the Navy was reluctant to divert effort to an untried project. By 1943 the outlook was better, and on 19 February of that year a Letter of Intent was issued for two XP2V prototypes based on the V-146 study. Even so, it was not until summer 1944 that project engineer Robert A .Bailey was able to assemble a design team. At last, on 17 May 1945, a test crew headed by Joe Towle made a very successful maiden flight from Lockheed Air Terminal.

The P2V Neptune was

designed for a crew of seven. As it had no airline ancestry the wing was mid-high, making possible a capacious internal bay for 8,000lb (3,629kg) of bombs, torpedoes, depth charges, mines and many other kinds of store. Defensive armament comprised paired 0.5in guns in the nose, tail and dorsal turret. The wings had an aspect ratio of 10, and were fitted with Fowler flaps and drooping ailerons, but no slots. The tail had a huge single fin, and a unique feature was that the fixed tailplanes carried hinged variable-camber surfaces, driven by irreversible screwjacks, to which the elevators were hinged. All leading edges were de-iced by combustion heaters. The 2,300hp Wright R-3350-8 engines drove four-blade propellers with alcohol de-icing.

Longevity

At the war's end orders were cut, but the P2V was to prove one of Lockheed's most enduring programmes; Lockheed built 1,051 in 20 years, and the last of an additional 82 came off Kawasaki's production line in Japan in March 1979. In 1946-47 Lockheed built 14

SP-2H (P2V-7S) Neptune

1 Nose compartment glazing
2 Course Indicator
3 Footrest
4 Observer's seat
5 Searchlight hand controller
6 Sliding seat rails
7 AS-578/ARA-25 antenna
8 Instrument consoles
9 ALR-3 antennae
10 Heater ducting
11 Cold air intake
12 Ditching panel
13 Cockpit/nose compartment bulkhead
14 ASR-3 amplifier
15 Temperature probe
16 Torque scissor links
17 Aft retracting nosewheel
18 Nose undercarriage leg strut
19 Nosewheel steering jack
20 ARR26 aerials
21 Nosewheel doors
22 Electrical system relay panels
23 Nose undercarriage hydraulic retraction jack
24 Cockpit floor level
25 Rudder pedals
26 Cockpit heater duct
27 Instrument panel
28 Instrument panel shroud
29 Windscreen wipers
30 Windscreen panels
31 Cockpit roof glazing
32 Overhead switch panel
33 Cockpit roof escape hatches

34 Sun visor
35 Copilot's seat
36 Aircraft captain's folding seat
37 Pilot's seat
38 Control column
39 Side console panel
40 Nosewheel bay
41 Entry doorway from lower wheel bay
42 Lower deck walkway
43 Retractable boarding ladder
44 Ventral radome
45 Hydraulic system panel
46 Tape recorder
47 Access hatch from lower deck
48 Parachute stowage
49 'Jezebel' operator's seat
50 AQA3 Indicator
51 Overhead instrument and control consoles
52 Sextant aperture
53 Astrodome/ escape hatch
54 Plotting board
55 Navigator's seat
56 Cabin window panel
57 Seat mounting rails
58 Electrical system distribution centre
59 Radar scanner drive unit
60 APS-203 search radar scanner
61 Radar electronics equipment bay
62 Electrical system secondary load centre
63 Tactical Commander's seat
64 ASA-16 indicator
65 AS-20 recorder
66 'Julie' operator's seat
67 ECM systems control panels
68 Cabin heater

69 Drift sight
70 Weapons bay door hydraulic jack
71 Weapons bay doors
72 Auxiliary fuel tank (two)
73 Parachute stowage
74 Hydraulic oil reservoir
75 Wing centre section carry-through
76 Roll stabilizer gyro
77 Front spar/fuselage main frame
78 Starboard wing inboard fuel tanks
79 Engine nacelle top fairings
80 Starboard engine nacelle
81 Exhaust duct
82 Engine cooling air exit louvre
83 Accessory equipment compartment
84 Exhaust driven power recovery turbine

85 Wright R-3350-32W Turbo-Compound 18-cylinder, two-row radial engine
86 Propeller reduction gearbox
87 Propeller hub pitch change mechanism
88 Spinner
89 Hamilton-Standard four-bladed variable pitch propeller
90 Engine cowling panels

91 Engine air intake duct
92 Starboard booster engine pod
93 Booster engine pylon
94 Underwing stores pylons (four)
95 Starboard outer wing panel fuel tanks

96 Starboard outer wing panel
97 Tip tank nose glazing
98 Remote control searchlight
99 Starboard wing tip tank
100 Tank stabilizing fin
101 Static dischargers
102 Starboard aileron
103 Aileron hinge control

104 Aileron tab
105 Starboard spoilers, open
106 Flap jacks
107 Outboard single-slotted Fowler-type flap
108 Outer wing panel bolted joint
109 Flap guide rails

110 Inboard flap/engine nacelle beaver tail fairing
111 ARC-1 antenna
112 Centre electronics rack
113 Liferaft
114 Emergency equipment
115 Rear spar/ fuselage main frame
116 Radio operator's station

117 Radio rack
118 Cabin window/escape hatch
119 Water tank
120 Rear electrical distribution centre

121 Rear cabin bulkhead
122 Dynamotor
123 Lower deck access steps
124 Oxygen bottles
125 Float light continers
126 Electronics equipment racks
127 HT-256/ARC antenna

128 Small sonobuoy stowage rack
129 Rear cabin skylight/escape hatch
130 Martin dorsal turret (initial production P2V-7 and all earlier models)
131 Two 0.50-in (12.7 mm)

132 Rear electronics equipment racks
133 Overhead sonobuoy stowage racks
134 Marine marker ejector
135 APA-69 antenna stowage

136 Observer's window/escape hatch port and starboard
137 Auxiliary electronics racks
138 Tailplane de-icing heater
139 Heater ram air intake

140 Starboard tailplane
141 Starboard two-segment 'Varicam' elevator
142 Remote compass transmitters
143 Fin construction
144 Fin tip aerial fairing
145 ADF loop aerial
146 Anti-collision light
147 Static dischargers
148 Rudder tab
149 Rudder construction
150 Elevator and rudder hinge controls

151 Compensator loop cables
152 Magnetic anomaly detector (MAD)
153 Tail navigation lights
154 Glassfibre MAD tail boom

155 Elevator tabs
156 Port two-segment elevator
157 'Varicam' elevator fore-section
158 Tailplane construction
159 Fin/tailplane attachment main frames
160 Tailplane leading-edge root fillet
161 Rear fuselage walkway
162 Tail bumper
163 AN/APR-9 antenna
164 Chemical toilet
165 Rear observer' s seats (two)
166 AN/APA-69 antenna
167 Aft ventral radome
168 Camera viewfinder
169 Pneumatic reservoir
170 Camera flasher mount
171 ECM aerials
172 Sonobuoy release relay panel
173 Small sonobuoy rack

174 AT-256/ARC antenna
175 S Sonobuoy launch tubes
176 Ladder
177 Oxygen bottles
178 Rear cabin ventral entry hatch
179 Large sonobuoy rack
180 Ventral Doppler aerial
181 Doppler electronics equipment rack
182 ALR-3 antenna
183 APR-26 aerials
184 Life raft
185 Emergency equipment stowage
186 Nacelle beaver tail fairing
187 Flap shroud ribs
188 Port single-slotted Fowler-type flaps
189 Port spoilers
190 Trailing edge ribs
191 Port aileron construction
192 Aileron tab
193 Tip tank stabilizing fin
194 Port wing tip fuel tank
195 Port navigation light
196 Tip tank nose fairing
197 Fuel filler cap
198 Outer wing panel rib construction
199 Lower wing skin/stringer panel
200 Leading edge nose ribs
201 Leading edge de-icing air duct
202 Port wing stores pylons (four)
203 5-in (12.7 cm) HVAR air-to-surface rockets
204 500-lb (227-kg) mines or 325-lb

calibre machine-guns

P2V-1s, with wing racks for 16 rockets. In September/October 1946 the specially modified Truculent Turtle set a non-stop record flying 11,236 miles (18,082 km) from Perth, Western Australia, to Washington DC. The 80 P2V-2s had R-3350-24W engines with water injection to give 2,800hp, driving Hamilton propellers with three "paddle" blades with electric de-icing. In the nose were six fixed 20mm cannon, and the last 72 aircraft had a different tail turret with two 20mm.

The P2V-3 had 3,090hp R-3350-26W engines with "jet stack" exhausts. Variants included the -3C intended as a carrier-based atom bomber and the -3W with APS-20 early-warning radar. The 52 P2V-4s were fitted with wingtip fuel tanks, and the final 27 were the first with R-3350-30W Turbo-Compound engines rated at 3,250hp. From this time onwards four-blade propellers were standard. The P2V-5 (redesignated P-2E in 1962) had bigger tip tanks (one housing a searchlight), an Emerson nose turret with two 20mm guns (progressively replaced by a plain plastic nose) and in

A US Navy P-2H returns from a patrol. Minus jet pods, Neptunes are today perfectly suited to operating as civilian fire bombers.

later versions a long tail "stinger" housing MAD (magnetic-anomaly detection) to find submarines. The P2V-5F added underwing 3,400lb (1,474kg) thrust Westinghouse J34 booster turbojets.

In 1952 production switched to the P2V-6 (P-2F), with increased fuel and equipment. Often all guns were removed, as was usually the case with the final Lockheed production version, the P2V-7 (P-2H), some of which originally had a twin-0.5in dorsal turret. Most had J34 jet pods, and the main engines were 3,700hp R-3350-32W Turbo-Compounds. Features included a raised flight deck with a clear bulged canopy and slimmer tip tanks. There were numerous conversions, including the Navy's OP-2E for delivery of land sensors to detect trucks in SE Asia, the AP-2H night interdictor, the EP-2H relay platform, the Army AP-2E COMINT/SIGINT surveillance

platforms and the USAF RB-69 electronic surveillance version.

Lockheed-built aircraft served with the RAF and seven other air forces and navies, and the very last version was the P-2J, developed by Kawasaki in Japan. This was powered by two 2,970shp General Electric T64-10 turboprops made by

IHI under licence, plus two J3 booster turbojets each of 3,417lb (1,550kg) thrust.

Features included a longer but lighter fuselage, APS-80 radar and twin-wheel main landing gears. Small numbers of Neptunes are still flying, a few having been converted to fight forest fires.

DATA FOR P2V–7 (P–2H):	
Span	103ft 10in (31.65m)
Length	91ft 8in (27.94m)
Wing area	1,000 sq ft (92.9m²)
Weight empty	49,935lb (22,650kg)
Maximum loaded	79,895lb (36,240kg)
Maximum speed	356mph (573km/h)
or with jets	403mph (648km/h)
Cruising speed	188mph (303km/h)
Service ceiling	22,000ft (6,700m)
Range, typically	2,500 miles (4,000km)
or with weapon-bay tanks	3,685 miles (5,930km)

MODEL 75 SATURN

FALSE DAWN

Towards the end of World War 2 almost all the US planemakers began making urgent plans to maximise their share of what was rightly foreseen as huge and expanding civil business. Lockheed carried out a nationwide survey and confirmed a need for a local-service transport "to do the big business for the little airline and the little business for the big airline", whilst "bringing air travel to Main Street" using short unpaved airstrips.

The result was two prototypes of the Saturn, the first of which was flown by Rudy Thoren and Tony LeVier on 17 June 1946. It was a very attractive aircraft, powered by two 600hp Continental GR9-A engines slung under a high-mounted wing. The unpressurized fuselage could be fitted with a movable bulkhead to convert it from all-cargo to all-passenger, seating up to 14 (the same as the Lodestar). Tricycle landing gear with twin-wheel main units put the floor horizontal at a convenient

height. Unlike earlier Lockheed transports there was a single vertical tail, with the newly fashionable dorsal fin.

Compared with the Lodestar the Model 75 Saturn had similar empty weight, lower gross weight, similar performance on much less power, full protection against icing, and far better accommodation, provisions for maintenance and fuel economy. Bad stall qualities were soon corrected, and engine-cooling problems were rectified in the second aircraft by fitting 800hp Wright 744C-7BA (R-1300 Cyclone) engines. This also considerably shortened the

takeoff, though performance was generally significantly below expectation.

More serious was that the huge effort Lockheed put into this aircraft had to be reflected in a price increase from $85,000 to $100,000. This was just what the project did not need, and in the event almost

The Saturn joined a growing list of aircraft which failed to compete with war surplus DC-3s.

all the potential customers bought ex-military transports for less than one-fifth of the price. The two prototypes were scrapped in 1948.

DATA FOR MODEL 75 SATURN:	
Span	**74ft 0in (22.555m)**
Length	**51ft 6in (15.70m)**
Wing area	**502 sq ft (46.64m²)**
Weight empty (Wright engines)	**11,361lb (5,153kg)**
Maximum takeoff weight	**16,000lb (7,258kg)**
Maximum cruising speed	**206mph (332km/h)**
Range	**600 miles (966km)**

"AIRPLANE ON GROUND"

In the final years before World War 2 Pan American held discussions with Boeing, Douglas and Lockheed – not, incidentally, with the builders of its great flying boats Martin and Sikorsky – regarding the future development of giant long-range landplanes. Such aircraft, operating from the long runways then being built around the world, promised to fly the Atlantic and Pacific faster and more efficiently than the seaplanes. After Pearl Harbor a ban was imposed on non-military aircraft development. Accordingly, the discussions centred on the Army and Navy, and in June 1942 the latter ordered two prototypes of the enormous Model 89, with Navy designation R6O-1 (changed to R6V-1 in 1950).

A crew led by Joe Towle and Tony LeVier made the first flight of the No 1 R6O (BuNo 85163) from Burbank to Lake Muroc (later called Edwards) on 9 November 1946. The sec-

ond (85164) did not follow until June 1948. The big problem was that such aircraft outstripped the power of available engines. It had been hoped to use turboprops, especially the 5,500shp Wright T35 Typhoon. Pending such engines, the only alternative was four Pratt & Whitney R-4360 Wasp Major piston engines. Initially the R-4360-18 was used, rated at

3,000hp and driving 19ft 2in (5.84m) Curtiss Electric reverse-pitch propellers, among the largest ever fitted to any aircraft. All engines were accessible in flight.

The wing was broadly scaled up from that of the Constellation. The whale-like fuselage was fully pressurized and was one of the first of the "double-bubbles" with two

A Model 12 gives scale to the gleaming Constitution. Spiral stairways connected the upper and lower decks. I'm Connie, fly me, might just have worked.

superimposed decks, each with a radius of 77in (1,956mm). The monster landed on four main legs each fitted with twin wheels, retracting inwards into

R60-1 CONSTITUTION

The Constitution really needed turboprops but had to manage on 14,000hp. It remains to this time the largest aircraft ever delivered to a US Navy squadron.

a bay in the most highly stressed part of the wing covered by a huge rectangular door. Uniquely, electric motors spun up the wheels to reduce tyre wear on touchdown (landings were so gentle a microswitch on one main leg illuminated a cockpit caption saying *AIRPLANE ON GROUND*. The twin-wheel steerable nose gear folded forwards into the extreme nose. The tail had a huge single fin,

and all flight-control surfaces were hydraulically boosted.

Flight testing was prolonged, with instrumentation almost filling the vast upper deck. In 1947 3,500hp R-4360-22W engines were fitted, with water injection (failure of which on Engines 3 and 4 almost caused a write-off). Eventually, in 1949 both aircraft were delivered to Navy transport squadron VR-44 at Alameda for use on the service

to Hawaii. Predictably, they proved underpowered and deficient in range, and though on one occasion No 85163 did

fly with 92 sailors on the upper deck, 76 on the lower and a crew of 12, these impressive aircraft spent most of their life on recruiting tours.

A few takeoffs were boosted by six rocket bottles clipped at the wing roots. They did a few Hawaiian runs in support of the Korean War, but were struck off charge in 1953.

By this time the Navy had the 5,550shp Pratt & Whitney T34 turboprop, about to be tested in a Navy R7V-2, and this could possibly have extended the life of these impressive machines.

DATA FOR R60-1:	
Span	189ft 11in (57.89m)
Length	156ft 1in (47.57m)
Wing area	3,610 sq ft (335.37m²)
Weight empty	114,575lb (51,971kg)
Maximum takeoff weight	184,000lb (83,462kg)
Cruising speed	269mph (433km/h)
Range	2,600 miles (4,184km)

T-33

TOP TRAINER
T33, T2V/T-1A

In late 1944 M. V. F. Short, vice-president military relations and the former V-P engineering at Vega, suggested that there would be a need for a jet trainer, and that the P-80 could serve as the basis of one. The reply was "Hell, Mac, the P-80 is the best fighter they've got; why make it a dodo ?" It was more than two years later that Lockheed risked $1 million of its own money carrying Short's idea into effect. On 22 March 1948 Tony LeVier made the first flight of the converted TP-80C from Van Nuys airport. Nobody expected his verdict: "It not only flies better than the single-seater, it's faster!"

Certainly nobody expected that, while Lockheed sold 1,718 F-80s, it would produce 5,691 of the trainer version, to which would be added 656 made by Canadair and 210 by Kawasaki.

The prototype was a P-80C, 48-356. Project engineer Don

Palmer added a 38.6in (98.04cm) plug ahead of the wing and a 12in (30.5cm) plug behind, but to accommodate the rear cockpit for the instructor it was still necessary to reduce fuselage tankage from 172.5gal (207 US gal, 784 litres) to 79.2gal (95 US gal, 360 litres).

Accordingly the wing tanks were just plain nylon bladders without self-sealing, giving a total internal capacity of 294gal (353 US gal, 1,336 litres), compared with the

354gal (425 US gal, 1,609 litres) of the F-80C. Standard F-80C external tanks were added under the wingtips.

The original engine was the 4,600lb (2,087kg) J33-23, but most later had the 5,400lb (2,449kg) J33-35. Dual controls were provided in the tandem cockpits under a one-piece canopy hinged up from the rear electrically. The pupil had a gunsight for the two 0.5in nose guns. Later the tip tanks were of the 192gal (230 US gal, 871 litre) type.

Like the first T-33s, Navy TV-2s initially came with F-80 tip tanks. The bare metal finish makes it easy to spot the fuselage plug ahead of the wing.

The TP-80C was restyled TF-80C in May 1948, three months before the first production trainer was accepted by the Air Force. On 5 May 1949 the designation changed again, to T-33A. The 5,691 aircraft were ordered in 28 production

Unlike the T2V flying chase, the T2V-1 SeaStar (foreground) was carrier-capable. The high profile canopy required a deep dorsal spine to restore rudder authority.

blocks funded in fiscal years 1948 to 1958 inclusive. They included 699 for the Navy, designated TV-2. Many aircraft were modified as RT-33 reconnaissance machines, AT-33 armed trainers, DT-33 drone directors, NT-33 test aircraft and, in the 1970s, QT-33 drones and targets. The airfame was remarkably adaptive.

In addition to all US armed forces the T-33A served with the air forces of 19 other countries. In 1998 a very small number were still active, and indeed in recent years various upgrade proposals have appeared.

In October 1952 Lockheed began a more thoroughgoing study into how the same basic design could be improved for the training role.

It repurchased a T-33A and rebuilt it into the Lockheed Trainer, registered N125D. First re-flown on 16 December 1953, this was in turn further improved as the first T2V-1 SeaStar for the Navy, cleared for deck landing. A total of 150 were built, powered by the 6,100lb (2,767kg) J33-24. Features included strengthened structure, blown flaps, slats, an enlarged tail, raised rear cockpit and new canopy, extensible nose leg and arrester hook. In 1962 the designation changed to T-1A.

DATA FOR T-33A:		
Span	**38ft 10.5in 11.85m**	
	(over tanks	42ft 10in, 13.055m)
Length	**37ft 9in (11.51m)**	
Wing area	**234.8 sq ft (21.8m²)**	
Weight empty	**8,365lb (3,794kg)**	
Maximum takeoff weight	**15,061lb (6,832kg)**	
Maximum speed	**600mph (966km/h)** at sea level	
Initial climb	**4,870ft (1,484m)/min**	
Service ceiling	**48,000ft (14,630m)**	
Range	**1,275 miles (2,052km)**	

Ordered by Northwest and PanAm off the drawing board, the success of the speedy Model 10 Electra ensured the survival of the Lockheed Aircraft Corporation. After being released by the airlines, many Model 10s continued to operate as executive transports and air taxis.

The retractable gear fitted to the Model 9 of 1931 was its only real fault: pilots kept forgetting to lower it for landing. The answer – panel lights and a warning horn – were pioneered with the Orion.

The 1937 Model 14 Super Electra (main picture) was at the leading edge of civil aircraft development. No other airliner could match it for sheer efficiency, though some pilots struggled to adjust to high wing loadings, Fowler flaps, feathering propellers and superchargers.

The Vega was the first in a pantheon of Lockheed greats. Rolled out of the company's Hollywood workshops on 4 July 1927, Vega No 1 vanished somewhere in the Pacific. This example (which lacks the wheel spats fitted to most Vegas), takes a bow for the camera at Burbank.

An upbeat 1945 publicity shot for the Big Dipper which, had it not crashed, could have rivalled more conventional designs. With its pusher propeller, the aircraft also had potential as a future *ab initio* military trainer.

The P-38's turbo-super-charged Allison V-1710 engines were amazingly quiet. With twin drop tanks (P-38F), they could fly 8-hr missions.

Opposite page top right: **Few warbirds are as complex as the P-38, or as satisfying to watch. Modern pilots find the view from the cockpit very restricted in every direction except straight ahead. (Photo: David Berryman)**

Opposite, main picture: **Also pictured on page 30, Lockheed's commemorative P-38J cruises over Burbank. With nose guns removed, YIPPEE was still operating from Van Nuys Airport in the mid 1960s.**

Left: **Busy scene at Burbank in 1950 as F-94A Starfire night/all-weather fighters are prepared for delivery. By this time electronics were having a serious impact on unit cost.**

Both XF-90 'heavy penetration fighters' were delivered to Edwards AFB for flight testing, which confirmed poor thrust from the twin J34 turbojets.

Martin-Baker GQ-7A ejection
seats became standard on the
F-104G for Nato.
(Photo: John Ailes)

Opposite, main picture: **F-104C fighter-bombers were equipped with FR probes and served briefly with Tactical Air Command, which provided KB-50J triple-hose tankers.**

Classic 'missile with a man in it' portrait of an F-104A pilot, complete with partial-pressure suit.

Spectacularly striped CF-104G of No 439 Sqn, Canadian Armed Forces, ready to pounce at a Nato Tiger Meet in the 1970s. (Photo: David Berryman)

The USAF's huge C-130 fleet includes a bewildering number of special versions. Most of the Hercules in service today are developments of the H model, which in 1964 was first put into production for the RNZAF. (The first export customer was the RAAF, which ordered 12 As in 1957.) The world's greatest tactical transport looks as good today as it did in 1954.

VOODOO HEX

In 1946 the USAF issued a specification for what it called a "penetration fighter", able to penetrate deep into hostile airspace either escorting bombers or attacking surface targets. Despite wild variations in the numerical requirements, Lockheed's advanced projects team, led in this case by XP-80 designers Don Palmer and Bill Ralston, not only competed but became one of the finalists with Lockheed Model 153 (the other was McDonnell, with the XP-88 Voodoo). In June 1946 a contract was received for two XP-90 prototypes, 46-687/8 (redesignated XF-90 in June 1948).

Having actually started to build a delta-wing aircraft, the design was almost started afresh and emerged as a traditional form but with swept-

Despite Lockheed's best efforts, the XF-90 failed to shine as a fighter but, as they say, 'provided much valuable data'.

XF-90

XF-90

back surfaces. The wing was swept at the fashionable 35°, and had a laminar profile of 8 per cent thickness. It was fitted with leading-edge slats (which stopped well away from the fuselage) and Fowler flaps inboard of hydraulically boosted ailerons. The tailplanes were swept at 40° and were fully powered, being mounted on pivots one-third of the way up the swept fin. A pitot boom was mounted on the pointed "needle nose" of the large fuselage, which had fixed sharp-lipped inlets to the two 3,000lb (1,361kg) Westinghouse J34-11 turbojets. The main landing gears resembled strengthened F-80 units, but the nose gear retracted forwards. Tanks between the engine ducts, in the wings and on jettisonable latches centred on the wingtips housed no less than 1,386.5gal (6,303 litres). Provision was made for six 20mm guns under the inlet ducts and for four underwing pylons, the inboard stations being stressed for 1,000lb (454kg) bombs. These loads combined with expected very high speeds resulted in widespread use of steel (for the sin-

gle main spars) and the new 75ST light alloy, with numerous heavy machined forgings.

Tony LeVier flew 46-687 at Edwards on 3 June 1949. Results were generally successful, though the heavy structure and inadequate engines resulted in poor flight performance. The second XF-90 was completed with J34-15 engines fitted with afterburners which increased thrust to 4,200lb (1,905kg), and these were retrofitted to the first aircraft. Eventually, with severe flight-control problems, the XF-90s were dived beyond Mach 1, a maximum of 1.12 being reached on 17 May 1950. Lack

of adequate engines made this visually attractive aircraft a non-starter. According to the 1950-51 Jane's the engines were "Westinghouse J46-3 . . . each rated at 6,000lb thrust". Such engines (and several other alternatives) were never fitted, and development was abandoned in September 1950.

Tony LeVier in 46-687, which he managed to push beyond Mach 1 when afterburners were fitted. The flight test programme would be terminated within just fifteen months of the first flight.

DATA FOR J34-15 ENGINES:	
Span (excluding tanks)	**39ft 2in (11.94m)**
Length	**56ft 2in (17.12m)**
Wing area	**345 sq ft (32.05m2)**
Weight empty	**18,050lb (8,187.5kg)**
Maximum takeoff weight	**31,060lb (14,089kg)**
Maximum speed	**668mph (1,075km/h)**
Range	**1,050 miles (1,690km)**

QUICK WORK

As related in the Introduction, Mac Short encountered well-meaning opposition when he suggested that the sleek F-80 should be turned into a trainer. Eventually USAF serial 48-356 took to the air on 22 March 1948 as the first T-Bird – the first of 6,637! Nobody expected this, and still less did they predict that 48-356 would make a third "first flight" on 16 April 1949 as the prototype YF-94 Starfire. (Unlike many Lockheed names, this was never written StarFire.)

Other unexpected events were the testing by the Soviet Union of an atomic bomb and the stately flypast over Red Square, Moscow, of copies of the B-29. These developments brought an obvious urgent need for a night and all-weather interceptor, but the Curtiss XF-87 had been rejected, the Northrop F-89 was years away, and the Air Force even evaluated the Navy F3D Skyknight. The interim answer was to emulate the RAF's lash-up Meteor and Vampire conversions and put radar into an established type. The

USAF invited Lockheed to try in December 1948, using the trainer (then called the TF-80C) as a basis, and requested the first production delivery within a year. Johnson assigned Russ Daniell as project engineer.

Afterburn

The YF-94 was a textbook exercise in rapid engineering. The most obvious change was to splice on a greatly enlarged nose to house the Hughes E-1 fire-control system, with APG-32 radar, whilst retaining the

six 0.5in guns. Flight controls in the rear cockpit were replaced by the radar operator's controls and displays. One of the bigger tasks, for Allison as well as Lockheed, was to fit an afterburning engine to retain performance despite the greater weight. Allison was already testing such engines, and with much help from Solar Aircraft at San Diego the J33-33 was quickly rated at 6,000lb (2,722kg) thrust for takeoff. The rear fuselage was enlarged to accommodate it, with a two-

The F-94B in its final configuration toting underwing gun pods, Fletcher tip tanks and APG-32 radar.

position nozzle with upper and lower eyelids worked by pneumatic rams. The engine drove a more powerful electric generator to supply current for the radar and fire-control.

"Proper" Development

Even before first flight the Air Force had ordered 110 F-94As. To reduce weight the Fletcher tip tanks were replaced by the underslung 137gal (165 US gal, 623-litre) pattern. Almost the only retrograde feature was that, to ease accommodation problems and get the centre of gravity in the right place, two guns had to be omitted. As promised, deliveries began in December 1949, and when war broke out in Korea in June 1950 the 319th All-Weather Fighter Squadron was working up. Backseaters learned how to give the pilot steering instructions, and on one of the first live practice interceptions a drone was shot down without the pilot ever seeing the target. Lockheed was keenly aware of the F-94's very limited endurance and modest firepower. It responded by delivering 357 F-94Bs with the Fletcher tanks restored and – usually after being passed to the Air National Guard in 1955 – a two-gun pod hung under each wing to double the firepower. Other upgrades included a Lear autopilot, ILS and a Zero Reader flight instrument to make the pilot's task much easier.

The F-94 had always been a quick lash-up to fill a temporary gap in the inventory.

Lockheed are an aggressive company, and decided to risk large sums seeing if they could develop this aircraft much further. To create the F-97A they constructed an extra F-94 fuselage and fitted it with a new wing with thickness/chord ratio reduced from 13 per cent to 10, with the structure almost completely "hogged" from solid metal. This raised critical Mach number from 0.8 to 0.85, and this in turn required that the horizontal tail should be swept back. Fuel capacity was increased to 1,270gal (1,526 US gal, 5,773 litres). To counter the great increase in weight Lockheed selected the Pratt & Whitney J48-5, rated with afterburner and water injection at 8,750lb (3,969kg). At first they could not get this Navy engine, so the YF-97 prototype first flew on 19 January 1950 with a Rolls-Royce Tay (from which the J48 was derived). During development Lockheed redesigned the speedbrakes, added a braking parachute and, after enormous effort, fitted the Hughes E-5 automatic fire control. This used the APG-40 radar to find a target and then steered the aircraft

automatically on a so-called "collision course", at the last moment firing a salvo of 24 Mighty Mouse rockets from four compartments round the nose, replacing the guns.

F-94C
From the YF-97 Lockheed developed the F-94C, of which 387 were delivered in 1952-54. Early in the production run

the radome was made more pointed, and in 1953 firepower was doubled by adding a 12-tube launcher under each wing. With a virtually unbreakable structure, F-94C pilots were cleared to dive beyond Mach 1, an unusual capability for an aircraft with a centrifugal engine. These remarkable aircraft did not leave the USAF and ANG until 1959.

DATA FOR F-94A & C:		
Span (ignoring tanks)	(A)	37ft 6in (11.43m)
	(C)	37ft 4in (11.38m)
Length	(A)	40ft 1in (12.22m),
	(C)	44ft 6in (13.56m)
Wing area	(A)	234.8 sq ft (21.81m²),
	(C)	232.8 sq ft (21.63m²)
Weight empty	(A)	9,572lb (4,342kg)
	(C)	12,708lb (5,764kg)
Maximum loaded weight	(A)	15,330lb (6,954kg)
	(C)	27,000lb (12,247kg)
Maximum speed	(A)	606mph (975km/h)
		at low level
	(C)	646mph (1,040km/h)
		at low level
		585mph (941km/h)
		at 35,000ft (10,668m)
Initial climb	(A)	11,274m (3,436m)/min
	(C)	7,980ft (2,432m)/min
Service ceiling	(A)	49,750ft (15,164m)
	(C)	51,400ft (15,667m);
Range, hi, drop tanks	(A)	1,079 miles (1,736km)
	(C)	1,275 miles (2,052km)

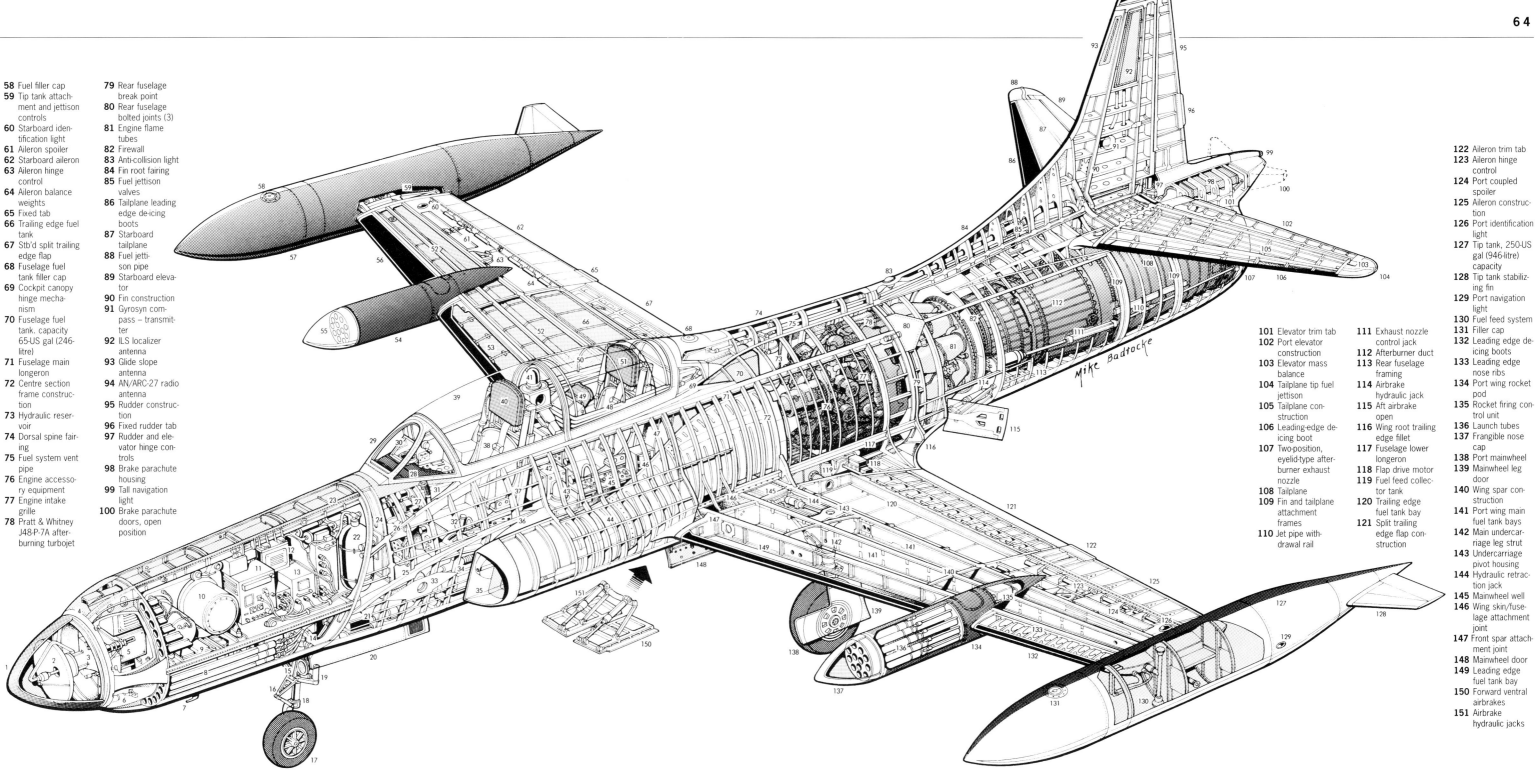

31 Control column
32 Engine throttle control
33 Pressure refu- elling connection
34 Air conditioning plant
35 Port engine air intake
36 Boundary layer bleed air duct
37 Cockpit framing
38 Pilot's ejection seat
39 Cockpit canopy cover
40 Ejection seat headrest
41 AN/ARN-6 radio compass loop antenna
42 Radar operator's AN/APG-40 indi- cator
43 Accelerometer
44 Intake ducting
45 Side console panel
46 Cockpit pressur- ization valve
47 Rear pressure bulkhead
48 Radar operator's blackout hood, folded
49 Radar viewing scope
50 Canopy mounted ADF sense aerial
51 Radar operator's ejection seat
52 Starboard wing main fuel tanks: total one-wing capacity (with 53 and 66). 129 US gal 488 litres)
53 Leading edge tank
54 Starboard wing rocket pod, 12x2.75-in (6.99-cm) rock- ets
55 Frangible nose cap
56 Leading edge de- icing boots
57 Tip tank.250-US gal (946-litre) capacity

58 Fuel filler cap
59 Tip tank attach- ment and jettison controls
60 Starboard iden- tification light
61 Aileron spoiler
62 Starboard aileron
63 Aileron hinge control
64 Aileron balance weights
65 Fixed tab
66 Trailing edge fuel tank
67 Stb'd split trailing edge flap
68 Fuselage fuel tank filler cap
69 Cockpit canopy hinge mecha- nism
70 Fuselage fuel tank. capacity 65-US gal (246- litre)
71 Fuselage main longeron
72 Centre section frame construc- tion
73 Hydraulic reser- voir
74 Dorsal spine fair- ing
75 Fuel system vent pipe
76 Engine accesso- ry equipment
77 Engine intake grille
78 Pratt & Whitney J48-P-7A after- burning turbojet

79 Rear fuselage break point
80 Rear fuselage bolted joints (3)
81 Engine flame tubes
82 Firewall
83 Anti-collision light
84 Fin root fairing
85 Fuel jettison valves
86 Tailplane leading edge de-icing boots
87 Starboard tailplane
88 Fuel jetti- son pipe
89 Starboard eleva- tor
90 Fin construction
91 Gyrosyn com- pass – transmit- ter
92 ILS localizer antenna
93 Glide slope antenna
94 AN/ARC-27 radio antenna
95 Rudder construc- tion
96 Fixed rudder tab
97 Rudder and ele- vator hinge con- trols
98 Brake parachute housing
99 Tall navigation light
100 Brake parachute- doors, open position

101 Elevator trim tab
102 Port elevator construction
103 Elevator mass balance
104 Tailplane tip fuel jettison
105 Tailplane con- struction
106 Leading-edge de- icing boot
107 Two-position, eyelid-type after- burner exhaust nozzle
108 Tailplane
109 Fin and tailplane attachment frames
110 Jet pipe with- drawal rail

111 Exhaust nozzle control jack
112 Afterburner duct
113 Rear fuselage framing
114 Airbrake hydraulic jack
115 Aft airbrake open
116 Wing root trailing edge fillet
117 Fuselage lower longeron
118 Flap drive motor
119 Fuel feed collec- tor tank
120 Trailing edge fuel tank bay
121 Split trailing edge flap con- struction

122 Aileron trim tab
123 Aileron hinge control
124 Port coupled spoiler
125 Aileron construc- tion
126 Port identification light
127 Tip tank, 250-US gal (946-litre) capacity
128 Tip tank stabiliz- ing fin
129 Port navigation light
130 Fuel feed system
131 Filler cap
132 Leading edge de- icing boots
133 Leading edge nose ribs
134 Port wing rocket pod
135 Rocket firing con- trol unit
136 Launch tubes
137 Frangible nose cap
138 Port mainwheel
139 Mainwheel leg door
140 Wing spar con- struction
141 Port wing main fuel tank bays
142 Main undercar- riage leg strut
143 Undercarriage pivot housing
144 Hydraulic retrac- tion jack
145 Mainwheel well
146 Wing skin/fuse- lage attachment joint
147 Front spar attach- ment joint
148 Mainwheel door
149 Leading edge fuel tank bay
150 Forward ventral airbrakes
151 Airbrake hydraulic jacks

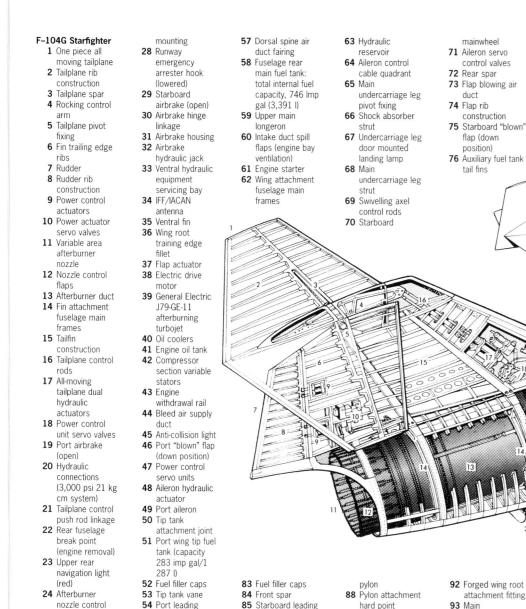

F–104G Starfighter

1 One piece all moving tailplane
2 Tailplane rib construction
3 Tailplane spar
4 Rocking control arm
5 Tailplane pivot fixing
6 Fin trailing edge ribs
7 Rudder
8 Rudder rib construction
9 Power control actuators
10 Power actuator servo valves
11 Variable area afterburner nozzle
12 Nozzle control flaps
13 Afterburner duct
14 Fin attachment fuselage main frames
15 Tailfin construction
16 Tailplane control rods
17 All-moving tailplane dual hydraulic actuators
18 Power control unit servo valves
19 Port airbrake (open)
20 Hydraulic connections (3,000 psi 21 kg cm system)
21 Tailplane control push rod linkage
22 Rear fuselage break point (engine removal)
23 Upper rear navigation light (red)
24 Afterburner nozzle control jacks
25 Brake parachute housing (open)
26 Lower rear navigation light (white)
27 Jet pipe thrust

28 Runway emergency arrester hook (lowered)
29 Starboard airbrake (open)
30 Airbrake hinge linkage
31 Airbrake housing
32 Airbrake hydraulic jack
33 Ventral hydraulic equipment servicing bay
34 IFF/IACAN antenna
35 Ventral fin
36 Wing root training edge fillet
37 Flap actuator
38 Electric drive motor
39 General Electric J79-GE-11 afterburning turbojet
40 Oil coolers
41 Engine oil tank
42 Compressor section variable stators
43 Engine withdrawal rail
44 Bleed air supply duct
45 Anti-collision light
46 Port "blown" flap (down position)
47 Power control servo units
48 Aileron hydraulic actuator
49 Port aileron
50 Tip tank attachment joint
51 Port wing tip fuel tank (capacity 283 imp gal/1 287 l)
52 Fuel filler caps
53 Tip tank vane
54 Port leading edge flap (lowered)
55 Wing pylon hardpoint
56 Port wing panel multi-spar construction

57 Dorsal spine air duct fairing
58 Fuselage rear main fuel tank: total internal fuel capacity, 746 Imp gal (3,391 l)
59 Upper main longeron
60 Intake duct spill flaps (engine bay ventilation)
61 Engine starter
62 Wing attachment fuselage main frames

63 Hydraulic reservoir
64 Aileron control cable quadrant
65 Main undercarriage leg pivot fixing
66 Shock absorber strut
67 Undercarriage leg door mounted landing lamp
68 Main undercarriage leg strut
69 Swivelling axel control rods
70 Starboard

71 Aileron servo control valves
72 Rear spar
73 Flap blowing air duct
74 Flap rib construction
75 Starboard "blown" flap (down position)
76 Auxiliary fuel tank tail fins

77 Starboard navigation light
78 Wing tip fuel tank
79 Starboard aileron
80 Aileron ten cylinder hydraulic actuator
81 Tip tank fuel connectors
82 Jettisonable tip tank attachment joint

83 Fuel filler caps
84 Front spar
85 Starboard leading edge flap (lowered)
86 Underwing fuel tank, capacity 283 Imp gal (1,287 l)
87 Starboard wing

mainwheel
pylon
88 Pylon attachment hard point
89 Starboard wing panel multi-spar construction
90 Leading-edge flap lock actuator and linkage
91 Wing root rib

92 Forged wing root attachment fittings
93 Main undercarriage hydraulic retraction jack
94 Wing root attachment longeron
95 Intake flank fuel

tanks
96 Access panels
97 Leading-edge flap electric actuator
98 Starboard position light
99 Intake ducting
100 Control cable runs
101 Fuel system piping

102 Gravity fuel filler cap
103 Port air intake duct
104 Fuselage access panels
105 Forward main fuel tank
106 Boundary layer spill duct
107 Starboard air intake duct framing
108 intake duct access door
109 Shock cone boundary layer

air ventral spill duct
110 Boundary layer air bleed slot
111 Fuselage centre line pylon
112 Practice bomb carrier
113 20-lb (9 8kg) practice bombs (four)
114 Starboard air intake
115 Fixed intake shock cone centre body
116 Forward auxiliary fuel tank

117 Auxiliary tank gravity filler
118 Ammunition bay hatch (open position)
119 Ammunition feed chute
120 M61 Vulcan 20-mm six-barrel rotary cannon
121 Cannon recoil mounting
122 Gun drive motor
123 Integrated IFF/UHF/TACAN aerial
124 Upper formation light (white)
125 Ammunition magazine (725 rounds)
126 Ram air turbine spring actuator

127 Ram air turbine door (open)
128 Emergency ram air turbine (hydraulic and electrical power)
129 Nose undercarriage shock absorber leg strut
130 Nosewheel (forward retracting)
131 LAU-3A rocket pack, 19x2.75-in (70-mm) FFAR
132 Kormoran air-to-surface anti-shipping missile
133 1,000-lb (454-kg) HE bomb
134 2.75-in (70mm) folding fin aircraft rockets (FFAR))
135 Nosewheel doors
136 Refrigeration unit ram air intake
137 Electrical equipment bay

M. Badrocke

UNFORGIVING MULTINATIONAL

The F-104 was like no other manned aircraft. Lockheed themselves called it "the missile with a man in it", and it was designed to fly the proverbial rings round any opponent. Unfortunately, its limitations in range, endurance, weapon capability and, above all, manoeuvrability made early versions of very limited value, except as a recruiting tool. Yet Lockheed's strength in marketing and diplomacy led to 2,578 being constructed.

It resulted from Johnson's visit to fighter pilots facing MiG-15s in Korea. To a man they said they would gladly do without such things as armour, an ejection seat, even a complex gunsight (one said "I'd settle for a piece of gum stuck on the windscreen") in order to outfly the Soviet aircraft. Johnson came back determined to give them unbeatable performance. He schemed the Model 83, later called the CL-246, Weapon System 303A and XF-104, named first StarFighter and finally Starfighter.

Engineering design began in November 1952, and the first XF-104, USAF 53-7786, was flown by Tony LeVier on 4 March 1954. Apart from the striking T-type tail it was virtually all fuselage. The tiny wing measured 7.5ft (2.29m) from the root, where it was bolted all the way along the numerous spars to fuselage rings, to the wingtip tank. It had a thickness/chord ratio of only 3.36 per cent, and the electrically powered drooping leading edge was so sharp as to be considered dangerous to ground crew. On the trailing edge were plain flaps blown with high-pressure air tapped from the engine, and ailerons driven by "piccolo" actuators with ten hydraulic rams all fitting into the available depth of just one inch (25.4mm).

The perfectly streamlined fuselage had an air inlet on each side to feed the Wright XJ65-6 (basically a British Sapphire) with afterburning thrust of 10,200lb (4,627kg). The body also housed the fuel, landing gears, a T-171 20mm "Gatling gun" and the cockpit

Italian F-104G with conventional stores, which are detailed overleaf.

**F-104S Starfighter
(Aeritalia)**
1 Pitot tube
2 Radome
3 Radar scanner
   dish
4 R21G/H multi-
   mode radar
   equipment
5 Radome
   withdrawal rails
6 Communications
   antenna
7 Cockpit front
   bulkhead
8 Infra-red sight
9 Windscreen
   panels
10 Reflector
   gunsight
11 Instrument panel
   shroud
12 Rudder pedals
13 Control column
14 Nose section
   frame
   construction
15 Control cable
   runs
16 Pilot's side
   console panel
17 Throttle control
18 Safety harness
19 Martin-Baker IQ-
   7A ejection seat
20 Face blind seat
   firing handle

21 Cockpit canopy
   cover
22 Canopy bracing
   struts
23 Seat rail support
   box
24 Angle of attack
   probe
25 Cockpit rear
   bulkhead
26 Temperature
   probe
27 Nosewheel doors
28 Taxying lamp
29 Nosewheel leg
   strut
30 Nosewheel
31 Steering linkage
32 AIM-7 Sparrow
   avionics
   (replacing M61
   gun installation of
   strike model)
33 Inertial platform
34 Avionics
   compartment
35 Avionics
   compartment
   shroud cover
36 Cockpit aft
   glazing

37 Ramair turbine
38 Emergency
   generator
39 Avionics
   compartment
   access cover
40 Fuselage frame
   construction
41 Pressure
   bulkhead
42 Ammunition
   compartment
   auxiliary fuel tank
   (101.6 Imp
   gal/462 litre
   capacity)
43 Fuel feed pipes
44 Flush-fitting UHF
   antenna panel
45 Anti-collision light
46 Starboard intake
47 Engine bleed air
   supply to air
   conditioning
48 Gravity fuel fillers

49 Fuselage main
   fuel tanks (total
   internal capacity
   746 Imp
   gal/3,391 litres)
50 Pressure
   refuelling adaptor
51 Intake shock
   cone centre body
52 De-iced intake lip
53 Port intake
54 Shock cone
   boundary layer
   bleed
55 Boundary layer
   bleed air duct
56 Auxiliary intake
57 Hinged auxiliary
   intake door

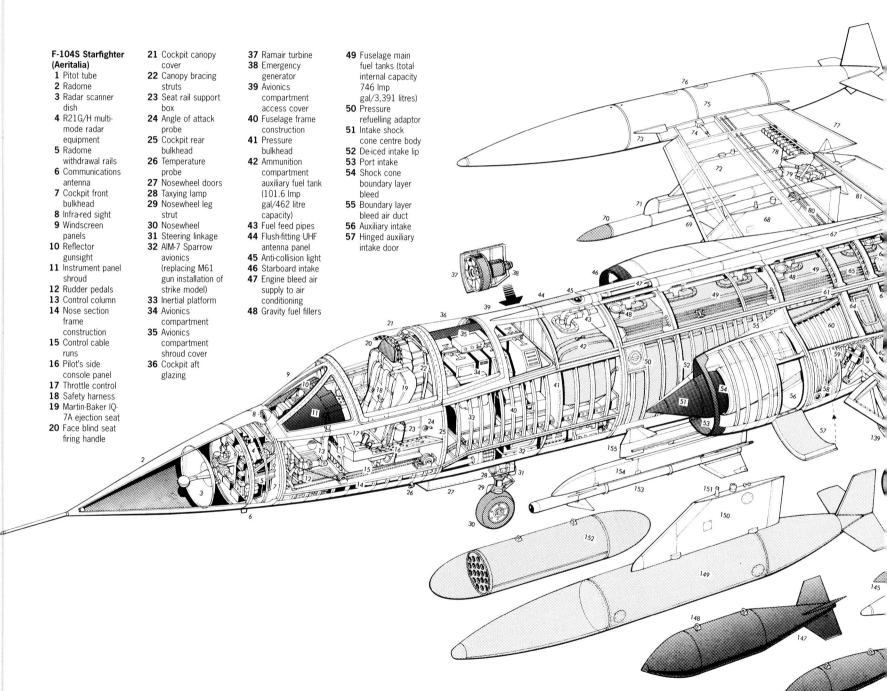

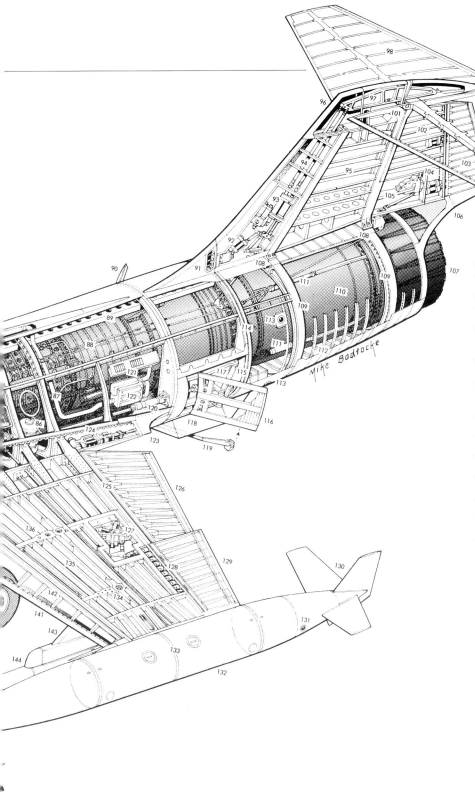

58 Navigation light
59 Leading edge flap jack
60 Intake trunking
61 Fuselage main longeron
62 Wing root attaching members
63 Intake flank fuel tanks
64 Wing-mounting fuselage mainframes
65 Control cable runs
66 Electrical junction box
67 Dorsal spine fairing
68 Starboard inboard pylon
69 Leading edge flap (lowered)
70 AIM-7 Sparrow AAM
71 Missile launch rail
72 Starboard outer pylon
73 Tip tank vane
74 Tip tank latching unit
75 Starboard wingtip tank
76 Fuel filler caps
77 Starboard aileron
78 Aileron power control jacks
79 Power control servo valves
80 Fuel lines to auxiliary tanks
81 Flap blowing duct
82 Starboard blown flap (lowered)
83 Engine intake compressor face

84 Intake spill flaps
85 Aileron torque shaft
86 Hydraulic reservoir
87 Air conditioning bleed air supply pipe
88 General Electric J79-GE-19 turbojet
89 Engine withdrawal rail
90 Starboard airbrake (open)
91 Fin root fillet
92 Elevator servo controls
93 Elevator/all moving tailplane hydraulic jacks
94 Push-pull control rods
95 Tailfin construction
96 Fin tip fairing
97 Tailplane rocking control arm
98 Starboard tailplane
99 One-piece tailplane construction
100 Tailplane spar
101 Tailplane spar central pivot
102 Fin trailing-edge construction
103 Rudder construction
104 Rudder power control jacks
105 Rudder servo valves
106 Exhaust shroud
107 Fully-variable afterburner exhaust nozzle

108 Fin attachment joints
109 Fin-carrying mainframes
110 Afterburner duct
111 Nozzle control jacks
112 Steel and titanium aft fuselage construction
113 Rear navigation lights
114 Aft fuselage attachment joint
115 Brake parachute housing
116 Port airbrake (open)
117 Airbrake scissor links
118 Fuselage strake (both sides)
119 Emergency runway arrester hook
120 Airbrake jack
121 Air exit louvres
122 Primary heat exchanger
123 Wing root trailing edge fillet
124 Flap hydraulic jack
125 Flap blowing slot
126 Port blown flap (lowered)
127 Aileron servo valves
128 Aileron power control jacks
129 Port aileron
130 Tip tank fins
131 Port navigation light
132 Port wing tip fuel tank (283 Imp gal/ 1287 litre capacity)

133 Fuel filler caps
134 Outboard pylon mounting rib
135 Wing multi-spar construction
136 Inboard pylon mounting rib
137 Main undercarriage leg door
138 Shock absorber strut
139 Swivel axle control rods
140 Port mainwheel
141 Leading edge flap (lowered)
142 Leading edge flap rib construction
143 Port outboard pylon
144 Missile launch rail
145 Port AIM-7 Sparrow AAM
146 Mk 82 500-lb (226-kg) bomb
147 Mk 83 1,000-lb (454-kg) bomb
148 Bomb-mounting shackles
149 Auxiliary fuel tank (163 Imp gal/740 litre capacity)
150 Port inboard wing pylon
151 Pylon attachments
152 LAU-3A 2 751n (70-mm) FFAR pod (19 rockets)
153 AIM-9 Sidewinder AAM
154 Missile launch rail
155 Fuselage stores pylon adaptor

with a seat which, because of the tail, ejected downwards. In the nose was an ASG-14 ranging radar linked to the MA-10 sight. Flight-test problems were numerous. On 17 February 1956 Herman 'Fish' Salmon made the first flight of the first of 15 YF-104As. This was also the first flight of an aircraft designed for the brilliant General Electric J79 engine, in this application with an afterburning rating of 14,800lb (6,713kg). Though it looked like a slightly enlarged XF, the YF was totally redesigned. Among other things the wingtips could exchange tanks for Sidewinder missiles, and the engine inlets were fitted with axially sliding half-cone centrebodies to control the hurricane of air that either entered the engine or left via the ejector ring round the variable afterburner nozzle. Performance was tremendous, but flight development was punctuated by accidents. It was small wonder that one of the 155 F-104As of Tactical Air Command set a world speed record at 1,404mph (2,259km/h) while an F-104C, with FR probe, three tank/bomb pylons and a J79-7 engine, zoomed to 103,396ft (31,515m). Mitsubishi made the similar F-104J, and the F-104B and D were dual trainer versions. But production might have stopped at 271 had Lockheed not been determined to develop the basic aircraft into the F-104G multirole tactical aircraft for the reborn Luftwaffe. Powered by the J79-11A rated at 15,600lb (7,076kg), the G had a strengthened airframe, larger powered rudder, Nasarr radar, inertial navigation, C-2 upward-ejection seat, combat manoeuvre flaps and five pylons to carry weapon loads up to 4,000lb (1,814kg). Huge production schemes embraced not only West Germany but also Canada, Belgium, the Netherlands and Italy. Among many versions were the RF-104G produced to map the NATO area to allow F-104Gs to drop nuclear weapons by inertial guidance alone.

Italy went on to develop the final version, the F-104S. This was an all-weather interceptor, with R21G radar and nine attachment points for a total load of external stores of 7,500lb (3,402kg), which could include Sparrow or Aspide radar-guided missiles. Powered by the J79-19 rated at 17,900lb (8,119kg), it took off at over 350mph (563km/h), with a wing loading of 158 lb/sq ft (772kg/m2). Aeritalia delivered 246 in 1968-79.

The abiding memory of the F-104 is of flashing performance gained at the cost of unforgiving handling. In the early 1960s the Luftwaffe suffered, on average, 139 writeoffs per 100,000 hours, and the definition of an optimist was "A Starfighter pilot worried about dying of cancer". Even in 1967 there was a total loss roughly every ten days, and to reduce the fatalities the seats were replaced by the Martin-Baker GQ-7, after four years of bitter opposition by Lockheed and the USAF.

There were numerous special versions, including the NF-104A trainers for NASA Astronauts fitted with booster rocket engines. Lockheed failed to market many others, notably the CL-704 jet-lift V/STOL project and the turbofan CL-1200 Lancer with a bigger wing.

DATA FOR F-104 STARFIGHTER:

Span		**21ft 9in (6.63m)**
Length		**54ft 8in (16.66m)**
Wing area		**196.1 sq ft (18.2m²)**
Weight empty	(A)	**12,562lb (5,698kg)**
	(G)	**13,996lb (6,349kg)**
	(S)	**14,900lb (6,759kg)**
Maximum takeoff weight	(A)	**19,600lb (8,891kg)**
	(G)	**29,038lb (13,172kg)**
	(S)	**31,000lb (14,062kg)**
Maximum speed, clean, at high		
altitude (except S) typically		**1,146mph (1,844km/h)**
	(S)	**1,450mph (2,333km/h)**
Initial climb	(A)	**60,395ft (18,408m)/min**
	(G)	**48,000ft (14,630m)/min**
	(S)	**55,000ft (16,764m)/min**
Normal range,		
hi, two tanks	(A)	**730 miles (1,175km)**
	(G)	**1,080 miles (1,738km)**
	(S)	**1,550 miles (2,494km)**

HALF-WAY HOUSE

After World War 2 numerous curious German projects led designers in several countries to study the problems of VTOL (vertical takeoff and landing) aircraft. Such aircraft could operate from secure bases in forests or even city centres, and also from many kinds of ship without needing a large flight deck. The start of the Korean war in June 1950 resulted in military budgets being sharply increased, and later in that year the Navy asked for proposals for a combat aircraft able to operate from small decks.

For the moment jet engines appeared not to offer sufficient ratio of thrust to weight, but this was not the case with turboprops. Convair and Lockheed responded with proposals for unique aircraft – basically seen as having the potential for development into fighters – built around the 7,500shp Allison T54, driving eight-blade contra-rotating propellers. The idea was that the aircraft should be parked in the vertical attitude, standing on four small wheels mounted on cruciform tail surfaces. The pilot would enter via a long ladder and strap into a pivoted seat. At full power the thrust would overcome the weight. The pilot would then progressively push the aircraft over into the horizontal attitude, with the weight supported by the wing. A normal aeroplane in combat, it would then recover to the ship by reducing speed and transferring lift from the wing to the upward thrust of the propellers. The pilot then had to juggle engine power whilst descending vertically, tail-first.

Two examples were ordered of Lockheed's Model 081-40, receiving Navy designation XFV-1 (V for Lockheed, not vertical). The stumpy fuselage terminated in the large cruciform tail mounted at 45°, with the movable surfaces combining to control the aircraft in partnership with ailerons on the short equi-tapered wings. Pending availability of the T54 engine, the first prototype was fitted with an Allison T40-6 with a brochure rating of 5,850hp but actually giving 5,100hp. Pods on the wingtips housed a proportion of the 423gal (1,923 litres) of fuel and

instrumentation. In a production aircraft they were to house either 48 rockets or four 20mm guns. Lacking adequate power for safe vertical flight, the first XFV-1 (BuNo 138657) was fitted with clumsy fixed landing gear for conventional flight testing from an Edwards runway. Herman "Fish" Salmon made a brief hop on 23 December 1953, but the first of 32 real flights took place on 16

The XFV-1 tail-sitter being erected. VTOL was never actually attempted, but hovering flight was achieved after conventional T.O.

June 1954. The idea was soon seen as a non-starter, though Salmon (see page 147) did manage brief hovers.

Cancelled in June 1955, No 138657 rests in the San Diego Aerospace Museum.

DATA FOR XFV-1:	
Span	30ft 10.15in (9.4m)
Length	36ft 10.25in (11.233m)
Wing area	246 sq ft (22.85m²)
Weight empty	11,599lb (5,261kg)
Maximum takeoff weight	16,221lb (7,358kg)
Maximum speed (estimated)	580mph (933km/h)
Range (estimated)	420 miles (676km)

U-2/TR-1

DRAGON LADY

In 1953 the Soviet Union tested its first thermonuclear weapon, and it was obvious to the USA that before long hostile strategic bombers and missiles would be armed with such devices. This underlined the urgent need for the ability to overfly the Soviet landmass in order to monitor progress. The task called for aircraft with unprecedented high-altitude capability, yet able to carry the giant cameras that were just becoming available. Largely because of the lobbying of 'Kelly' Johnson, and his promise of a prototype within eight months, the task was given to Lockheed's Skunk Works.

The customer was the Central Intelligence Agency; the USAF continued to fund the rival Bell X-16. As a cover the Lockheed project, the CL-282, was given the utility designation of U-2, though nothing was disclosed publicly. It was expected that several would be built and

used for a brief period (Johnson thought about two years). In the utmost secrecy the work went ahead at the end of 1954. At the remote airfield at Groom Lake, Nevada, Tony LeVier made a brief hop in the prototype U-2 (Article 341) on 1 August 1955, following with the first real flight four days later. The U-2 resembled a large jet-propelled glider. The fuselage was an enlarged version of that of the XF-104, with bays for cameras in the nose and behind the cockpit, a twin-wheel main landing gear and tiny twin tailwheels, and a Pratt & Whitney J57-37 turbo-

jet of 10,500lb (4,763kg) thrust. The most striking feature was the wing, with an aspect ratio of 10.6. Like the rest of the aircraft, weight was pared to the bone, and only the most gentle manoeuvres were permitted.

To save weight, not only was the airframe designed to a lower factor than any other jet aircraft but the cockpit was unpressurized and fitted with an ordinary seat, occupied by a pilot inside a full-pressure suit. The centreline landing gear was augmented by simple "pogo units" under the wings which were jettisoned after

Most U-2Rs have received new engines and sensor upgrades to become U-2Ss.

takeoff. The aircraft landed on the centreline gears, and at the end of the landing run rocked gently over on to one of its downturned wingtips. Flight controls were manual, and the side-hinged canopy was opened by hand.

In 1956, with ten aircraft flying, it was announced that the U-2 was "A simple research aircraft of the National Advisory Committee for Aeronautics". A photograph was released in February 1957 with "NACA 320" painted on the tail.

Instead of a handful of aircraft serving for about two years, the U-2 proved so useful that the prototype has been followed by 104 further aircraft which have served in many versions and in many roles all over the world. The first 55, built in 1955-58, included 35 for the USAF (the rest being covert CIA aircraft). Most were initially powered by the Pratt & Whitney J57 turbojet, initially the J57-37 of 10,500lb thrust and later the J57-31A of 11,200lb (5,080kg). In 1958 growth in the weight of sensor payloads, including new cameras and various electronic sensors, resulted in aircraft being upgraded to U-2B and various later standards with the J75-13 rated at 15,800lb (7,167kg), later increased in stages to 18,500lb (8,392kg). One, 56-6693, was shot down over Sverdlovsk on 1 May 1960. This blew the cover and temporarily reduced U-2 activity.

At that time 21 aircraft had been lost from various causes, and there was an urgent need for more, with greater payload capability. The situation was complicated by existence of the rival RB-57F and Lockheed's own Oxcart (A-12) programme, but, cutting a long story short, eventually 12 larger aircraft designated U-2R were ordered. The first, 68-10329, flew on 28 August 1967. In 1981-89 Lockheed delivered a further batch comprising seven U-2Rs, a U-2RT trainer, 25 TR-1As, two dual-control TR-1Bs and two ER-2 Earth-Resource aircraft for the civilian agency NASA (which for a time operated a third, originally a TR-1A). In October 1991 the TR-1 designation was dropped, all aircraft being restyled U-2R.

These aircraft have operated with more than 40 sensor installations for many purposes. Most are equipped with large wing pods to supplement the available sensor volume. The largest payloads are the ASARS-2 (Advanced Synthetic-Aperture Radar System) and Senior Span in a giant container mounted on a pylon above the fuselage.

In 1969 one aircraft successfully completed carrier qualification from USS *America*, but, so far as is known, this capability has not yet been used operationally. Whereas the J75 engine was the key to the later enlarged aircraft, this engine was increasingly seen as heavy and inefficient (it dated from 1949) and in 1989 Lockheed began testing an aircraft re-engined with a derivative of the General Electric F101.

Today many surviving aircraft (not all) have been brought up to U-2S standard, powered by the GE F118-101 turbofan rated at 17,000lb (7,711kg). This engine is lighter and more fuel-efficient than the J75. To this day the "Dragon Lady" continues to play a vital role in many military and civilian tasks, most involving some form of high-altitude surveillance.

Operations over Iraq have hit the headlines, but there are many others. NASA is even considering extending the wings of its ER-2s in order to reach 80,000ft (24,384m). There are four dual-control aircraft designated TR-1S which continue to train pilots for service into the next millenium.

DATA FOR U-2A:

Span	80ft 2in (24.435m)
Length	49ft 9in (15.16m)
Wing area	565 sq ft (52.49m²)
Weight empty	12,480lb (5,661kg)
Maximum takeoff weight	22,100lb (10,025kg)
Typical operating condition	400mph (644km/h) at 65,000ft (19,812m)
Range	2,880 miles (4,635km)

DATA FOR TR-1S:

Span	103ft 0in (31.39m)
Length (most)	62ft 9in (19.13m)
Wing area about	995 sq ft (92.44m²)
Weight empty (typical)	15.200lb (6,895kg)
Maximum takeoff weight	41,000lb (18,598kg)
Typical operating condition	440mph (708km/h) at 72,000ft (21,946m)
Range about	4,800 miles (7,725km)

U-2R/TR-1

1 Radome
2 Side-looking radar antenna
3 Radar mounting
4 Interchangeable nose section, SLAR installation shown
5 Radar transmitting and receiving equipment
6 ADC equipment
7 TACAN
8 Autopilot equipment
9 Pitot head, port and starboard
10 Downward vision periscope/driftsight
11 Cockpit front pressure bulkhead
12 Underfloor control linkages
13 Cockpit pressure floor
14 Rudder pedals
15 Circuit breaker panel
16 Instrument panel
17 Instrument panel shroud
18 Windscreen panels
19 Periscope/driftsight viewer
20 Control column handwheel
21 Canopy hinged to port
22 Rear view mirror
23 Canopy ultra-violet shield
24 Cockpit air circulation fan
25 Pilot's ejection seat
26 Engine throttle lever
27 Side console panel
28 Cockpit rear bulkhead
29 Q- bay mission equipment space
30 Q-bay lower pressurised hatch

31 Equipment air conditioning
32 Forward fuselage frame construction
33 Astro – inertial navigation system equipment package
34 Q-bay upper pressurised hatch
35 Starboard air intake
36 Q- bay rear pressurised bulkhead
37 E-bay hatch
38 UHF equipment
39 Boundary layer air duct
40 Liquid oxygen converter
41 Air conditioning system ram air intake
42 Intake duct framing
43 Intake spill air louvres
44 Mainwheel doors
45 Hydraulic retraction jack
46 Twin nosewheels
47 Main undercarriage leg strut
48 Landing/taxying lamps
49 Main undercarriage pivot fixing
50 Engine bay fireproof bulkhead
51 Intake compressor face
52 Hydraulic pumps
53 Fuselage upper longeron
54 Cockpit air conditioning plant
55 Heat exchanger air outlet
56 UHF aerial
57 Inner wing tank fuel filler cap

58 Starboard wing inner integral fuel tank
59 Starboard wing equipment pod
60 Equipment pod interchangeable sections
61 TR1 B trainer variant, nose section
62 Instructor's raised canopy
63 Wing leading - edge retractable stall strip
64 Outrigger "Pogo" wheel unit, jettisoned on take-off
65 Dry bay
66 Outer wing tank filler cap
67 Starboard wing outboard integral fuel tank
68 Wing tip folding section hinge rib, manual folding
69 Outer wing panel dry bay
70 Wing tip landing skid
71 Starboard navigation light
72 Wing tip sensor pod (TR-1)
73 Starboard wing tip folded position, ground handling
74 Starboard aileron
75 Aileron tab
76 Fuel jettison
77 ECM aerial
78 Starboard spoilers/lift dumpers, open
79 Three-segment plain flap, down position
80 Starboard ELINT (electronic intelligence) alternative wing pod
81 Equipment pod tail fairing
82 Inboard two-segment plain

flap, down position
83 Centre fuselage frame construction
84 Engine oil tank
85 Engine bleed air blow-off valve
86 Wing root attachment rib
87 Engine bay sump tanks (two)
88 Wing panel attachment joints
89 Machined fuselage main frames
90 Fuel pumps and flowmeters
91 Wing root trailing-edge fillet
92 Pratt & Whitney J75- P – 138 nonafterburning turbojet
93 Anti -collision light
94 Fuselage skin panelling
95 Rear fuselage break point, engine removal
96 Cooling air scoop
97 Communications equipment bay
98 Elevator control rod
99 Fin root fillet
100 Tailplane leading-edge skin external stiffeners
101 Starboard trimming tailplane
102 Starboard elevator
103 Leading – edge HF aerial
104 Tailfin construction
105 Tail navigation light
106 Fin tip sensors
107 Rudder horn balance
108 Rudder rib construction
109 Fixed rudder tab

110 Fin/tailplane attachment joint
111 Tailplane sealing plate
112 Rudder and elevator control linkages
113 Trimming tailplane jack
114 Tailcone ECM equipment bay
115 Elevator trim tab

116 Port elevator construction
117 Elevator horn balance
118 Tailplane construction
119 Convergent-divergent augmentor exhaust nozzle
120 Tail assembly attachment main frame

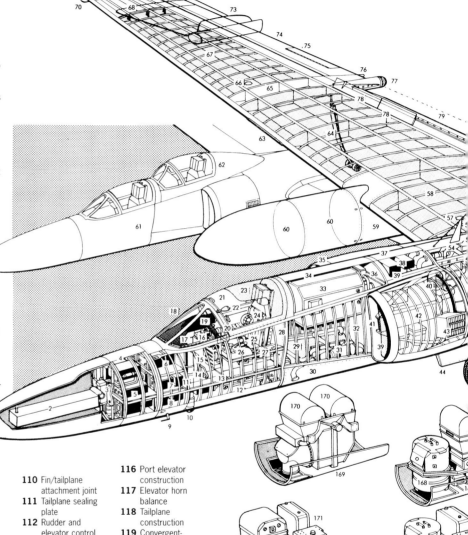

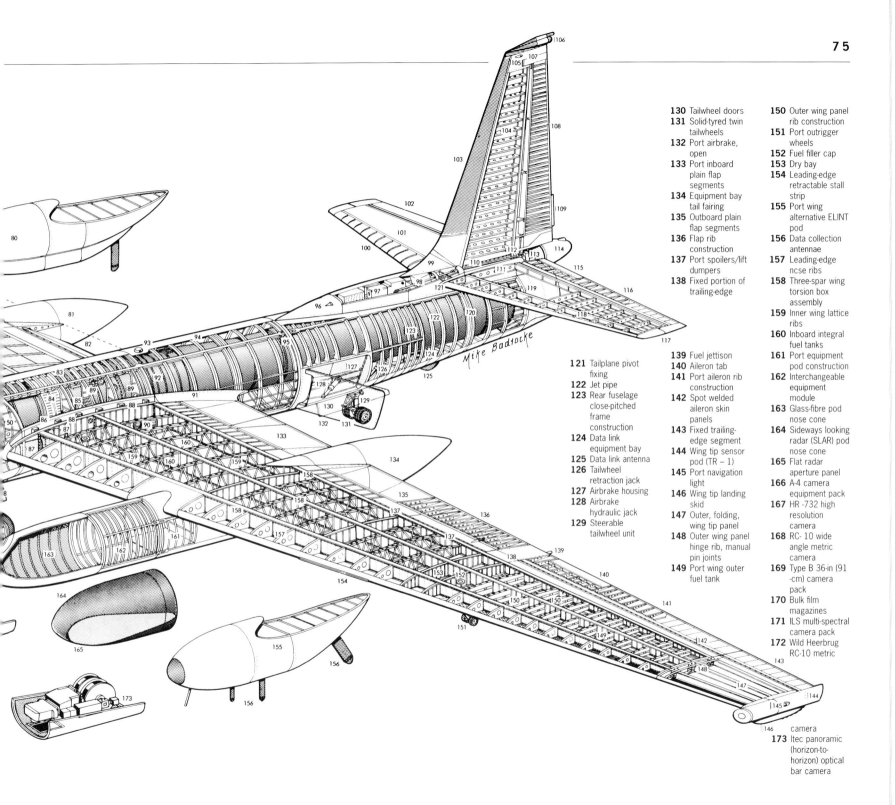

130 Tailwheel doors
131 Solid-tyred twin tailwheels
132 Port airbrake, open
133 Port inboard plain flap segments
134 Equipment bay tail fairing
135 Outboard plain flap segments
136 Flap rib construction
137 Port spoilers/lift dumpers
138 Fixed portion of trailing-edge

121 Tailplane pivot fixing
122 Jet pipe
123 Rear fuselage close-pitched frame construction
124 Data link equipment bay
125 Data link antenna
126 Tailwheel retraction jack
127 Airbrake housing
128 Airbrake hydraulic jack
129 Steerable tailwheel unit

139 Fuel jettison
140 Aileron tab
141 Port aileron rib construction
142 Spot welded aileron skin panels
143 Fixed trailing-edge segment
144 Wing tip sensor pod (TR – 1)
145 Port navigation light
146 Wing tip landing skid
147 Outer, folding, wing tip panel
148 Outer wing panel hinge rib, manual pin joints
149 Port wing outer fuel tank

150 Outer wing panel rib construction
151 Port outrigger wheels
152 Fuel filler cap
153 Dry bay
154 Leading-edge retractable stall strip
155 Port wing alternative ELINT pod
156 Data collection antennae
157 Leading-edge ncse ribs
158 Three-spar wing torsion box assembly
159 Inner wing lattice ribs
160 Inboard integral fuel tanks
161 Port equipment pod construction
162 Interchangeable equipment module
163 Glass-fibre pod nose cone
164 Sideways looking radar (SLAR) pod nose cone
165 Flat radar aperture panel
166 A-4 camera equipment pack
167 HR -732 high resolution camera
168 RC- 10 wide angle metric camera
169 Type B 36-in (91 -cm) camera pack
170 Bulk film magazines
171 ILS multi-spectral camera pack
172 Wild Heerbrug RC-10 metric camera
173 Itec panoramic (horizon-to-horizon) optical bar camera

MODEL 329 JETSTAR

NEW AGE TRAVEL

After World War 2 the market for corporate and executive aircraft grew rapidly, fed largely by conversions of small transports and, especially, high-speed wartime medium bombers. It was obvious that such vehicles would one day be swept away by turboprops and jets, and in 1956 the chance came with the announcement by the USAF that, when the budget permitted, it was interested in aircraft meeting the UCX specification for a multi-role small jet able to carry up to ten passengers or urgent cargo, or trainee navigators, to fly 2,000 miles at 500mph. At company risk Lockheed built two Model 329 prototypes, flying the first on 4 September 1957.

Power was provided by two 4,850lb Bristol Orpheus turbojets (planned to be produced in the USA as the Wright TJ37) hung on the sides of the rear fuselage, The wing had 30° sweep at quarter-chord, lead-

ing-edge flaps, and double-slotted trailing-edge flaps. The fully pressurized fuselage provided a passenger cabin 28ft 2.5in (8.6m) long and 74.5in (1,892mm) wide, with a speed brake hinged under the rear. The main landing gears had twin wheels and retracted inwards hydraulically. Flight controls were hydraulically boosted, and the tailplane incidence could be adjusted for trimming by pivoting the fin.

Flight testing was exceptionally successful, but the Orpheus was never made in the USA, so for the production Model 1329 Lockheed switched to four 3,000lb Pratt & Whitney JT12A-6 turbojets, in side-by-side pairs fitted with thrust reversers.

Other changes included addition of rubber-boot wing and tail de-icers, a twin-wheel nose gear and addition of prominent 470gal (565 US gal,

The Model 329 was in a class of its own for room, range and rapidity; fan-powered JetStars rival later-generation Gulfstreams and Falcons.

2,138 litre) non-jettisonable tanks centred on the wings.

Lockheed had the nerve to put the JetStar into production, as the Model 1329 JetStar 6, at what was then the company's Georgia Division. It picked up orders which eventually included the USAF and Navy for various versions of C-140. From No 97 the aircraft became the JetStar 8, with 3,300lb JT12A-8 engines. In 1974 AiResearch refitted a Jet-Star 6 with its TFE731 geared turbofan engine, rated at 3,700lb and offering major advantages in fuel economy and reduced noise. Many aircraft were converted, and Lockheed switched to the TFE731 in the Model 2329 Jet-Star II.

This also featured a fuel capacity increased from 2,215gal (2,660 US gal, 10,069 litres) to 2,237gal (2,686 US gal, 10,168 litres) despite the slipper tanks being underslung and faired off under the wing.

Lockheed produced 204 Jet-Stars, most of which were still flying after various upgrades in 1998. On 5 September 1986 AAI flew the prototype FanStar, re-engined with two General Electric CF34-1A engines derated from their usual 8,650lb to about 7,500lb, but this remained a prototype. Though Lockheed were certainly pointing the way forward.

DATA FOR JETSTAR:

Span	54ft 5in (16.59m)
Length	60ft 5in (18.415m)
Wing area	542.5 sq ft (50.40m²)
Weight empty	24,750lb (11,227kg)
Maximum takeoff weight	44,500lb (20,185kg)
Cruising speed	504mph (811km/h)
Range	2,995 miles (4,820km)

Four jets and mid-wing external fuel tanks make JetStars unique amongst business jets. In service, few pilots would contemplate this kind of manoeuvre – it might spill the gin and tonic.

ILL-STARRED TURBOPROP

L-188 ELECTRA

In the early 1950s Lockheed studied various jet and turboprop civil transports, without eliciting interest from US airlines. In 1954 Capital Airlines asked if Lockheed could produce a rival to the British Viscount, but Lockheed saw no obvious market. Capital accordingly bought 60 Viscounts, and this cerainly helped jolt the US carriers out of their lethargy. Late in 1954

American issued a specification for an aircraft powered by four turboprops and seating 75, to which Lockheed offered the CL-310. After repeated revisions to increase capacity, speed and range, American signed for 35 Electras on 8 June 1955 (the first order for a US turbine-engined civil transport), followed by 40 for Eastern nearly four months later.

The first L-188 Electra made its maiden flight at Burbank on 6 December 1957, and FAA certification was granted ahead of schedule on 22 August 1958. The engines were four Allison 501D-13s each rated at 3,460shp (3,750ehp) driving Aeroproducts reversing propellers with four "paddle" blades (the only European customer, KLM, chose Hamilton propellers). These engines had a power section similar to the T56, but the propeller gearbox

was below the axis of the engine instead of above; thus, the air inlet was above the spinner instead of below. Each engine was mounted high on the wing, with the jetpipe going straight over the top to the trailing edge.

Trans-Australia Airlines (TAA) bought the modified Electra II. Soon replaced as passenger aircraft, Electras excelled as freighters.

The wing was of remarkably short span, and featured machined skins, boosted ailerons and Fowler flaps. The twin-wheel main landing gears and steerable nose unit all retracted forwards hydraulically. Integral tanks held 4,596gal (5,515 US gal, 20,892 litres) of fuel. Unlike the Constellation, the fuselage had a constant circular section of 11ft 4in (3.45m) diameter, seating 66-98 passengers, with an integral airstairs door.

Eastern flew the first service on 12 January 1959. By this time major carriers were more interested in jets. Moreover, within 14 months three Electras had crashed. The FAA ordered a reduction in cruising speed to 295mph (475km/h), and it was discovered that the cause was a whirl mode oscillation of the propeller and engine which within a few seconds could lead to wing flexure causing separation of the complete wing at the root. Lockheed redesigned the structure, but by this time the Electra was unsaleable.

Total sales comprised 116 L-188As and 54 L-188Cs with slightly greater fuel capacity. Fortunately for Lockheed, the same airframe served as the basis for the P-3 Orion.

When the Electra first flew turboprops seemed logical for short/medium routes.

DATA FOR L-188:		
Span		99ft 0in (30.18m)
Length		104ft 6in (31.85m)
Wing area		1,300 sq ft (120.77m2)
Weight empty	(A)	57,300lb (25,990kg)
	(C)	57,400lb (26,037kg)
Maximum takeoff weight	(A)	113,000lb (51,257kg)
	(C)	116,000lb (52,618kg)
Cruising speed		373mph (600km/h)
Range	(A)	2,770 miles (4,458km)
		with 18,000lb (8,165kg) payload
	(C)	3,500 miles (5,630km)
		with 11,200lb (5,080kg) payload

P-3 ORION

SUB BUSTER

In 1957 the US Navy issued a requirement for a long-range land-based ASW (anti-submarine warfare) and maritime patrol aircraft. Lockheed's proposal for an aircraft based on the Electra was an easy winner. Not only did the company have unrivalled experience with the Neptune, but a derivative aircraft promised reduced risk, lower costs and quicker development.

The YP3V-1 first flew on 19 August 1958. This was little more than the third Electra modified with a dummy weapons bay and MAD (magnetic-anomaly detection) boom projecting behind the tail. The first production Model 185, designated P3V-1 until September 1962 and P-3A thereafter, flew on 15 April 1961. Compared with the Electra it had Allison T56-10W engines rated at 4,180shp (4,500ehp) with water injection, driving Hamilton propellers. The fuselage remained fully pressurized, but it was shortened ahead of the wing, and instead of putting in a capacious Nimrod-type

weapon bay the decision was taken to incorporate a shallow bay ahead of the wing and add eight pylons under the outer wings and two under the wing roots to bring the total weapon load up to 20,000lb (9,072kg). The wing is de-iced by engine bleed and the tail by electric heaters. Typically the P-3 is flown by a flight crew of five, the centre fuselage forming the tactical compartment with a separate five-man mission crew. At the extreme rear is a dinette and two folding bunks.

Lockheed built 157 of the initial P-3A version, which entered service in August 1962. Among the host of navaids and sensors were the APS-80 search radar in the nose, the ASQ-10 MAD in the tip of the tail boom and an ASR-3 detector sensitive to the exhaust of snorkelling submarines. These items are among many which were later updated, and most P-3As were later converted into CP-3A transports, EP-3A/-3B/-3E electronic monitoring and surveillance aircraft, RP-3A

Normally solitary, P-3Cs of the RAN demonstrate how to fly box formation. No 4 is stepped down to stay clear of turbulence.

oceanographic platforms, TP-3A trainers, VP-3A VIP transports and WP-3A weather reconnaissance aircraft.

The Model 185 P-3B introduced the T56-14 engine, rated at 4,591shp (4,910ehp). Sensors and systems were uprated, and 144 of this version were delivered, many still serving in the original role. In September 1968 Lockheed began testing the YP-3C, prototype of the Model 285 P-3C. Again powered by T56-14 engines, this has become the standard maritime and ASW aircraft not only of the US Navy but also of almost every air force equipped with such aircraft (the Netherlands even used it to replace the Atlantic, which had been designed as a "clean sheet of paper" aircraft).

In recent years the most common variant has been the P-3C Update III, major items of which include the APS-115 radar, ASA-64 MAD, a battery of sonobuoys in the rear fuselage ejected by cartridge (eliminating the previous pneumatic system), an improved auxiliary power unit and, among 22 types of dropped store, two Harpoon cruise missiles. Like earlier versions it is possible to have a surveillance camera on gimballed mounts in a glass chin gondola as an alternative to a retractable turret housing a FLIR (forward-looking infrared) detector. The pylons under the wing roots can carry such devices as the ALQ-78 ESM (electronic surveillance mea-

sures) or AXR-13 LLTV (low-light TV).

The Update IV aircraft incorporate a further group of new items, including the ALR-77 tactical passive ESM in the wingtips. Among many other versions the most electronically dissimilar is the CP-140 Aurora of the Canadian Armed Forces, 20 of which were delivered, which is based around the avionics and data processors of the S-3A Viking. In 1984 Lockheed began testing an AEW&C version called P-3 Sentinel, with a 24ft (7.32m) revolving rotodome which in a production version might house an APS-138 (Hawkeye) radar. To meet the RAF need for a replacement for the Nimrod MR.2 Lockheed and vari-

ous partners offered upgrades, Orion 2000 and Valkyrie.

Various minor differences characterise the Model 785 P-3C made under licence by Kawasaki in Japan. In 1998 this is the only version in low-rate production, a total of 110 hav-

Accepted at Patuxent River NAS, Maryland, on 13 August 1962, this is the very first P3V-1 (P-3A). The P-3 is a multiple record breaker, including 19min 42.2sec. from takeoff to 12,000m (39,370ft) in 1971.

ing been so far funded in P, EP and various UP versions. Lockheed's total production amounted to 641 aircraft, the last delivered in September 1985. Various further upgrades and new-generation successors are being studied. Among P-3C conversions are the RP-3D atmospheric and magnetic research aircraft (closed circuit distance record holder, 6,278 miles, 1972) and two WP-3Ds for weather reconnaissance.

DATA FOR P-3 ORION:		
Span		99ft 8in (30.38m);
Length (with MAD)		116ft 10in (35.61m)
Wing area		1,300 sq ft (120.77m²)
Weight empty	(A)	60,060lb (27,243kg)
	(C)	61,491lb (27,892kg)
Maximum takeoff weight	(A)	127,500lb (57,834kg)
	(C)	142,000lb (64,411kg).
Maximum cruising speed		378mph (608km/h)
Patrol speed		237mph (381km/h)
Range (maximum fuel)		4,765 miles (7,668km)
Mission radius		1,550 miles (2,494km)
		(3h on station at low level)

ITALIAN SUCCESS

LASA-60

This light utility transport had a convoluted history. It was designed by the Mooney brothers for Lockheed-Georgia, where two US-registered prototypes were constructed (the first aircraft designed at Marietta). It was the intention that production would be undertaken by Lockheed-Azcárate in Mexico and Lockheed-Kaiser in Argentina, under the name Santa Maria. But things didn't work out.

Powered by a 250hp Continental IO-470R engine, the first aircraft resembled a Cessna 185, with a similar six-seat cabin, but the wing was larger and fitted with Fowler flaps for STOL (short takeoff and landing) and the landing gears were of the levered-suspension nosewheel type.

The first prototype was flown at Marietta on 15 September 1959, and FAA certification was granted on 5 April 1960. Eventually 18 were built in Mexico, but the programme was abandoned in April 1962. Argentina never even got start-

ed. This is surprising, because Aermacchi in Italy built large numbers under licence, as the AL-60 followed by the AL-60B and C with more powerful engines.

With further development Atlas in South Africa continued major production as the Bosbok, which in turn was developed into the Kudu. Somewhere along the way, Lockheed lost interest.

Polished like a mirror, the first Lockheed-Azcarate Model 60. Designed for maximum utility, the aircraft could be easily converted.

DATA FOR ORIGINAL LASA-60:	
Span	39ft 4.4in (12.0 m)
Length	28ft 1in (8.56m)
Wing area	210 sq ft (19.5m2)
Weight empty	2,024lb (918kg)
Maximum takeoff weight	3,752lb (1,702kg)
Cruising speed	130mph (209km/h)
Range	550 miles (885km)

FORERUNNER

In the 1950s Lockheed began a low-key investigation into helicopters, which on 2 November resulted in the start of flight trials of this experimental machine. Powered by a 140hp Lycoming VO–360 piston engine, its main purpose was to explore the design of a rigid main rotor. Such rotas were already being investigated by others, and promised to offer many advantages. For the CL–475 the design team, led by Irvin Culver, began with a rotor with two blades of laminated wood, stabilized by two masses held on arms at 90° to the blades and attached to the control swashplate by springs.

The simple airframe was made of welded tube covered in fabric, and had side-by-side seats in the nose.
Gradually severe vibration and control problems were overcome, and by mid-1960 the XH–475 was flying well, with a rotor with three metal blades (supplied by Parsons) stabilized by a heavy gyroscopic ring

The gyroscopic ring used to stabilize the rotor blades is clearly visible as N6940C hovers for landing.

attached rigidly to the swashplate. This machine led to the Models 186 and 286.

DATA FOR CL-475:	
Diameter of main rotor	32ft 0in (9.75m)
Length of fuselage	29ft 6in (9.0m)
Weight empty	1,625lb (737kg)
Loaded weight	2,000lb (907kg)
Maximum speed	90mph (145km/h)
Cruising speed	128mph (206km/h)
Range	75 miles (121km)

C-130 HERCULES

THE BEST

Beyond doubt the greatest military transport aircraft in history, the Model 82 was designed to meet a tough USAF requirement of February 1951, at the height of the Korean war. The chief demands were to carry 90 troops or a 30,000lb (13,608kg) payload, operate from short unpaved strips and drop paratroops at 144mph (232km/h). Lockheed won in July 1951. 53-3397's maiden flight at Burbank was on 23 August 1954.

Powered by four 3,250shp Allison T56-1 turboprops driving three-blade Curtiss propellers, the YC-130 had the flight performance of a World War 2 fighter, and almost the same agility. At a time when other airlifters had tailwheels, and cruised at half the speed, the Lockheed had a capacious hold 10ft 3in (3.13m) wide and 9ft 3in (2.8m) high, 41.5ft long, fully pressurized yet provided with a full-section rear ramp opening to a level floor at "truck bed" height. Other features included a modern flight deck with all-round vision, main gears with tandem low-

pressure tyres retracting into side blisters (one housing a gas-turbine auxiliary power unit), Fowler flaps and a modern airframe with 2024 high-strength alloy, machined panels in the wings and cargo floor and titanium in the nacelles and flap skins.

The whole programme was moved to the Georgia plant, where the first C-130A, powered by T56-9 engines rated at 3,460shp (3,750ehp), flew on 7 April 1955. It was the first US production aircraft with turbine engines. From the 28th aircraft the bluff nose was replaced by a projecting radome. The Curtiss propellers were replaced by Aeroproducts, and in the heavier C-130B, with T56-7 engines rated at 3,755shp (4,050ehp) and increased fuel capacity, a propeller problem was at last cured with a four-blade type. The C-130E increased fuel tankage a second time, to 5,796gal (6,960 US gal, 26,347 litres), plus two large external tanks. For many years the basic type was the C-130H, with T56-15 engines rated at 4,591shp (4,910ehp) normally flat-rated at 4,508ehp. The RAF bought 66 C-130Ks, basically

an H with British content, designated Hercules C.1.

These basic versions sold all over the world in a profusion of sub-types. These include AC-130 "gunships" of various kinds with night sensors and devastating side-firing artillery; DC-130 drone/RPV direction aircraft; various types called EC-130 for surveillance, battlefield control, Tacamo communications and electronic warfare; HC-130 search/rescue aircraft; JC-130 test aircraft, including versions for satellite recovery; KC-130 aerial tankers; ski-equipped LC-130s for Antarctica; MC-130 Combat Talon aircraft with a host

of special equipment for clandestine missions at night (often at treetop level); RC-130 reconnaissance platforms and special sub-variants for night search/rescue missions; and several types of WC-130 weather-recon aircraft.

On 20/21 April 1964 the prototype L-100 civil Hercules made a first flight. This version was followed by the L-100-20 with with stretched fuselage. The main civil version is the L-100-30, with a further stretch, increasing available volume from 4,500 cu ft (127.4m^3) of the original aircraft to 6,057 cu ft (171.52m^3). From 1979 to '85, 30 of the RAF Hercules C.1

DATA FOR C-130 VARIANTS:		
Span		132ft 7in (40.41m)
Length		97ft 9in (29.79m)
(stretch)		112ft 9in (34.37m)
Wing area		1,745 sq ft (162.12m²)
Weight empty	(A)	59,328lb (26,911kg)
	(H)	76,780lb (34,827kg)
	(J)	75,562lb (34,274kg)
	(J-30)	79,291lb (35,966kg)
Maximum takeoff weight	(A)	124,200lb (56,337kg)
	(H, J, J-30)	175,000lb (79,380kg)
Cruising speed	(A)	328mph (528km/h)
	(H)	355mph (571km/h)
	(J)	390mph (628km/h)
Range	(A)	2,090 miles (3,363km) with 35,000lb (15,876kg) payload
	(H)	2,745 miles (4,418km) with 45,000lb (20,412kg) payload

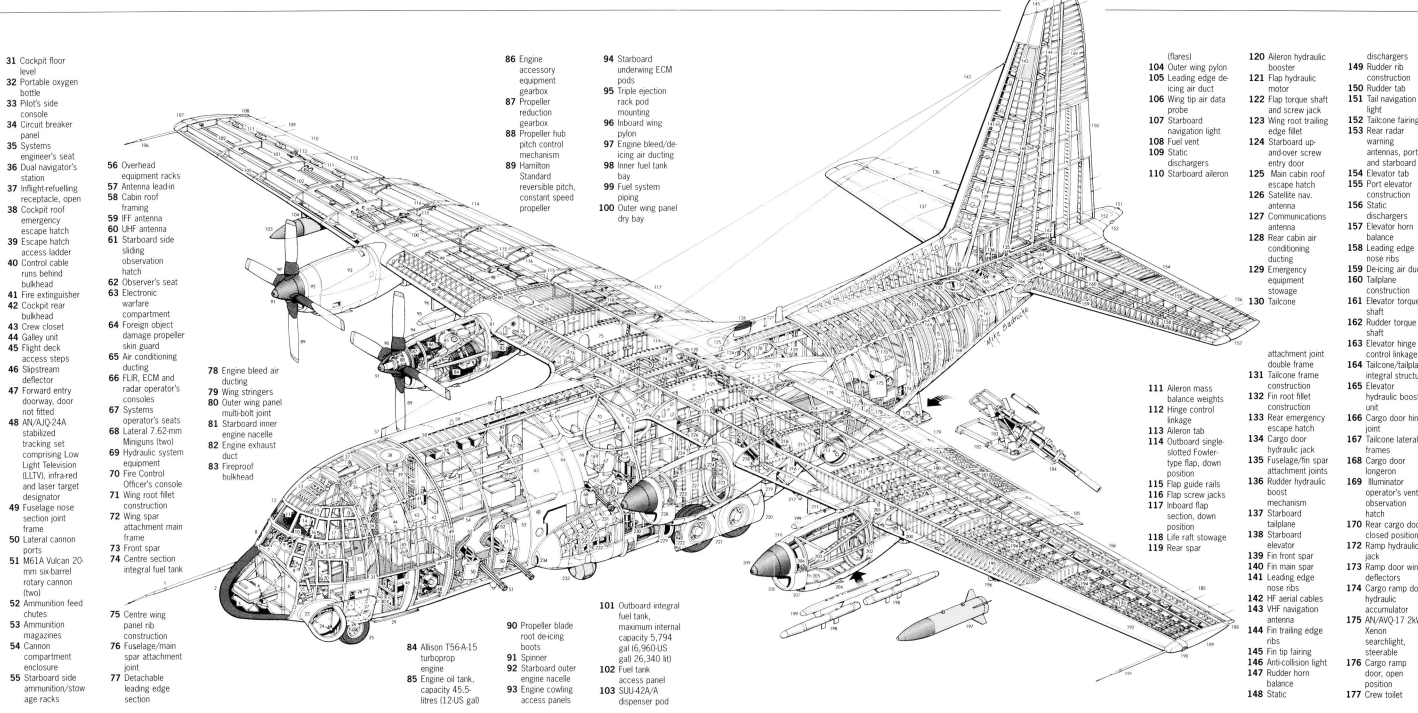

31 Cockpit floor level
32 Portable oxygen bottle
33 Pilot's side console
34 Circuit breaker panel
35 Systems engineer's seat
36 Dual navigator's station
37 Inflight-refuelling receptacle, open
38 Cockpit roof emergency escape hatch
39 Escape hatch access ladder
40 Control cable runs behind bulkhead
41 Fire extinguisher
42 Cockpit rear bulkhead
43 Crew closet
44 Galley unit
45 Flight deck access steps
46 Slipstream deflector
47 Forward entry doorway, door not fitted
48 AN/AJQ-24A stabilized tracking set comprising Low Light Television (LLTV), infra-red and laser target designator
49 Fuselage nose section joint frame
50 Lateral cannon ports
51 M61A Vulcan 20-mm six-barrel rotary cannon (two)
52 Ammunition feed chutes
53 Ammunition magazines
54 Cannon compartment enclosure
55 Starboard side ammunition/stowage racks

56 Overhead equipment racks
57 Antenna lead-in
58 Cabin roof framing
59 IFF antenna
60 UHF antenna
61 Starboard side sliding observation hatch
62 Observer's seat
63 Electronic warfare compartment
64 Foreign object damage propeller skin guard
65 Air conditioning ducting
66 FLIR, ECM and radar operator's consoles
67 Systems operator's seats
68 Lateral 7.62-mm Miniguns (two)
69 Hydraulic system equipment
70 Fire Control Officer's console
71 Wing root fillet construction
72 Wing spar attachment main frame
73 Front spar
74 Centre section integral fuel tank
75 Centre wing panel rib construction
76 Fuselage/main spar attachment joint
77 Detachable leading edge section

78 Engine bleed air ducting
79 Wing stringers
80 Outer wing panel multi-bolt joint
81 Starboard inner engine nacelle
82 Engine exhaust duct
83 Fireproof bulkhead

84 Allison T56-A-15 turboprop engine
85 Engine oil tank, capacity 45.5-litres (12-US gal)

86 Engine accessory equipment gearbox
87 Propeller reduction gearbox
88 Propeller hub pitch control mechanism
89 Hamilton Standard reversible pitch, constant speed propeller

90 Propeller blade root de-icing boots
91 Spinner
92 Starboard outer engine nacelle
93 Engine cowling access panels

94 Starboard underwing ECM pods
95 Triple ejection rack pod mounting
96 Inboard wing pylon
97 Engine bleed/de-icing air ducting
98 Inner fuel tank bay
99 Fuel system piping
100 Outer wing panel dry bay

101 Outboard integral fuel tank, maximum internal capacity 5,794 gal (6,960-US gal) 26,340 lit)
102 Fuel tank access panel
103 SUU-42A/A dispenser pod

(flares)
104 Outer wing pylon
105 Leading edge de-icing air duct
106 Wing tip air data probe
107 Starboard navigation light
108 Fuel vent
109 Static dischargers
110 Starboard aileron

111 Aileron mass balance weights
112 Hinge control linkage
113 Aileron tab
114 Outboard single-slotted Fowler-type flap, down position
115 Flap guide rails
116 Flap screw jacks
117 Inboard flap section, down position
118 Life raft stowage
119 Rear spar

120 Aileron hydraulic booster
121 Flap hydraulic motor
122 Flap torque shaft and screw jack
123 Wing root trailing edge fillet
124 Starboard up-and-over screw entry door
125 Main cabin roof escape hatch
126 Satellite nav. antenna
127 Communications antenna
128 Rear cabin air conditioning ducting
129 Emergency equipment stowage
130 Tailcone

attachment joint double frame
131 Tailcone frame construction
132 Fin root fillet construction
133 Rear emergency escape hatch
134 Cargo door hydraulic jack
135 Fuselage/fin spar attachment joints
136 Rudder hydraulic boost mechanism
137 Starboard tailplane
138 Starboard elevator
139 Fin front spar
140 Fin main spar
141 Leading edge nose ribs
142 HF aerial cables
143 VHF navigation antenna
144 Fin trailing edge ribs
145 Fin tip fairing
146 Anti-collision light
147 Rudder horn balance
148 Static

dischargers
149 Rudder rib construction
150 Rudder tab
151 Tail navigation light
152 Tailcone fairing
153 Rear radar warning antennas, port and starboard
154 Elevator tab
155 Port elevator construction
156 Static dischargers
157 Elevator horn balance
158 Leading edge nose ribs
159 De-icing air duct
160 Tailplane construction
161 Elevator torque shaft
162 Rudder torque shaft
163 Elevator hinge control linkage
164 Tailcone/tailplane integral structure
165 Elevator hydraulic boost unit
166 Cargo door hinge joint
167 Tailcone lateral frames
168 Cargo door longeron
169 Illuminator operator's ventral observation hatch
170 Rear cargo door, closed position
172 Ramp hydraulic jack
173 Ramp door wind deflectors
174 Cargo ramp door hydraulic accumulator
175 AN/AVQ-17 2kW Xenon searchlight, steerable
176 Cargo ramp door, open position
177 Crew toilet

178 Urinal
179 Port double-slotted Fowler-type flaps, extended
180 Flap shroud ribs
181 Flap rib construction
182 Cabin floor rib mounting
183 Gun elevation mechanism
184 105-mm howitzer (retrofit to late production aircraft)
185 Static dischargers
186 Aileron tab
187 Port aileron construction
188 Fuel vent
189 Wingtip fairing
190 Port navigation light
191 Port wing tip air data probe
192 Leading edge skin panelling
193 Outer wing panel rib construction
194 Port wing integral fuel tankage
195 Leading edge nose ribs
196 Outer wing pylon
197 SUU-42A/A dispenser pod (chaff)
198 AN/ALQ-87 ECM pods
199 Triple ejecter rack ECM pod mounting
200 Infra-red exhaust suppression mixing air duct
201 Nacelle mounting framework
202 Port outer engine nacelle construction
203 Engine mounting beam
204 Oil cooler exhaust flap
205 Oil cooler
206 Gearbox mounting sub-frame

207 Oil cooler air intake
208 Engine air inlet
209 Spinner
210 Detachable cowling panels
211 Inner wing pylon
212 Inboard fuel tank bay rib construction
213 AN/APQ-150 sideways looking tracking radar
214 Port entry door, inoperative
215 Outer wing panel multi-bolt joint rib
216 Lateral gun ports
217 Cannon barrels
218 40-mm Bofors cannon (two), one gun replaced by 105-mm howitzer in later aircraft
219 Gun port air deflector
220 Mainwheel door
221 Twin tandem mainwheels
222 Landing/taxiing lamp
223 Main landing gear leg struts
224 Retraction screw jacks
225 Main landing gear retraction hydraulic motor and torque shaft
226 Engine fire extinguisher bottles
227 Main landing gear wheel bay
228 Port inner engine nacelle
229 APU exhaust
230 Gas turbine auxiliary power unit (APU)
231 Extended landing gear sponson fairing construction
232 Sensor equipment units
233 Forward-looking infra-red (FLIR) ball turret
234 Cooling air intake

fleet were stretched 15ft (4.57m) to C.3 standard. For the Falklands campaign in 1982 various RAF aircraft were fitted with hose-drum units as tankers and/or probes to receive fuel. In 1983-88 Lockheed tested a High Technology Test Bed with numerous upgrades. In 1991 Lockheed began development of a more conventional Hercules II, which became the C-130J. The obvious modification is that the engines are Allison AE2100D3 with thermodynamic power of 6,000shp but flat-rated at the same 4,591shp as in earlier aircraft, driving six-blade Dowty R591 propellers. In fact, the J is new throughout, with upgraded structure, digital avionics and new self-defence systems.

An RAF Hercules flight-tested the new propulsion system in the No 1 (port outer) position, and the programme was launched by an RAF order in December 1994 for 15 stretched Hercules C.4 and 10 standard-length C.5. By 1998 it was expected that this largely new aircraft would add not less than 800 aircraft, including AEW&C, tanker/transport, psy-war, weather, possibly including the L-100J civil model (on offer) and a catamaran seaplane version. No. 4,000 might be delivered in 2020!

Lockheed Martin C–130J Hercules

1 Fixed in-flight refuelling probe
2 Upward hinging radome
3 Westinghouse MODAR 4000 full-colour weather/nav radar scanner
4 Glide slope antenna
5 Radar transmitters and receivers
6 Scanner rotating mounting
7 Radome hinges
8 Front pressure bulkhead
9 Forward missile (AAR-47) and radar (ALR-56M) warning antenna, port and starboard
10 Instrument panel with four full-colour multifunction LCD primary displays
11 Monochrome command and control LCD displays
12 Flight Dynamics head-up-displays
13 Instrument panel shroud
14 Windscreen wipers
15 Windscreen panels
16 Overhead systems control panels
17 Cockpit eyebrow windows
18 Co-pilot's seat
19 Pilot's seat, basic two-crew flight deck
20 Control column
21 Downward vision window
22 Underfloor liquid oxygen converter

23 Dual pitot heads, port and starboard
24 Nose undercarriage wheel bay
25 Ground intercom socket
26 Twin nosewheels forward retracting
27 Battery bay
28 Ground power socket
29 Underfloor avionics equipment racks, cabin air conditioning system on starboard side
30 External door handle
31 Crew door with integral stairs
32 ALE-47 chaff/flare launcher
33 Internal stairway
34 Crew galley unit
35 Augmented crew member's seat
36 Augmented crew station, flight refuelling and defensive systems controls
37 TCAS antenna
38 Cockpit emergency exit hatch
39 Upper crew rest bunk
40 Lower bunk/triple seat unit
41 Safety equipment stowage
42 Main cabin bulkhead
43 Crew equipment stowage locker
44 Toilet with pull-round curtain (2)
45 Loadmaster's seat
46 Main cargo deck
47 Stowable troop seats
48 Overhead avionics equipment rack

49 Fuselage close pitched frame structure
50 Upper main longeron
51 Starboard emergency exit hatch
52 Cabin soundproofing and insulating lining
53 Cargo deck support structure
54 Lower main longeron
55 Port emergency exit hatch
56 Cabin windows
57 Wing/engine inspection light
58 Detachable roller conveyors, cargo handling
59 Cargo hold air conditioning system in starboard main landing gear fairing

60 Propeller debris guard skin doubler
61 Conditioned air distribution ducting
62 No 1 GPS/INS antenna
63 Dual ADF antenna
64 UHF antenna
65 Conditioned air delivery and mixing unit

66 Wing root leading edge fairing
67 Front spar
68 Centre section bag type auxiliary fuel tank bay
69 Wing root attachment rib
70 Wing inboard integral fuel tank
71 Engine bleed air ducting
72 Engine mounting support ribs
73 Starboard inboard engine nacelle
74 Ventral exhaust duct

75 Engine bay firewall
76 Allison AE2100D3 turboprop engine
77 Engine oil tank
78 Intake ducting
79 Propeller hub pitch control mechanism
80 Dowty R391 six bladed all composite propeller
81 Propeller blade root de-icing
82 Leading edge erosion sheath
83 Starboard outer engine nacelle
84 Leading edge de-icing air ducts

85 Starboard intermediate integral fuel tank
86 Dry bay
87 Fuel venting tanks and delivery pipes
88 Starboard outboard integral fuel tank
89 Tank access panels
90 Starboard navigation light
91 Fuel jettison
92 Starboard aileron
93 Aileron hinge control link
94 Aileron trim tab
95 Outboard single-slotted flap segment
96 Flap guide rails
97 Shaft driven flap operating screw jack
98 Outer wing panel bolted joint
99 Life raft stowage with automatic inflation bottles

100 Starboard inboard single-slotted flap segment
101 Wing root trailing edge fillet
102 Aileron hydraulic booster
103 Flap drive hydraulic power unit
104 Cargo bay ditching hatch
105 Rear overhead avionics equipment rack
106 IFF antenna

107 No 2 GPS/INS antenna
108 VHF antenna
109 Up-and-over paratroop door, port and starboard
110 Starboard side toilet with pull around curtain (1)
111 Equipment Stowage lockers
112 Tailcone joint frame
113 Fin root fillet frame structure
114 Tailcone ditching hatch

115 Cargo door hydraulic jack
116 Elevator dual hydraulic boosters
117 Rudder hydraulic booster
118 Fin spar root attachment joint
119 HF SSE antenna
120 Emergency Locator Transmitter (ELT) antenna
121 Starboard tailpipe
122 Starboard elevator
123 Fin leading edge de-icing
124 Fin leading edge structure
125 Two-spar fin torsion box structure
126 Fin ribs

127 VOR/LOC antenna
128 Anti-collision beacon
129 Rudder horn balance
130 Static dischargers
131 Rudder rib structure
132 Rudder trim tab
133 Rear missile (AAR-47) and radar (ALR-56M) warning antenna
134 Tailcone aft fairing
135 Rudder hinge control link and mass balance weight

136 Elevator hinge control links and mass balance weights
137 Elevator trim tab
138 Port elevator rib structure
139 Static dischargers
140 Elevator horn balance
141 Tailplane two-spar torsion box structure
142 Tailplane leading edge de-icing
143 Rear ALE-47 chaff/flare launcher
144 Cargo door hinge mounting
145 Tailplane root fairing
146 Rear cargo door open position
147 Tailcone frame structure
148 Paratroop static line reel, port and starboard
149 Detachable vehicle loading ramps
150 Cargo ramp door hydraulic jacks
151 Auxiliary hydraulic reservoir
152 Drinking water containers
153 Equipment stowage lockers
154 Cargo door aperture vertical and diagonal braces
155 Cargo ramp door
156 Port inboard single-slotted flap segment
157 Inboard flap segment all-composite structure
158 Port paratroop doorway
159 Flap operating screw jack drive shaft
160 Wing rear spar
161 Flap shroud ribs

composite trailing edge skin panels
162 Port outboard flap segment
163 Outer flap segment rib structure
164 Aileron trim tab
165 Port aileron rib structure
166 Static dischargers
167 Port wing tank fuel jettison
168 Wing tip fairing
169 Port navigation light
170 Outer wing panel rib structure
171 Outer integral fuel tank bay
172 Leading edge ribs
173 Port outboard engine nacelle
174 Nacelle mounting struts
175 Engine mounting beam structure
176 Ventral oil cooler
177 Oil cooler air intake
178 Engine air intake
179 Propeller spinner
180 Detachable engine cowling panels
181 Hinged paratroop door and deflector
182 ALE-47 chaff/flare launcher
183 ALQ-157 Infra-Red counter-measures unit
184 Position of pressure refuelling point on starboard side
185 Port outer wing panel bolted joint
186 Port inboard nacelle mounting structure
187 Engine fire extinguisher bottles
188 Fuselage/wing attachment and

P-3C Orion; on 27 January 1971 a P-3C set a turboprop straight-line speed record of 500.89mph (806.1kmh). Photo: John Ailes

Inset top: **The elegance of the Super Constellation survived its conversion into the WV-2 (EC-121K) radar picket for the US Navy.**

Inset middle: **Magnificently complex, the AH-56 attack helicopter had a profound influence on the design of the Russian Mi-24.**

Now part of Air Combat Command, C-141B StarLifters were formerly the backbone of MAC. (Photo: Nick Hall)

Both the SR-71 and U-2S can operate at altitudes in excess of 85,000ft (26,000m); crews' David Clark S-1031A pressure suits are similar to those worn by Shuttle astronauts.

Combining stealth, supercruise capability, maximum agility and AMRAAMs, the Raptor has no equal in air combat. As it lands the YF-22 shows its humped but narrow canopy, sharp chine and enormous vertical tails. Viewed from above, the Raptor reveals its remarkable wing, which tapers sharply at the leading edge. Outboard ailerons, inboard flaps and full-span leading-edge droop flaps provide variable camber in combat. Combined with 2D vectoring nozzles, these give the Raptor incredible manoeuvrability and STOL performance.

Top left: **Ground crew prepare to pull the chocks as an F-117A begins a characteristically noctural mission. The name Nighthawk was not officially confirmed by the USAF until 24 June 1994.**

Far left, below: **Rare view of a Nighthawk 'uncloaked' at Palmdale; the starboard inlet is without its radar defeating grille and associated faceting.**

Left: **The only unstealthy part of a Nighthawk mission: flight refuelling. In combat, careful route planning and EW support is used to obscure the tanker's presence.**

Below: **The unmanned DarkStar could be the USAF's next strategic reconnaissance vehicle.**

Bottom: **This is how Lockheed's ATF concept looked in 1985; its configuration is markedly different to today's F-22.**

October 1992, and the F-117 and P-38 meet at
Peterson AFB, Colorado Springs, for the dedication
of a Lightning memorial at the USAF Academy.

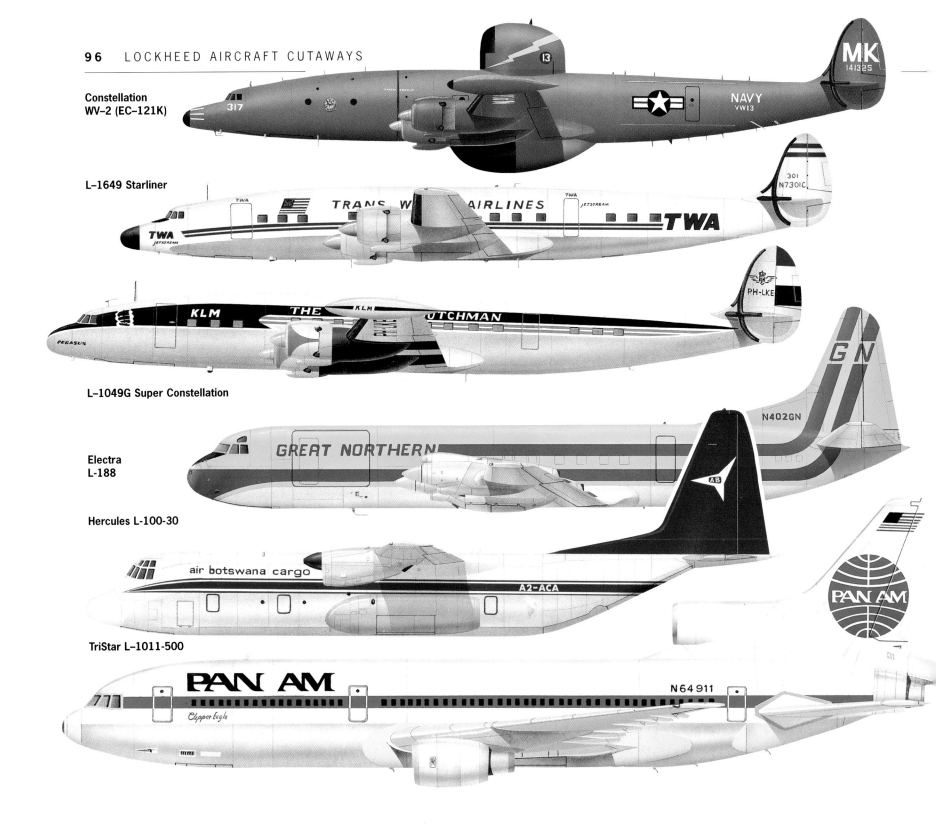

Constellation
WV–2 (EC–121K)

L–1649 Starliner

L–1049G Super Constellation

Electra
L-188

Hercules L-100-30

TriStar L–1011-500

BLACK ARTS
YF–12 AND SR–71

In 1957 the CIA's Richard Bissell asked various organisations, especially Lockheed's Skunk Works, to study the speed, altitude and RCS (radar cross-section) of an aircraft to replace the U-2, which was thought to be vulnerable to Soviet defences. On 29 August 1959 Lockheed's submission designated A-12 was accepted, and Project Oxcart was launched in the greatest secrecy (see Introduction).

Compared with today's fighters, the A-12 was designed to fly three times as fast and twice as high. It remains to this day the fastest air-breathing manned aircraft ever built. Most of the family were painted radar-absorbent black, resulting in the popular nickname of Blackbird. Propulsion was by two Pratt & Whitney J58-1 (JT11D-20) single-shaft

'Kelly' Johnson's masterpiece: the SR-71. At Mach 3.2 the spike inlets are much less prominent and provide more than half the thrust.

A-12

turbojets with an afterburner which in supersonic flight is augmented by air fed through six bypass pipes. While at take-off all the thrust (32,500lb) was provided by the engine, at the design cruise speed of Mach 3.2, 54 per cent of the thrust was provided by the axially sliding spike inlet and 28.4 per cent by the convergent/divergent variable nozzle, only 17.6 per cent coming from the engine, burning special JP-7 fuel.

The long body had a sharp chine along each side which blended into the delta wing over the aft half of the aircraft. Well outboard on each side were the large propulsion nacelles, outboard of which was a small wingtip which, with the outer half-nacelle, could hinge up for access to the engines. The trailing edge comprised four elevons, whose limits of travel were sharply restricted above Mach 0.5. The design load factors for the airframe were much lower than those of highly manoeuvrable fighters. Above the centre of each nacelle was a one-piece powered rudder inclined inwards. Each main landing gear had three small wheels

**Lockheed
SR-71A Blackbird**
1 Pitot tube
2 Air data probe
3 Radar warning antennae
4 Nose mission equipment bay
5 Panoramic camera aperture
6 Detachable nose cone joint frame
7 Cockpit front pressure bulkhead
8 Rudder pedals
9 Control column
10 Instrument panel
11 Instrument panel shroud
12 Knife-edged windscreen panels
13 Upward hinged cockpit canopy covers
14 Ejection seat headrest
15 Canopy actuator
16 Pilot's Lockheed 'zero-zero' ejection seat
17 Engine throttle levers
18 Side console panel
19 Fuselage chine close-pitched frame construction
20 Liquid oxygen converters
21 Side console panel
22 Reconnaissance Systems Officer's (RSO) instrument display
23 Cockpit rear pressure bulkhead
24 RSO's Lockheed 'zero-zero' ejection seat
25 Canopy hinge point

26 SR71B dual control trainer variant, nose profile
27 Raised instructor's rear cockpit
28 Astro navigation star tracker
29 Navigation and communications systems electronic equipment
30 Nosewheel bay
31 Nose undercarriage pivot fixing
32 Landing and taxiing lamps
33 Twin nosewheels (forward retracting)
34 Hydraulic retraction jack
35 Cockpit environmental system equipment bay
36 Air refuelling receptacle (open)
37 Fuselage upper longeron
38 Forward fuselage frame construction
39 Forward fuselage integral fuel tanks

40 Palletized, interchangeable reconnaissance equipment packs
41 Fuselage chine member
42 Forward/central fuselage joint ring frame
43 Centre fuselage integral fuel tanks: total system capacity 46182 litres (12.200 US gal)
44 Beta B. 120 titanium alloy skin panelling
45 Corrugated wing skin panelling
46 Starboard main undercarriage stowed position

47 Intake centre-body bleed air louvres
48 By-pass duct suction relief louvres
49 Starboard engine air intake
50 Movable intake conical centre-body
51 Centre-body retracted (high speed) position
52 Boundary layer bleed air holes
53 Automatic intake control system air data probe
54 Diffuser chamber
55 Variable inlet guide vanes

56 Hinged engine cowling/ outerwing panel
57 Pratt & Whitney JT11D-20B (J58) single spool turbo-ramjet engine
58 Engine accessory equipment
59 By-pass duct suction relief doors
60 Compressor bleed air by-pass ducts
61 Afterburner fuel manifold
62 Tailfin fixed root section

63 Starboard outerwing panel
64 Under-cambered leading edge
65 Outboard, roll control, elevon
66 All-moving starboard fin
67 Continuously operating afterburning duct
68 Afterburner nozzle
69 Engine bay tertiary air flaps
70 Exhaust nozzle ejector flaps
71 Variable area exhaust nozzle

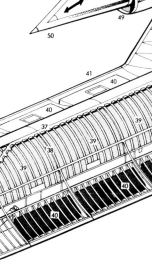

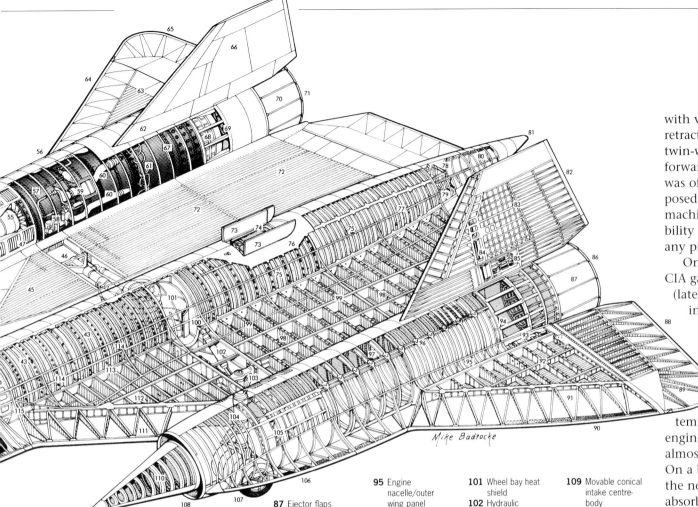

Mike Badrocke

with very high pressure tyres, retracting inwards, and the twin-wheel nose gear retracted forwards. Most of the structure was of titanium alloys, and posed more difficulties – with machine tools and incompatibility of materials – than with any previous aircraft in history.

On 30 January 1960 the CIA gave the go-ahead for 12 (later 15) A-12 aircraft, including one dual-control trainer with a raised rear instructor cockpit.

Lou Schalk made the first hop in 60-6924 at Groom Lake on 24 April 1962, temporarily using J75 engines. The aircraft proved almost impossible to handle. On a brief flight two days later the non-structural radar-absorbent fillets on the left wing were shed. Full flight testing from 30 April was more encouraging, though punctuated by violent yaws and other uncommanded manoeuvres caused by difficulty in precisely controlling the inlet shock-waves.

The A-12 was used by the USAF to fly reconnaissance missions over North Vietnam and other sensitive areas. The

72 Starboard wing integral fuel tank bays
73 Brake parachute doors, open
74 Ribbon parachute stowage
75 Aft fuselage integral fuel tanks
76 Skin doubler
77 Aft fuselage frame construction

78 Elevon mixer unit
79 Inboard elevon torque control shaft
80 Tailcone
81 Fuel vent
82 Port all-moving fin
83 Fin rib construction
84 Torque shaft hinge mounting
85 Fin hydraulic actuator
86 Port engine exhaust nozzle

87 Ejector flaps
88 Port outboard elevon
89 Elevon titanium alloy rib construction
90 Under-cambered leading edge
91 Leading edge diagonal rib construction
92 Outer wing panel titanium alloy construction
93 Outboard elevon hydraulic actuator
94 Engine bay tertiary air flaps

95 Engine nacelle/outer wing panel integral construction
96 Engine cowling/ wing panel hinge axis
97 Port nacelle ring frame construction
98 Inboard wing panel integral fuel tank bays
99 Multi-spar titanium alloy wing construction
100 Main undercarriage wheel bay

101 Wheel bay heat shield
102 Hydraulic retraction jack
103 Main undercarriage pivot fixing
104 Mainwheel leg strut
105 Intake duct framing
106 Outer wing panel/nacelle chine
107 Three-wheel main undercarriage bogie, inward retracting
108 Port engine air intake

109 Movable conical intake centre-body
110 Centre-body frame construction
111 Inboard leading edge diagonal rib construction
112 Inner wing panel integral fuel tank
113 Wing root/fuselage attachment root rib
114 Close-pitched fuselage titanium alloy frames
115 Wing/fuselage chine blended fairing panels

last two A-12s were modified as A-12(M) aircraft to carry and launch hypersonic D-21 reconnaissance drones, one of which brought about the destruction of the last aircraft, 60-6941.

The A-12s were followed by three YF-12A experimental interceptors for the USAF, meeting Specific Operational Requirement 220 to follow the F-106. These aircraft, numbered 60-6934/6936 in the middle of the A-12 block, were single seaters with Hughes ASG-18 radar, an infra-red sensor at the front of each chine and four large Hughes AIM-47A missiles carried in an internal bay. A shallow fin was added under the rear of each nacelle, and a large side-folding fin under the centreline. The first began flight testing on 8 August 1963, and on 1 May 1965 the third aircraft set records for sustained height (80,257.86ft, 24,468.86m) and various speed classes which included the 15/25km straight run (2,070.101mph, 3,331.41km/h). NASA used the YF-12 to test ramjets.

In 1962 Lockheed told the USAF that the A-12 could also be developed into a reconnaissance/strike aircraft. The result was the RS-12, later called B-12, B-71, RS-71 and finally SR-71, the first of which (64-17950) was flown by Robert Gilliland on 23 December

Lockheed spent ages trying to perfect a paint for the Blackbird's national markings, which had to survive temperatures of several hundred degrees C.

1964. Compared with earlier Blackbirds the SR-71 was slightly larger, with a rear cockpit for an RSO (reconnaissance systems officer), considerably greater fuel capacity (and thus

heavier weights), fuselage chines extended to the sharp flattened nose (enabling the ventral fins to be omitted), a lengthened fuselage tail and completely new and capacious bays in the nose and along the fuselage chines for a wide variety of reconnaissance sensors for optical surveillance, Elint (electronic intelligence) and advanced synthetic-aperture radar. The strike role was never activated. Lockheed delivered 31 SR-71s (64-17950/17980), including two dual-control SR-71B trainers ('956, '957), plus a 31st aircraft, the dual-control SR-71C ('981), assembled from a static-test forward fuselage grafted on a YF-12A. In service the SR-71A operational aircraft were supported by KC-135Q tankers dispensing the special JP-7 fuel. The main operating base was Beale AFB, California, but actual operations were first mounted from Kadena, Okinawa, to cover south-east Asia and eastern Siberia. Extremely long missions over the Middle East were flown from the USA, with multiple air refuellings, many more were flown from Mildenhall, England, and three aircraft were operated by NASA.

An SR-71A receives its special brew of JP-7 fuel from a KC-135Q tanker. The Lockheed Martin Tactical Communications Division data link now adds to the SR-71's utility.

The SR-71A was retired on 6 March 1990, but in 1995 two were recalled to active duty. Lockheed Martin assisted in the refurbishment of '967 and '971, which in 1998 continue to render valuable service. Among records gained by the SR-71 one which still stands is speed over a 15/25km straight course of 2,193.167mph (3,529.464 km/h).

DATA FOR A-12:

Span	**55ft 7in (16.94m)**
Length	**102ft 0in (31.09m)**
Wing area	**1,795sq ft (166.76m²)**
Weight empty	**43,900lb (19,913kg)**
Maximum takeoff weight	**110,000lb (49,896kg)**
Maximum speed	**Mach 3.2**
(also maximum cruising speed)	**2,114mph (3,402km/h)**
Range	**4,120nm (4,741miles, 7,630km)**

DATA FOR SR-71A:

Length increased to	**107ft 5in (32.74m)**
(64-17959 had additional sensor bays in an extended tail giving a length of about 114ft, 34.75m)	
Weight empty	**67,500lb (30,618kg)**
Maximum takeoff weight	**172,000lb (78,019kg)**
Performance similar to A-12 except range (classified) considerably increased	

VZ-10

VTOL AGAIN
VZ-10, XV-4 HUMMINGBIRD

In 1956 Lockheed-Georgia began a prolonged investigation of ejector-jet systems for VTOL (vertical takeoff and landing). The concept was based on the fact that a high-velocity jet can entrain a large flow of fresh air around it. By 1960 the company felt ready to propose construction of a manned free-flight research vehicle, and in September 1961 work began against a $2.5 million US Army contract for two VZ-10 Hummingbirds, with service designation XV-4 and serial numbers 62-4503/4.

(Interest in VTOL at that time saw a variety of projects from several sources, the VJ -101C monoplane from the German Entwicklungsring Sud research group for example, with six RB.108 jets.) On each side of the stressed-skin fuselage of the VZ-10 was installed a Pratt & Whitney JT12A-3LH turbojet with a nominal rating of 3,000lb (1,361kg). The jetpipes were fitted with diverter valves which for VTOL could switch the flow to 20 high-velocity nozzles blowing downwards

inside an ejector duct forming the mid-section of the fuselage. The airflow thus induced entered through dorsal doors and was ejected through the bottom of the duct, which was inclined 12° aft. This accelerated the aircraft forward; at 90mph (145km/h) one engine was switched to forward thrust, and at 145mph

(233km/h) the second engine was switched, the duct doors then being closed and lift provided solely by small wings.

Features included a nose cockpit with side-by-side seats, leading- and trailing-edge flaps, retractable nosewheel landing gears and a T-type tail. From 7 July 1962 the first XV-4 was tested as a conventional aero-

Intake and exhaust doors open, the first Hummingbird hovers in front of curious onlookers. It was not in the same league as its ornithological namesake and little thrust augmentation was produced. Genuine VTOL was yet to be achieved.

plane without the ejector system. This was then fitted and from November 1962 the aircraft was subjected to hazardous and unsatisfactory tethered tests. After many modifications, as the XV-4A, free VTO was achieved on 28 May 1963, followed by transition from VTO to forward flight and back to a VL on 20 November 1963. Both aircraft were handed to the Army in February 1964, but the first soon crashed and 62-4504 was transferred to NASA Ames.

Lockheed then received USAF support for a near-total reconstruction of the surviving machine as the XV-4B Hummingbird II direct-lift testbed for the Flight Dynamics Laboratory. The mid-fuselage was enlarged to house two 3,015lb (1,368kg) General Electric J85-19 turbojets mounted vertically. At takeoff these were augmented by two more J85-19 engines mounted above the wing roots replacing those originally fitted, with diverter valves to direct the jets downwards or aft. Powerful air-bleed control jets were added at the

The rebuilt XV-4B as delivered to the USAF. Unusually for a jet aircraft, it was flown with the canopy removed – possibly to facilitate escape.

wingtips, nose and tail, and fuel capacity was increased from 237 to 616gal (from 1,079 to 2,801 litres). Flight testing began in August 1968, but the XV-4B was destroyed in a crash on 14 March 1969.

DATA FOR XV-4A:

Span	**25ft 8in (7.82m)**
Length	**32ft 8in (9.95m)**
Wing area	**104 sq ft (9.66m²)**
Weight empty	**4,995lb (2,266kg)**
Maximum takeoff weight	**7,200lb (3,266kg)**
Maximum speed	**518mph (834km/h)**

DATA FOR XV-4B:

Span over tip nozzles	**27ft 1in (8.26m)**
Length	**33ft 9.6in (10.3m)**
Weight empty	**7,463lb (3,385kg)**
Maximum takeoff weight	**12,580lb (5,706kg)**
Maximum speed	**463mph (745km/h)**

MODEL 186 AND 286

NO TAKERS
186, 286, XH–51A

By 1961 Lockheed had tamed the rigid helicopter rotor, and the CL-475 test-bed had been flown by many pilots from the military as well as NASA and the FAA. The company failed to win the big contract for an Army LOH (light observation helicopter), but in February 1962 it received a joint Navy/Army contract for two prototypes of a rigid-rotor machine with high flight performance. The first Model 186, with Service designation XH-51A and Navy BuNo 151262, began flight testing on 2 November 1962.

It was a much more advanced machine than the CL-475, with a stressed-skin fuselage and fin, with a fixed tailplane, retractable skids and a four-seat cabin (in fact occupied by two seats and test instrumenta-

The four blade main rotor was a big improvement over three. The original streamlined shape can be seen hiding behind the turbojet on the stumpy fixed wing.

tion), overall streamlining being superior to any previous helicopter. The main rotor had three Parsons blades of stainless steel wrapped over a bonded aluminium-honeycomb core. The engine was a 550shp Pratt & Whitney Canada PT6B-9 turboshaft, and to reduce drag further the swashplate was inside the fuselage and its control rods were brought up inside the rotor drive shaft. Instead of a gyro ring the main rotor was stabilized by three masses on radial arms mounted just above the hub.

Behaviour was improved by switching to a four-blade main rotor, with four stabilizing arms. To explore the limits of performance the second machine was modified under Army contract as a compound helicopter with a small fixed wing of 16ft 11in (5.16m) span carrying a 2,900lb thrust Pratt & Whitney J60-2 turbojet mounted close against the left side of the fuselage, balanced by a mass on the opposite tip. In this condition the XH-51A Compound reached 302.6mph (486.9km/h) in level flight on 29 June 1967.

In June 1964 NASA ordered a third Model 186, called NASA 531 and designated XH-51N. Fitted with a three-blade main rotor and five-seat cabin, it was used as a versatile test vehicle. Finally Lockheed built two Model 286 helicopters as company demonstrators. Almost identical to the 186, with a five-seat interior, these were fully certificated and demonstrated their agility and speed (almost double that of an Alouette on similar power) but without attracting customers.

Seen in its final form with stub wings and J60 turbojet, the XH-51A Compound set new standards for speed and manoeuvrability. But the price was too steep.

DATA FOR ORIGINAL XH-51A:

Diameter of main rotor	**35ft 0in (10.67m)**
Length of fuselage	**34ft 9in (10.59m)**
Weight empty	**2,640lb (1,197.5kg)**
Maximum takeoff weight	**4,100lb (1,860kg)**
Maximum speed	**174mph (280km/h)**
(in very slight descent, 206mph, 332km/h)	
Range	**260 miles (418km)**

ANOTHER MAC WINNER

C-141 STARLIFTER

By the start of the 1960s there was an urgent need to re-equip the US Military Air Transport Service which, apart from a small fleet of C-133 turboprops, was entirely piston-engined. This is all the more surprising when it is remembered that Strategic Air Command had ordered the KC-135 in 1954, and from 1957 had been receiving these jet tankers at the rate of 20 per month. Accordingly, in May 1960 Specific Operational Requirement was issued calling for a jet transport capable of carrying a 60,000lb (27,216kg) payload for 3,500 nautical miles (6,486km).

Following a four-way competition Lockheed-Georgia was selected on 13 March 1961. The first C-141A StarLifter began flight testing on 17 December 1963. By February 1968 the Marietta plant delivered 284 almost identical aircraft, plus one civil example used for infra-red research by NASA. Approximately 61 per cent of each aircraft, including major parts of structure, was

subcontracted. Compared with the contemporary 707 and C-135 the C-141 had a high-mounted wing with less sweep and thus greater span, giving shorter takeoff and landing at the expense of slower cruising speeds.

A major (and erroneous) decision was to base the fuselage cross-section on that of the C-130, though capacity was

increased to 6,530.5 cu ft (184.92m³) by increasing available length ahead of the rear ramp door to 70ft (21.34m).

The wing had 1.2° anhedral, a fixed leading edge with hot-air de-icing, Fowler flaps driven by a single hydraulic motor in the fuselage, fully powered ailerons, and hydraulically driven spoilers ahead of the flaps used as

The press release boasts "New C-141 shows growth of AF Airlift ... twice as much capacity as C-130."

airbrakes and lift dumpers. Well inboard were hung the propulsion pods, each housing a Pratt & Whitney TF33-7 turbofan rated at 21,000lb (9,525kg) thrust and fitted with a reverser. The main wing box, supplied by Avco, formed a series of 12 integral tanks with a capacity of 19,645 gal (23,592 US gal, 89,306 litres). A pressure-fuelling connection was provided in the fairing over the starboard four-wheel main landing gear. On top of the large swept fin and one-piece powered rudder was pivoted the slightly swept tailplane, driven both hydraulically and electrically for trimming purposes and with an electrically heated leading edge, carrying the fully powered elevators.

The fixed nose housed weather radar, the flight deck was fitted with tape instruments and housed an all-weather landing system, and the cargo floor incorporated a powered system for loading and positioning ten pallets containing up to 62,717lb (28,448kg) of cargo. Other loads could include 80 litters plus 23 seats for casualties and medical attendants, or aft-facing seat pallets for 138 troops or side-facing seats for 124 fully equipped paratroops. A small number of aircraft were fitted with strengthened structure to carry the 86,207lb

(39,103kg) load of a Minuteman ICBM in its transport/erector container. These aircraft were restricted to a 2.25g load factor instead of the usual 2.5g.

The C-141A entered service with the first of 14 Air Transport Squadrons just as the transpacific airlift to support the Vietnam war was beginning in earnest. Such was the effort that, within four months of entry to service, average daily utilization was to reach 5.5 hours; later this was to be almost doubled. By 1972 the StarLifters had flown 6,000 medevac (medical evacuation) missions from SE Asia, as well as many hundreds bringing back the bodies of personnel killed in action. Another 421 round trips were flown in support of Israel's Yom Kippur war.

Virtually all missions were flown with a full load, yet because of lack of space the average cargo payload on ten pallets was only 46,000lb (20,866kg). Moreover, the flights to Israel (with most European staging posts politically unavailable) had demonstrated the need for air-refuelling capability. Lockheed proposed a fuselage stretch,

plus an air-refuelling receptacle, but the C-5 history had left Lockheed-Georgia with few friends. After a fight to re-establish credibility, the company was given a contract for a single YC-141B, and this began flight trials on 24 March 1977.

Lockheed spliced in a "barrel section" or "plug" ahead of and behind the wing, increasing usable volume by nearly 75 per cent to 11,399 cu ft (322.8m^3). Above the fuselage behind the cockpit was added a boom receptacle. The result was brilliant. In 1979-82 the

Marietta plant redelivered 270 aircraft, for a total price of $650 million, in effect adding an extra 90 aircraft to the Military Airlift Command inventory. Indeed, thanks to air refuelling, the effect was even greater.

Today 202 C-141B StarLifters remain active, 64 of them flown by Air National Guard squadrons. Lockheed did not succeed in selling the civil L-300, nor a variety of military variants such as a refuelling tanker, AWACS and cruise-missile carrier.

DATA FOR C-141:		
Span		**159ft 11in (48.74m)**
Length	(A)	**145ft 0in (44.2m)**
	(B)	**168ft 3in (51.29m)**
Wing area		**3,228 sq ft (299.9m²)**
Weight empty	(A) initially	**133,773lb (60,678kg)**
	later	**136,900lb (62,097kg)**
	(B) initially	**148,120lb (67,186kg)**
	later	**153,350lb (69,558kg)**
Maximum takeoff weight	(A)	**316,600lb (143,600kg)**
	(B) 2.5g	**323,100lb (146,556kg)**
	(B) 2.25g	**343,000lb (155,585kg)**
Cruising speed (both)		**478mph (769km/h)**
Takeoff run at maximum weight	(B)	**6,420ft (1,957m)**
Range with maximum payload	(A)	**62,717lb (28,448kg)**
		4,155 miles (6,687km)
	(B)	**94,508lb, (42,869kg)**
		3,150 miles (5,069km)

C–141 STARLIFTER

C-141B StarLifter
1 Radome
2 Weather radar scanner
3 ILS glideslope aerial
4 Radar tracking mechanism
5 Front pressure bulkhead
6 Windscreen panels
7 Instrument panel shroud
8 Rudder pedals
9 Crew oxygen reservoir
10 Twin nosewheels
11 Nose undercarriage leg
12 Flight deck floor level
13 Control column
14 Pilot's seat
15 Direct vision opening, side window panel
16 Centre console
17 Co-pilot's seat
18 Overhead switch panel
19 Flight engineer's station
20 Navigator's station
21 Folding jump-seat stowage
22 Underfloor radio and electronics racks
23 Nosewheel leg door
24 Crew galley
25 Relief crew rest area seating
26 cockpit doorway
27 Escape ladder
28 Rest bunks
29 Cockpit roof escape hatch
30 Aerial refuelling director lights
31 Flight refuelling receptacle
32 IFF aerial
33 Fuel delivery piping
34 Troop transport aft facing seating
35 Crew entry door, open
36 Fire extinguisher bottles
37 Wing leading-edge inspection light
38 Cargo loading floor
39 Six-abreast troop seating
40 Cargo hold forward escape hatch
41 Escape ladder stowage
42 UHF (2) aerial
43 Refuelling line fairing
44 Forward fuselage stretch plug section
45 Fuselage skin panelling
46 Cargo hold insulating wall panels
47 Crew walkway
48 Fuselage plug section splice joint
49 Floor beam construction
50 Starboard emergency exit
51 Fuselage frame and stringer construction
52 Cargo floor roller conveyors
53 Port emergency exit
54 463L cargo pallets (13)
55 Wing spar/fuselage main frame
56 Air system vents
57 Ram air intake
58 Wing root
leading-edge fairing
59 UHF(I) aerial
60 Air conditioning plant
61 Wing centre-section carry-through structure
62 Fuel transfer's system piping
63 Starboard wing integral fuel tank bays; total fuel system capacity 23,592 US gal (89305 litres)
64 Engine bleed air ducting
65 Starboard engine nacelles
66 Nacelle Pylons
67 Leading edge de-icing air ducts
68 Fuel system piping
69 Starboard navigation light
70 Wing tip fairing
71 Static dischargers
72 Starboard aileron
73 Aileron tab
74 Fuel jettison pipe
75 Flap guide rails
76 Outboard spoilers, open
77 Starboard outer flap, down position
78 Starboard inboard flap, down position
79 Inboard spoilers, open
80 Flap screw jacks
81 VHV (2) aerial
82 Central flap motor
83 Aileron and spoiler drive mechanism
84 Life raft stowage
85 Emergency equipment packs
86 Wing root trailing edge fillet
87 Flush ADF sense aerials
88 Starboard side ditching hatch
89 Aft fuselage stretch plug section
90 Air system ducting
91 Recirculation air fan
92 Escape ladder stowage
93 Rear escape hatch
94 Aft fuselage upper decking
9S Cargo ramp pressure door upward opening
96 Rear pressure bulkhead
97 Cabin pressurization outflow valves
98 Aft fuselage framing
99 Fin root fillet
100 Tailfin construction
101 Fin internal maintenance ladders
102 VOR aerial
103 All-moving tailplane pivot fixing
104 Tailplane trim screw jack
105 HF probe antenna
106 HF aerial
107 Starboard tailplane
108 Static dischargers
109 Starboard elevator
110 Elevator hydraulic control jacks
111 Anti-collision light
112 Fin/tailplane bullet fairing
113 Elevator tabs
114 Port elevator rib construction
115 Elevator horn balance
116 Port tailplane construction
117 Rudder tabs
118 Rudder rib construction
119 Tailcone air vent
120 Rudder hydraulic control jacks
121 Fin mounting frames
122 Door strut

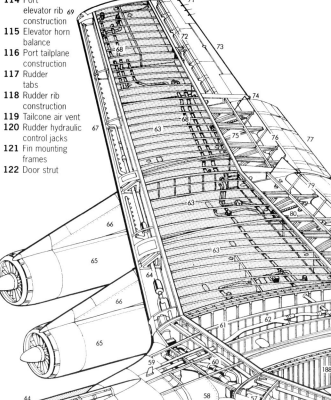
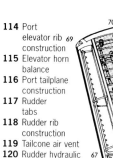

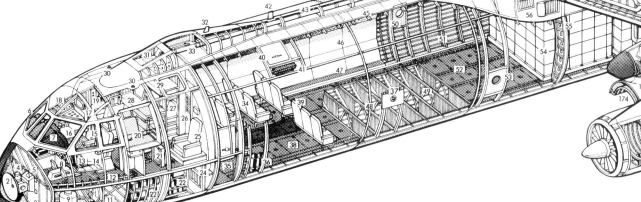

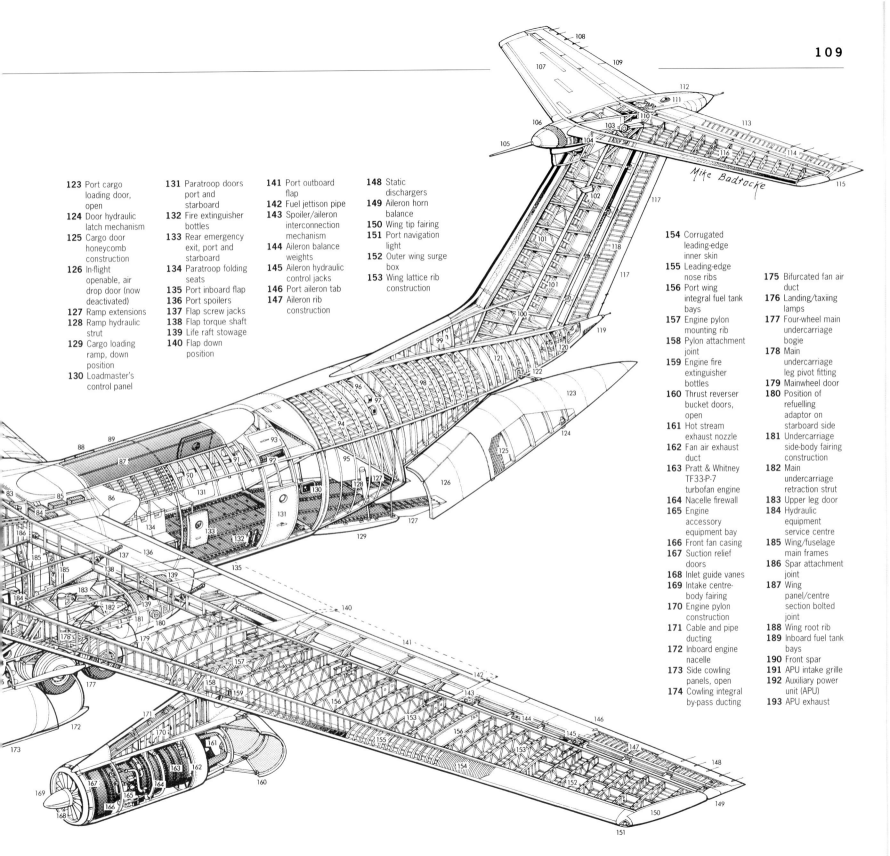

123 Port cargo loading door, open
124 Door hydraulic latch mechanism
125 Cargo door honeycomb construction
126 In-flight openable, air drop door (now deactivated)
127 Ramp extensions
128 Ramp hydraulic strut
129 Cargo loading ramp, down position
130 Loadmaster's control panel

131 Paratroop doors port and starboard
132 Fire extinguisher bottles
133 Rear emergency exit, port and starboard
134 Paratroop folding seats
135 Port inboard flap
136 Port spoilers
137 Flap screw jacks
138 Flap torque shaft
139 Life raft stowage
140 Flap down position

141 Port outboard flap
142 Fuel jettison pipe
143 Spoiler/aileron interconnection mechanism
144 Aileron balance weights
145 Aileron hydraulic control jacks
146 Port aileron tab
147 Aileron rib construction

148 Static dischargers
149 Aileron horn balance
150 Wing tip fairing
151 Port navigation light
152 Outer wing surge box
153 Wing lattice rib construction

154 Corrugated leading-edge inner skin
155 Leading-edge nose ribs
156 Port wing integral fuel tank bays
157 Engine pylon mounting rib
158 Pylon attachment joint
159 Engine fire extinguisher bottles
160 Thrust reverser bucket doors, open
161 Hot stream exhaust nozzle
162 Fan air exhaust duct
163 Pratt & Whitney TF33-P-7 turbofan engine
164 Nacelle firewall
165 Engine accessory equipment bay
166 Front fan casing
167 Suction relief doors
168 Inlet guide vanes
169 Intake centre-body fairing
170 Engine pylon construction
171 Cable and pipe ducting
172 Inboard engine nacelle
173 Side cowling panels, open
174 Cowling integral by-pass ducting

175 Bifurcated fan air duct
176 Landing/taxiing lamps
177 Four-wheel main undercarriage bogie
178 Main undercarriage leg pivot fitting
179 Mainwheel door
180 Position of refuelling adaptor on starboard side
181 Undercarriage side-body fairing construction
182 Main undercarriage retraction strut
183 Upper leg door
184 Hydraulic equipment service centre
185 Wing/fuselage main frames
186 Spar attachment joint
187 Wing panel/centre section bolted joint
188 Wing root rib
189 Inboard fuel tank bays
190 Front spar
191 APU intake grille
192 Auxiliary power unit (APU)
193 APU exhaust

Mike Badrocke

QT-2

QUIET REVOLUTIONS
QT-2,Q–STAR AND YO–3A

The extreme difficulty of detecting Viet Cong guerrillas in the dense jungles of south-east Asia led to the development of special low-altitude sensor-carrying aircraft, including various versions of Neptune and Warning Star. **In early 1966 Lockheed Missiles & Space Co began investigating what could be achieved using as the carrier platform an almost noiseless light aircraft intended to fly at low level.**

First, flown in July 1967, came two QT-2 rebuilds of Schweizer SGS 2-32 metal sailplanes, fitted with a 100hp Continental O-200A engine in a sound-proof bay behind the tandem-seat cockpit with a long shaft driving a very quiet, slow-running four-blade propeller above the nose. They proved effective in Vietnam, operating at heights around 100ft (30m) above ground level without alerting the enemy. One later became the X-26B of the Naval Test Pilot School.

A year later came the Q-Star, again based on an SGS 2-32 but with many changes includ-

As a sensor platform the YO-3A was unique, with near-silent operation and excellent slow flying characteristics; cockpit view was superb.

ing normal tailwheel landing gear. This flew with nine different propellers, from 1969 driven by a 185hp Curtiss-Wright RC2-60 rotary (Wankel) engine.

In July 1968 Lockheed received an Army contract for 14 YO-3A aircraft, again based on the SGS 2-32 but with a 210hp Continental IO-360D engine in the nose driving a six-blade slow-running propeller, wing-mounted inwards-retracting main landing gears and a one-piece upward-hinged windscreen/canopy unit.

They had improved sensors, mainly using infra-red wavelengths, under the nose and rear fuselage. In 1970-72 the last 13 operated over Vietnam, later serving in the USA, quite effectively, against poachers, and also as NASA quiet research aircraft and in various other roles.

DATA FOR QT-2:

Span	**57ft 1in (17.4m)**
Length	**30ft 10in (9.4m)**
Wing area	**180 sq ft (16.72m²)**
Weight empty	**1,576lb (714.9kg)**
Maximum takeoff weight	**2,182lb (989.8kg)**
Operating speed typically	**75mph (121km/h)** but selected from 50 to 90 kt
Range	**350 miles (563km)**

DATA FOR YO-3A:

Span	**57ft 0in (17.37m)**
Length	**29ft 4in (8.94m)**
Wing area	**205 sq ft (19.04m2)**
Weight empty	**3,129lb (1,419kg)**
Maximum takeoff weight	**3,800lb (1,724kg)**
Operating speed (quietest)	**71mph (114km/h)** but selected from 50 to 120kt
Range	**480 miles (772km)**

TOO MUCH TOO SOON

Experience over Vietnam quickly showed the urgent need for an escort/attack helicopter equipped with night and bad-weather sensors and heavy armament. In October 1964 the Army issued a requirement for the advanced aerial fire-support system (AAFSS), calling for such a helicopter. Despite severe demands, such as a speed of 253mph and ferry range of 2,417 miles, 12 submissions were received. Lockheed was announced winner in November 1966, with 10 AH-56A development helicopters ordered. Flight testing began (with the second machine, 66-8827) on 21 Sept 1967.

The difficult dynamic parts were naturally extrapolated from Lockheed's previous rigid-rotor helicopters. The main rotor had four blades made by Parsons, with a stainless-steel skin wrapped over a bonded honeycomb core, but this time with an added U-section spar of titanium alloy forming the leading edge. Approximately 39,000 strands of high-tension steel wire formed tension/tor-sion packs joining the blades to the massive titanium-alloy hub, above which was the four-spoke stabilizing unit. Uniquely, the tail driveshaft was geared not only to the usual anti-torque rotor but also to a three-blade reverse-pitch pusher propeller. In high-speed flight this propeller absorbed almost all the power from the single 3,925shp General Electric T64-16 engine, a mere 300shp being fed to the feathered main rotor to counter windmilling drag.

The stressed-skin airframe included a low wing with sharp dihedral, with the main wheels retracting into fairings at the roots. The tail comprised a fixed tailplane and a ventral fin with a tailwheel. The crew comprised a copilot/gunner in

The 1960s high speed gunship is personified in the AH-56; but by the early 1970s survivability became a higher priority.

the nose and the pilot seated higher up in the rear. They managed one of the most complex avionics systems ever created up to that time, with

AH-56A CHEYENNE

The Cheyenne had more sensors and weaponry than many jet combat aircraft.

1,000 lines more software than the B-52H. This incorporated night-vision equipment and helmet-mounted sights, and managed navigation, flight control and targeting for the planned armament, comprising an undernose gun in a powered turret – a 30mm cannon, 7.62mm Minigun or 40mm grenade launcher – plus

six TOW anti-armour missiles or 2.75in rockets.

Unfortunately, development proved a nightmare. Not only was the avionics/weapon system never debugged, but the basic helicopter suffered from serious stability problems. Shortly before planned delivery of a production AH-56A the production programme was cancelled. Lockheed continued to strive, and gradually made the Cheyenne a fast and agile machine able to aim weapons accurately, but the

programme was terminated in August 1972 when the belief that the job could be done by a less complex and costly machine won the day; (enter the Cobra and Apache).

Two tail rotors were not enough to ensure stability and were potentially hazardous to health on the ground.

DATA FOR AH-56A:	
Diameter of main rotor	**50ft 4.75in (15.36m)**
Length (fuselage)	**54ft 7in (16.64m)**
(overall)	**60ft 0.875in (18.31m)**
Weight empty	**12,961lb (5,879kg)**
Maximum takeoff weight	**25,880lb (11,739kg)**
Maximum speed	**253mph (407km/h)**
Range (external tank)	**875 miles (1,408km).**

BIG BUDGET, HEAVY METAL

In 1962 farsighted General Bernard 'Benny' Schriever organised Project Forecast to try to determine the needs of the US Air Force for at least 25 years ahead. One of the results was recognition that gas-turbine technology made it possible to build a new species of engine, a very large turbofan of high bypass ratio, with a take-off thrust in the order of 40,000lb (18,144kg). In turn, this made it possible to create a huge military airlift transport, much bigger than anything seen previously.

Lockheed was building the C-141, but this was unable to carry anything that would not fit into a C-130. There was an obvious need to be able to transport large radars and many other kinds of load, and eventually the CX-4 specification was issued for an aircraft with a cargo hold 19ft 5.79 m) wide and up to 13 ft 6 in (4.11m) high. One of the loads was the M60 battle tank, weighing over 50 short tons. Eventually the demand included the ability to carry 250,000 lb (113,400kg) over a "coast-to-coast" range, and 125,000lb (56,700kg) for 8,000 miles (12,875km). Another demand was to bring such loads to an upaved 4,000-ft (1,220-m) front-line airstrip.

In August 1965 GE won the $459,055,000 contract for the TF39 engine, and two months later Lockheed won the "Total Package" contract for the C-5

One of the original C-5As delivered to MAC between 1968-73. The Galaxy was the world's largest aircraft until deposed by the similar An-124.

C-5 GALAXY

Lockheed C-5B Galaxy
1 Radome
2 Multi-mode radar scanner colour weather display and ground mapping facilities
3 Radar mounting bulkhead
4 Kevlar composite nose plug section
5 Front pressure bulkhead
6 Station keeping antenna
7 Doppler antenna
8 Inertial platform
9 Visor nose, open
10 Nose section frame construction
11 Visor nose guide rail
12 Cockpit overhead systems switch panel
13 Windscreen panels
14 Instrument panel shroud
15 Windscreen wipers
16 Cockpit nose section framing
17 Rudder pedals
18 Visor nose hydraulic drive motor
19 Cargo ramp folding toe plates
20 Forward cargo ramp extension
21 Forward cargo loading ramp
22 Cockpit floor level
23 Opening (direct vision) side window panel
24 Pilot's seat
25 Co-pilot's seat
26 Observer's seat
27 Flight engineer's station
28 Circuit breaker panels

29 Navigator's station (special missions use only)
30 Crew work bag stowage
31 Visor nose hinge point
32 Crew entry lobby
33 Folding access ladder from lower deck
34 Forward entry doorway
35 Folding airstairs
36 Four-wheel nose undercarriage bogie, with kneeling facility
37 Nosewheel bay doors
38 Hydraulic steering jacks
39 Nosewheel pivot fixing
40 Nose undercarriage wheel bay
41 Lower deck air conditioning ducting
42 Cargo loading deck
43 Upper deck level
44 Avionics equipment racks
45 Cockpit roof escape hatch and ladder
46 IFF antenna
47 UHF antenna
48 Relief crew rest area, six bunks
49 Crew baggage compartment
50 TACAN antenna
51 UHF antenna
52 Wardrobe
53 Toilet compartment
54 Relief crew seating compartment, seven seats
55 Folding table
56 Service door/emergency exit
57 Lower deck palletized troop seating option,

270-seats, 10 abreast
58 Wing inspection light
59 Floor beam construction
60 Recirculating air duct
61 Cargo deck side walkway
62 Fuselage lower lobe frame and stringer construction
63 Wing root fillet framing
64 Escape slide stowage
65 Baggage compartment
66 Life raft automatic ejector
67 Cabin roof escape hatch
68 Starboard side galley unit
69 Anti-collision light
70 Courier compartment, eight seats
71 AC power distribution rack
72 Forward cabin rear bulkhead
73 Wardrobe
74 Baggage compartment
75 Electrical equipment rack
76 Heat exchanger air exhaust
77 Wing spar attachment fuselage main frame
78 Ground cooling fan
79 Air system intake plenum
80 Air conditioning plant
81 Conditioned air distribution box
82 Upper fuselage light
83 Wing centre section construction
84 Wing panel bolted joint

85 Inboard wing integral fuel tanks
86 Fuel system piping
87 Leading-edge slat drive shaft
88 Slat screw jacks
89 Inboard slat aerodynamic seals
90 Inboard leading edge slat segments, open
91 Starboard engine nacelles
92 Nacelle pylons
93 Outboard leading edge slat segments, open
94 Outer wing integral fuel tanks; system capacity 42,342 gal (50,850 US gal, 192,488 lit)
95 Surge tank
96 Wing tip fairing
97 Aileron mass balance
98 Starboard navigation light
99 Static dischargers
100 Starboard aileron
101 Aileron hydraulic actuators
102 Outboard spoilers, open
103 Fuel jettison
104 Outboard single-slotted Fowler-type flaps, down position
105 Inboard flap segments
106 Flap track fairings
107 Inboard spoilers
108 Flap guide rails
109 Flap screw jacks
110 Drive shaft
111 Air system distribution ducting
112 Central flap drive hydraulic motor
112 Nitrogen pressurizing bottles (two)
114 Rear cabin front

bulkhead
115 Toilet compartments (two)
116 D/F loop aerials
117 Rear upper cabin troop seating, 76 seats, six abreast
118 Trailing-edge fillet framing
119 Emergency exit, port and starboard
120 Wing root trailing-edge fillet
121 Fuselage upper lobe frame and stringer construction
122 ADF sense "towel rail" antennas
123 Escape chute stowage
124 VHF antenna
125 Life raft stowage
126 Emergency exit/service door, port and starboard
127 Hatchway to lower deck
128 External ladder stowage
129 Rear fuselage

upper deck
130 Galley unit
131 Wardrobe
132 Pressure relief door/access hatch
133 Rear pressure bulkhead
134 Fuselage skin panelling
135 Aft fuselage frame and stringer construction
136 Centre cargo door screw jacks
137 Aft fuselage service deck
138 Service ladder
139 HF transceiver
140 HF flush antenna
141 Fin front spar
142 Rendezvous beacon and antennas, port and starboard
143 Tail unit internal access ladder
144 Fin rib construction
145 VOR antenna
146 Tailplane pitch trim actuator
147 Tailplane chine fairing

148 Fin/tailplane bullet fairing
149 Starboard tailplane
150 Tailplane structure access panels
151 Static dischargers
152 Two-segment elevators
153 Tailplane pivot attachment
154 Service access hatch
155 Anti collision light
156 Air data/crash recorder
157 Tail navigation lights
158 Elevator rib construction
159 Elevator hydraulic actuators
160 Port tailplane rib construction

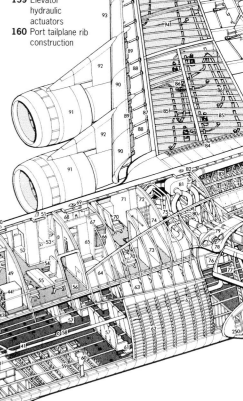

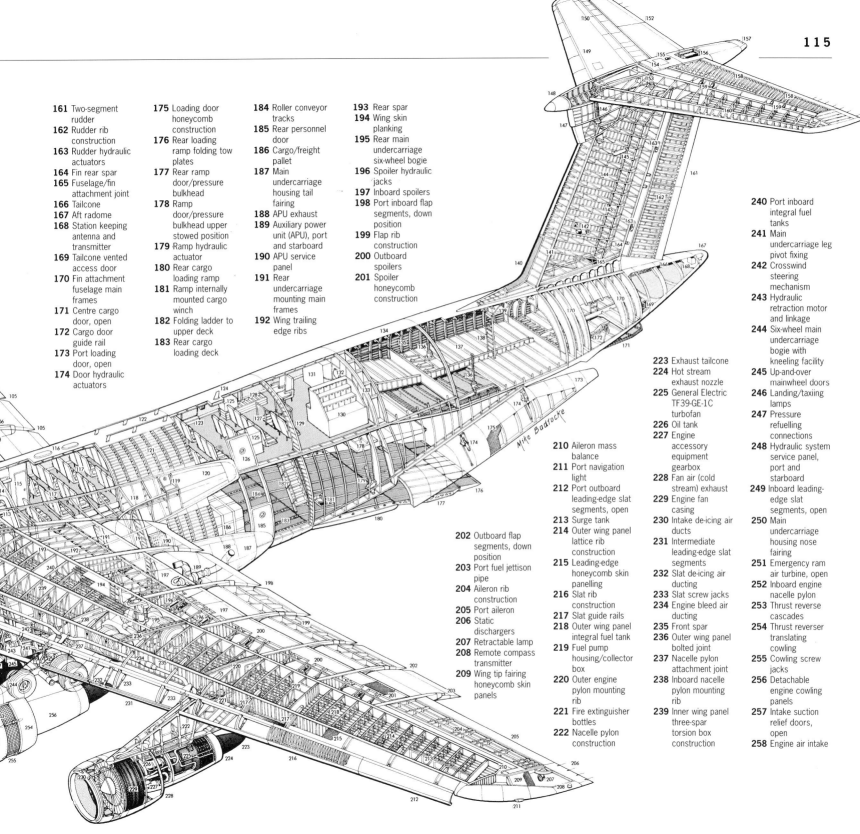

161 Two-segment rudder
162 Rudder rib construction
163 Rudder hydraulic actuators
164 Fin rear spar
165 Fuselage/fin attachment joint
166 Tailcone
167 Aft radome
168 Station keeping antenna and transmitter
169 Tailcone vented access door
170 Fin attachment fuselage main frames
171 Centre cargo door, open
172 Cargo door guide rail
173 Port loading door, open
174 Door hydraulic actuators

175 Loading door honeycomb construction
176 Rear loading ramp folding tow plates
177 Rear ramp door/pressure bulkhead
178 Ramp door/pressure bulkhead upper stowed position
179 Ramp hydraulic actuator
180 Rear cargo loading ramp
181 Ramp internally mounted cargo winch
182 Folding ladder to upper deck
183 Rear cargo loading deck

184 Roller conveyor tracks
185 Rear personnel door
186 Cargo/freight pallet
187 Main undercarriage housing tail fairing
188 APU exhaust
189 Auxiliary power unit (APU), port and starboard
190 APU service panel
191 Rear undercarriage mounting main frames
192 Wing trailing edge ribs

193 Rear spar
194 Wing skin planking
195 Rear main undercarriage six-wheel bogie
196 Spoiler hydraulic jacks
197 Inboard spoilers
198 Port inboard flap segments, down position
199 Flap rib construction
200 Outboard spoilers
201 Spoiler honeycomb construction

202 Outboard flap segments, down position
203 Port fuel jettison pipe
204 Aileron rib construction
205 Port aileron
206 Static dischargers
207 Retractable lamp
208 Remote compass transmitter
209 Wing tip fairing honeycomb skin panels

210 Aileron mass balance
211 Port navigation light
212 Port outboard leading-edge slat segments, open
213 Surge tank
214 Outer wing panel lattice rib construction
215 Leading-edge honeycomb skin panelling
216 Slat rib construction
217 Slat guide rails
218 Outer wing panel integral fuel tank
219 Fuel pump housing/collector box
220 Outer engine pylon mounting rib
221 Fire extinguisher bottles
222 Nacelle pylon construction

223 Exhaust tailcone
224 Hot stream exhaust nozzle
225 General Electric TF39-GE-1C turbofan
226 Oil tank
227 Engine accessory equipment gearbox
228 Fan air (cold stream) exhaust
229 Engine fan casing
230 Intake de-icing air ducts
231 Intermediate leading-edge slat segments
232 Slat de-icing air ducting
233 Slat screw jacks
234 Engine bleed air ducting
235 Front spar
236 Outer wing panel bolted joint
237 Nacelle pylon attachment joint
238 Inboard nacelle pylon mounting rib
239 Inner wing panel three-spar torsion box construction

240 Port inboard integral fuel tanks
241 Main undercarriage leg pivot fixing
242 Crosswind steering mechanism
243 Hydraulic retraction motor and linkage
244 Six-wheel main undercarriage bogie with kneeling facility
245 Up-and-over mainwheel doors
246 Landing/taxiing lamps
247 Pressure refuelling connections
248 Hydraulic system service panel, port and starboard
249 Inboard leading-edge slat segments, open
250 Main undercarriage housing nose fairing
251 Emergency ram air turbine, open
252 Inboard engine nacelle pylon
253 Thrust reverse cascades
254 Thrust reverser translating cowling
255 Cowling screw jacks
256 Detachable engine cowling panels
257 Intake suction relief doors, open
258 Engine air intake

C-5 GALAXY

Mike Badrocke

Galaxy, having undercut Boeing and Douglas with a bid of $1.9 billion. In effect all the first modern High By-Pass Ratio (HBPR) turbofans stemmed ftom the C-5A. GE's ambitious propulsion design had a by-pass ratio of 8, which limited speed; the 1.25 stage fan with pressure ratio of 1.55 and the variable-stator compressor which reached 16.8 meant an overall compression ratio of 26.04. Work went ahead on the C-5A at the Marietta plant under extreme pressure, and the design of the wing was subcontracted to CDI, a group of British engineers made redundant by cancellation of the HS.681, HS.1154 and TSR.2.

Each wing had anhedral, full-span slats and six sections of track-mounted flaps. The

The C-5A can carry a variety of armoured vehicles, including the M60 main battle tank about to climb the ramp (and its replacement, the M1 Abrams). A total of 28 tyres spread the load. Lockheed won the order by underbidding, but their estimates were way off.

huge fuselage had radar in an upward-hinged nose, allowing cargo to pass under the high flight deck, and full-section rear ramp doors. The landing gear comprised four nose-wheels and four main units each with six wheels. The TF39 engines were rated at 41,000 lb (18,598 kg), and fitted with reversers.

Triple inertial systems were installed, as well as a multi-function fault-detection system and a flight-refuelling socket.

The first C-5A took off from Dobbins AFB, beside the Marietta factory, on 30 June 1968. Things went wrong from the start. It was obvious that Lockheed's costs had been non-sense, and instead of 115 aircraft for $1.9 billion the Air Force finally got 81 C-5A aircraft for an initial $5.2 billion. Lockheed suffered from media hype of a succession of faults – for example, a wheel fell off – and a major US publisher produced a book entitled *The C-5A Scandal*. More serious was that the wing was under-strength. Cracks appeared, and despite retrofitting active ailerons to reduce stress the design airframe life had to be reduced from 30,000 hours to a mere

8,000. Worse, except in a national emergency, payload was limited to 50,000 lb (22,680 kg), one-fifth of the design figure.

Despite this, the Galaxy's unrivalled capacity enabled it to play a useful role in the Vietnam and Israeli Yom Kippur wars. (Those 28 wheels – four more even than the mighty Antonov AN-124 – dealt with the necessity for access to unpaved airstrips.) Lockheed picked round the edges with a succession of corrective programmes, and finally in 1978 the Air Force accepted the need for Avco Aerostructures to manufacture completely new wing boxes using a different detail design and thicker skins in new alloys. For the second time, Canadair supplied new slats, ailerons and flap tracks. In 1982-87 all 77 surviving aircraft of the 60th Military Airlift Wing at Travis, the 436th at Dover and the 443rd at Altus were rotated back to Lockheed-Georgia to have new wings fitted. There was still a need for more aircraft in this class. Congress wanted the Air Force to buy used 747s, but Lockheed's proposal to build a "no

faults" aircraft called C-5N was accepted. From 1985, at a contract price just over $8 billion, Lockheed delivered 50 aircraft designated C-5B, powered by TF39-1C engines rated at 43,000 lb (19,505 kg). Externally almost indistinguishable from a C-5A, these improved aircraft incorporate numerous modifications all intended to enhance overall service life. For example, the main landing gears have disc brakes of carbon instead of beryllium, and the number of gearboxes in the drives to the doors closing off the wheel bays has been reduced from 48 to 2. Like the refurbished C-5As these aircraft are painted in Europe 1 camouflage, and today Combat

Command squadrons fly a mix of A and B aircraft.

The C-5B was the Reagan administration's choice in preference to the McDonnell Douglas C-17. In 1994 the C-17 was in production, but in deep trouble with cost overruns and a shortfall in performance. Congress ordered the USAF to investigate alternatives, one of which was the proposal for a C-5D. This would have been powered by CF6-80C2 engines, and been a wholly digital aircraft with a modern cockpit and avionics almost identical to those of the C-130J. Eventually, Douglas dramatically improved the C-17 programme, fending off the challenge from the C-5D.

DATA FOR C-5A & B:		
Span		**222ft 8.5in (67.88m)**
Length		**247ft 10in (75.54m)**
Wing area		**6,200sq ft (576m²)**
Weight: empty	(C-5A)	**337,937lb (152,285kg)**
	(C-5B)	**374,000lb (169,646kg)**
Maximum takeoff	(A)	**769,000lb (348,810kg)**
	(B)	**840,000lb (381,025kg)**
Performance: cruising speed		**518mph (833km/h)**
Range with maximum payload	(A)	**2,729 miles (4,391km)**
		with 220,000lb (99,792kg)
	(B)	**3,435 miles (5,528km)**
		with 261,000lb (118,390 kg)

L-1011 TRISTAR

ENGINE TROUBLE

In 1963 Lockheed-California studied a large shore-based ASW aircraft powered by turbofan engines, to succeed the P-3 Orion. One of the twin-engined designs was so attractive the project team under W.M. 'Bill' Hannan studied a wide-body commercial version. The big ASW aircraft was never ordered, and in 1966 Boeing beat Lockheed for the SST contract (see Introduction), putting some 1,200 engineers out of work. With the Electra programme over, and no other commercial business, Lockheed went all out to win

an order from American Airlines for an "air bus" to carry 250 passengers out of constricted NY La Guardia on routes up to about 1,800 miles. La Guardia had short runways, and could not accept aircraft weighing over 270,000lb (122,470kg).

Launched by British Airways, the long-range L-1011-500 was also ordered by PanAm. Lockheed pioneered many new concepts on the TriStar, including (on the -500) active ailerons.

LOCKHEED TRISTAR K MK 1
1 Fixed Mk 8 flight refuelling probe
2 Radome
3 Dual VOR localiser aerials
4 Radar scanner dish
5 Dual ILS glideslope aerials
6 Front pressure bulkhead
7 Curved windscreen panels
8 Windscreen wipers
9 Instrumental panel shroud
10 Rudder pedals
11 Cockpit floor level
12 Ventral access door
13 Avionics equipment bay
14 Pitot heads
15 Observer's seat
16 Captain's seat
17 Centre control pedestal
18 Second pilot's seat
19 Pilots' overhead panel and circuit breaker panel
20 Flight engineer's station
21 Closed circuit television and refuelling control panel
22 Cockpit roof escape hatch
23 Refuelling probe floodlights
24 Cockpit air conditioning ducting
25 Crew toilet
26 Flight deck doorway
27 Galley unit
28 Nose undercarriage wheel bay
29 Forward entry door
30 Crew rest
31 Starboard service
32 Refuelling pipe pressure sealing box
33 UHF/VHF aerial
34 Curtained cabin divider
35 Interphone
36 Wardrobe
37 Air system heat exchanger
38 Nose undercarriage leg strut
39 Twin nosewheels
40 Hydraulic steering jacks
41 Nosewheel doors
42 Air conditioning plant, port and starboard
43 Fuel venting system air intake
44 Cabin window panel
45 Floor beam construction
46 Baggage containers
47 Cabin wall trim panelling
48 Dual IFF aerials
49 Fuel venting air duct
50 Cabin floor baggage handling system
51 Forward underfloor fuel cells: additional fuel load 100,000 lb (45 360 kg)
52 Forward underfloor cargo hold C2
compartment, 12 seats
53 Lower lobe frame and stringer construction
54 Fuel pump/collector box
55 Wing root fillet
56 Taxying and runway turn-off lamps
57 Bleed air system ducting
58 Escape chute and life raft stowage
59 Passenger door L2
60 Galley unit
61 Ball mats
62 Passenger door R2
63 UHF aerial
64 Dual anti collision lights
65 Fuselage/front spar attachment main frame
66 Dry bay
67 Centre section fuel tanks
68 Floor beam construction
69 Centre fuselage frame and stringer construction
70 TACAN aerial
71 Starboard wing inboard fuel tank bay
72 Thrust reverser cascades, open
73 Starboard engine nacelle
74 Nacelle pylon
75 Fixed portion of leading edge
76 Fuel surge box and boost pump reservoir
77 Fuel system piping
78 Outboard fuel tank bay
79 Pressure refuelling ground connections
80 Screw jack drive shaft
81 Slat screw jacks
82 Leading-edge slat segments, open
83 Mk 32 Flight Refuelling pod
84 Wind driven power turbine
85 Refuelling pod pylon adaptor
86 Outboard slat segments
87 Fuel vent compartment
88 Wing tip fairing
89 Starboard navigation (green) and forward strobe (white) lights

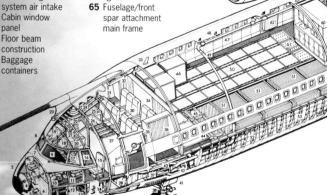

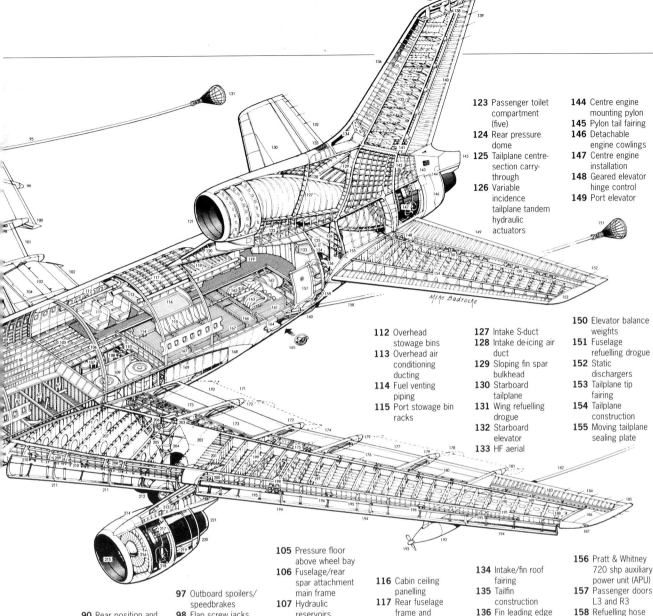

123 Passenger toilet compartment (five)
124 Rear pressure dome
125 Tailplane centre-section carry-through
126 Variable incidence tailplane tandem hydraulic actuators

144 Centre engine mounting pylon
145 Pylon tail fairing
146 Detachable engine cowlings
147 Centre engine installation
148 Geared elevator hinge control
149 Port elevator

165 Ventral closed-circuit television camera (CCTV)
166 Fuel pump collector box
167 Rear underfloor fuel cells
168 Wing root trailing edge fillet
169 Rear underfloor cargo hold C3
170 Port inboard double slotted flap
171 Flap down position
172 Flap track fairings
173 Inboard spoilers lift dumpers
174 Inboard (high speed) aileron
175 Aileron hydraulic actuators
176 Outboard spoilers/speedbrakes
177 Outboard double slotted flap
178 Flap down position
179 Flap track fairings
180 Outboard roll control spoilers
181 Fuel jettison pipe
182 Refuelling hose
183 Port aileron
184 Static dischargers
185 Rear position and strobe lights (white)
186 Port wing tip fairing
187 Port navigation (red) and forward strobe (white) lights
188 Fuel vent compartment
189 Rear spar
190 Fuel tank bay access
191 Front spar
192 Mk 32 Flight Refuelling pod
193 Wind-driven power turbine

194 Outboard leading-edge slat segments, open
195 Slat guide rails
196 Screw jacks
197 Wing rib construction
198 Pressure refuelling ground connections
199 Port wing integral fuel tank bay
200 Slat de-icing air duct
201 Wing stringers
202 Wing skin panelling
203 Main undercarriage pivot fixing
204 Main undercarriage leg strut
205 Undercarriage leg side breaker struts
206 Hydraulic retraction jack
207 Inboard integral fuel tank bay
208 Bleed air ducting
209 Screw jack drive shaft
210 Slat screw jacks
211 Inboard leading-edge slat segments, open
212 Four-wheel main undercarriage bogie
213 Port engine pylon
214 Detachable engine cowlings
215 Port engine intake
216 Rolls-Royce RB.211-524B turbofan
217 Oil cooler
218 Engine accessory gearbox
219 Thrust reverser cascades
220 Fan air (cold stream) exhaust duct
221 Core engine (hot stream) exhaust nozzle

112 Overhead stowage bins
113 Overhead air conditioning ducting
114 Fuel venting piping
115 Port stowage bin racks

127 Intake S-duct
128 Intake de-icing air duct
129 Sloping fin spar bulkhead
130 Starboard tailplane
131 Wing refuelling drogue
132 Starboard elevator
133 HF aerial

150 Elevator balance weights
151 Fuselage refuelling drogue
152 Static dischargers
153 Tailplane tip fairing
154 Tailplane construction
155 Moving tailplane sealing plate

105 Pressure floor above wheel bay
106 Fuselage/rear spar attachment main frame
107 Hydraulic reservoirs
108 Centre section service bay
109 Main undercarriage retracted position
110 Hydraulic flap drive motors
111 Rear cabin passenger seating, 204-seat layout

116 Cabin ceiling panelling
117 Rear fuselage frame and stringer construction
118 Cabin ceiling lighting panels
119 Cabin attendant's folding seat
120 Noise attenuating intake fairing
121 Centre engine intake
122 Intake support structure

134 Intake/fin roof fairing
135 Tailfin construction
136 Fin leading edge
137 Dual VOR aerials
138 Rudder mass balance
139 Static discharges
140 Rudder rib construction
141 Rudder hydraulic actuators
142 Engine bleed air system ducting
143 Bleed air spill duct

156 Pratt & Whitney 720 shp auxiliary power unit (APU)
157 Passenger doors L3 and R3
158 Refuelling hose
159 Refuelling signal lights
160 Drogue housing tunnel fairing
161 Hose drum unit pressure box
162 Hydraulic fuel pumps housing
163 Dual hose drum units
164 Cooling ram air intake fairing

90 Rear position and strobe lights (white)
91 Static dischargers
92 Starboard "active control" aileron
93 Aileron hydraulic-actuators
94 Fuel jettison pipe
95 Refuelling hose
96 Outboard roll control spoilers
97 Outboard spoilers/speedbrakes
98 Flap screw jacks
99 Flap track fairings
100 Outboard double slotted flap, down position
101 Inboard (high speed) aileron
102 Inboard double slotted flap, down position
103 Flap vane
104 Inboard spoilers/lift dumpers

Hannan led a team which quickly began to offer the airlines an attractive twin-jet. It was soon evident that American had to relax the 270,000lb limit, and by June 1967 the project had become the L-1011-365, from 365,000lb, with three engines to take care of loss of an engine over the Rockies. Soon the weight went to 385,000 and then 410,000lb. It was a serious blow when in February 1968 American ordered the rival DC-10, but a month later Lockheed announced launch orders for 144 L-1011 TriStars from Eastern, TWA and a British group called Air Holdings. Air Holdings was an offset to help get the project off the ground, and defuse protests over Lockheed's selection of the British Rolls-Royce RB.211 engine.

The L-1011 had a low wing with quarter-chord sweep of 35°, full-span slats, double-slotted flaps, inboard all-speed ailerons, outboard ailerons locked inoperative at high indicated airspeeds, and six sections of spoiler on each wing with the four inner surfaces also used as speedbrakes. All flight controls were powered, the horizontal tail com-

prising a pivoted tailplane with elevators added to increase camber. The RB.211 engines were intended to give 40,000lb (18,144kg) and were hung under each wing and centred in the rear fuselage fed by an S-duct. Bogie main landing gears retracted inwards and the twin-wheel nose gear forwards. Body diameter was 19ft 7in (5.97m), enabling up to 400 passengers to be seated up to 10-abreast.

The RB.211 engine proved to have been underpriced. More seriously, it suffered from unacceptable deficiencies, and none could be delivered. The result was Rolls-Royce's bankruptcy on 4 February 1971. Flight-test engines derated to 34,000lb (15,422kg) enabled a crew led by Hank Dees to fly the first TriStar at Palmdale on 16 November 1970, but the situation brought Lockheed itself near bankruptcy. At last, an L-1011-1, powered by RB.211-22 engines of 42,000lb (19,051kg) thrust, was delivered to Eastern for crew training on 4 April 1972, with FAA certification following on 14 April and the first passenger flight on the following day. Lockheed built 162 L-1011-1 aircraft, many of

Lockheed TriStar 500
1 Radome
2 VOR localiser aerial
3 Radar scanner dish
4 ILS glideslope aerial
5 Front pressure bulkhead
6 Curved windscreen panels
7 Windscreen wipers
8 Instrument panel shroud
9 Rudder pedals
10 Cockpit floor level
11 Ventral access door
12 Forward underfloor radio and electronics bay
13 Pitot tubes
14 Observer's seat
15 Captain's seat
16 First officer's seat
17 Overhead panel
18 Flight engineer's station
19 Cockpit roof escape hatch
20 Air conditioning ducting
21 Forward galley units
22 Starboard service door
23 Forward toilet compartments
24 Curtained cabin divider
25 Wardrobe
26 Forward passenger door
27 Cabin attendant's folding seat
28 Nose undercarriage wheel bay
29 Ram air intake
30 Heat exchanger
31 Nose undercarriage leg strut
32 Twin nosewheels
33 Steering jacks
34 Nosewheel door
35 Air conditioning plant, port and starboard
36 Cabin window panel
37 Six abreast first class seating 24 sears
38 Forward underfloor freight hold
39 Forward freight door
40 VHF aerial
41 Curtained cabin divider
42 Overhead stowage bins
43 Nine-abreast tourist class seating, 222 seats
44 Baggage/freight containers, twelve LD3 containers forward
45 Fuselage frame and stringer construction
46 Wing root filler
47 Taxying lamp
48 Bleed air system ducting
49 Escape chute and life raft stowage
50 Mid-section entry door
51 Centre section galley units
52 Fuselage centre section construction
53 Wing centre section carry-through structure
54 Dry bay
55 Centre section fuel tanks, capacity 6,711 Imp gal (30.510 l)
56 Floor beam construction
57 Fuselage/front spar attachment main frame
58 Anticollision lights

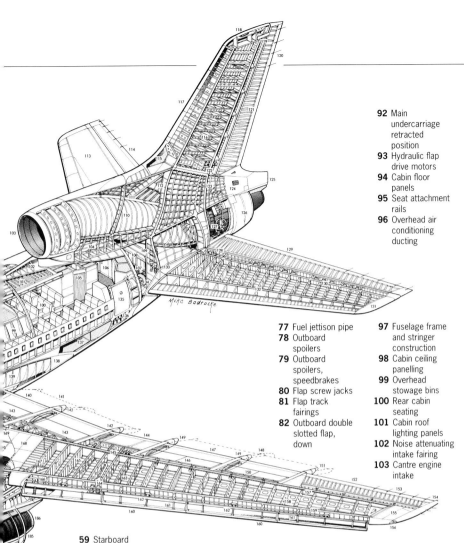

Mike Badrocke

L-1011 TRISTAR

92 Main undercarriage retracted position
93 Hydraulic flap drive motors
94 Cabin floor panels
95 Seat attachment rails
96 Overhead air conditioning ducting

77 Fuel jettison pipe
78 Outboard spoilers
79 Outboard spoilers, speedbrakes
80 Flap screw jacks
81 Flap track fairings
82 Outboard double slotted flap, down

97 Fuselage frame and stringer construction
98 Cabin ceiling panelling
99 Overhead stowage bins
100 Rear cabin seating
101 Cabin roof lighting panels
102 Noise attenuating intake fairing
103 Cantre engine intake

59 Starboard inboard fuel tank bay, capacity 6,649 Imp gal (30,226 l)
60 Thrust reverser cascade, open
61 Starboard engine nacelle
62 Nacelle pylon
63 Fixed portion of leading edge
64 Fuel surge box and boost pump reservoir
65 Fuel system piping
66 Outboard fuel tank bay capacity 3,169 Imp gal (14,407 l)

67 Pressure refuelling connections
68 Screw jack drive shaft
69 Slat screw jacks
70 Leading-edge slat segments open
71 Extended wing tip fairing
72 Starboard navigation light
73 Wing tip strobe light
74 Static dischargers
75 Starboard active control aileron
76 Aileron hydraulic jacks

83 Inboard aileron
84 Inboard double slotted flap, down
85 Flap vane
86 Inboard spoilers/ speedbrakes
87 Fuselage/rear spar attachment main frame
88 Cabin trim panels
89 Pressure floor over wheel bay
90 Hydraulic reservoirs
91 Centre section service bay

104 Intake duct support structure
105 Atf galley units
106 Rear toilet compartments (5)
107 Rear pressure dome
108 Tailplane centre section
109 Variable incidence tailplane hydraulic jacks
110 Intake S-duct
111 Intake de-icing air supply
112 Sloping fin spar bulkhead

113 Starboard tailplane
114 Starboard elevator
115 HF aerial
116 Tail fin construction
117 Fin leading edge
118 VOR aerial
119 Rudder mass balance
120 Static dischargers
121 Rudder construction
122 Rudder hydraulic jacks
123 Engine bleed air system
124 Centre engine pylon mounting
125 Tail fairing
126 Detachable engine cowlings
127 Centre engine installation
128 Geared elevator hinge control
129 Port elevator
130 Elevator balance weights
131 Tailplane tip fairing
132 Tailplane construction
133 Moving tailplane seating fairing
134 Pratt & Whitney Canada auxiliary power unit
135 Rear cabin door
136 Aft electronics bay
137 Underfloor cargo compartment
138 Wing root trailing edge filler
139 Aft underfloor freight compartment, seven LD3 containers
140 Port inboard double slotted flap
141 Flap down position
142 Flap track fairings
143 Inboard spoilers/ speedbrakes

144 Inboard aileron
145 Aileron hydraulic jacks
146 Outboard spoilers/speedbrakes
147 Outboard double slotted flap
148 Flap down position
149 Flap track fairings
150 Outboard spoilers
151 Fuel jettison pipe
152 Port 'active control' aileron
153 Static dischargers
154 Port wing tip strobe lights
155 Extended wing tip fairing
156 Port navigation light
157 Rear spar
158 Fuel tank bay access panels
159 Front spar
160 Outboard leading edge slat segments, open
161 Slat guide rails
162 Screw jacks
163 Wing rib construction
164 Pressure refuelling connections
165 Wing integral fuel tank bays, capacity 3,169 Imp gal (14,407l)
166 Slat de-icing air duct
167 Stringer construction
168 Wing skin plating
169 Undercarriage pivot fixing
170 Main undercarriage leg strut
171 Undercarriage side struts
172 Inboard integral fuel tank bay, capacity 6,649 Imp gal (30,336 l)

173 Bleed air ducting
174 Screw jack drive shaft
175 Slat screw jacks
176 Inboard leading edge slat segments, open
177 Four-wheel main undercarriage bogie
178 Port engine pylon
179 Detachable engine cowlings
180 Port engine

181 Rolls-Royce RB.211 524B turbofan engine
182 Oil cooler
183 Engine accessory gearbox
184 Thrust reverser cascades, closed
185 Fan air exhaust duct
186 Hot stream exhaust nozzle

intake

which subsequently being brought up to later standards.

Lockheed soon suffered from the inability of Rolls-Royce to offer a more powerful engine; it could not match the heavier DC-10-30 and -40 and progressively fell behind in orders. The L-1011-100 was cleared to a maximum takeoff weight increased from 430,000lb (195,048kg) to 466,000lb (211,378kg); 14 were delivered. The L-1011-200 had 48,000lb (21,773kg) RB.211-524 engines, 24 being delivered for "hot and/or high" operations. Delta upgraded six Dash-1 aircraft to L-1011-250 standard, with -524B4 engines rated at 50,000lb (22,680kg) and extra fuel.

The final new-build version was the L-1011-500. This attempted to meet DC-10 performance (notably in range) by combining the engines, tankage and weights of the L-1011-250 with a shorter fuselage

L-1011 TRISTAR

seating 246-300. The -500 first flew on 16 October 1978, and later aircraft (initially for PanAm) were fitted with a long-span wing with active ailerons automatically driven to relieve wing loads and reduce drag. Lockheed delivered 50 of the -500 version, to bring total production up to 250, ending in August 1983.

Once settled down in service the TriStars proved to be excellent aircraft. Their reliability made them popular with the airlines and their customers. Lockheed has supplied kits for updating early examples to -250 standard and also to the -150 (470,000lb, 213,192kg) standard with extra tankage. In the UK Marshall of

TriStar KC1

1 Flight refuelling probe
2 Weather radar
3 Avionics equipment racks
4 Pitot heads
5 Cockpit roof escape hatch
6 Television monitor and refuelling control panel
7 Air conditioning pack, single port, dual starboard
8 Nose undercarriage bay
9 Fuel venting air intake
10 Relief crew rest compartment, 12-seats
11 9G cargo restraint net
12 104in x 140in (2.64m x 3.56m) cargo door
13 Forward underfloor fuel cells, total additional fuel load 100,000 lb (45,360 kg)

14 Upper deck cargo compartment, maximum allowable palletised load 98,110 lb (44,500 kg)
15 Taxying and runway turn-off lamps
16 Fuel collector box
17 Centre section integral fuel tanks
18 Central hydraulic equipment service bay
19 Main undercarriage stowage
20 Wing box integral fuel tankage
21 Rolls-Royce RB.211-524B turbofan engines
22 Thrust reverser cascades
23 Pressure refuelling connections
24 Leading edge slats
25 Mk 32 flight refuelling pod
26 Wing tip vent tank

27 Navigation light
28 Rear position light
29 Outboard active control aileron
30 Fuel jettison
31 Outboard double-slotted flap segment
32 Inboard (high speed) aileron
33 Inboard double-slotted flap segment
34 Air driven turbine, port and starboard
35 Rear underfloor fuel cells
36 Fuel collector box
37 Equipment cooling air scoop
38 Dual Mk 17T hose-drum units (HDU)
39 Ventral closed

circuit television camera
40 Drogue housing tunnel fairings
41 Refuelling traffic lights
42 Hydraulic fuel pump housing
43 Rear pressure bulkhead
44 Auxiliary Power Unit (APU)
45 Centre engine installation
46 All-moving tailplanes and elevators
47 Rudder
48 Trailed refuelling hoses
49 Refuelling drogues

Cambridge have become experienced in offering a range of upgrades. The experience was gained initially by converting TriStars into tanker/transports for the RAF.

Work began with six L-1011-500s purchased in 1982 from British Airways. Four were initially rebuilt as TriStar K.1 tankers cleared to 540,000lb (244,940kg), with a fuel capacity of 313,300lb (142,111kg), two Mk 17T Fight-Refuelling hose-drum units and a flight-refuelling probe above the flight deck. All six are now to KC.1 standard, which add a large cargo door, pallet-handling system and the ability also to carry passengers.

Three TriStar C.2(K) aircraft are ex-PanAm L-1011-500s used mainly as transports but also fitted with high-flow Mk 32 flight-refuelling pods.

DATA FOR TRISTAR VARIANTS:						
Span	(most)	**155ft 4in (47.345m)**	Cruising speed		
	(-500)	**164ft 4in (50.09m)**		(commercial)	**484mph (779km/h)**
Length	(most)	**178ft 8in (54.46m)**		(RAF)	**553mph (889km/h)**
	(-500)	**164ft 2.5in (50.05m)**	Range	(-1)	**4,465 miles (7,185km)**
Wing area	(most)	**3,456 sq ft (321.06m²)**			with maximum payload of 40,000lb (18,144kg)
	(-500)	**3,541 sq ft (328.96m²)**		(-500)	**4,310 miles (6,936km)**
Weight empty	(-1)	**234,275lb (106,267kg)**			with maximum payload of 74,960lb (34,001kg)
	(-500)	**242,967lb (110,210kg)**	(TriStar K.1)	**4,834 miles (7,780km)**
Maximum takeoff weight	(-1)	**430,000lb (195,048kg)**			with maximum payload of 95,000lb (43,092kg)
	(-500)	**496,000lb (224,986kg)**			
	(TriStar K.1)	**540,000lb (244,944kg)**			

NOT BEFORE TIME

By the 1960s the menace of the Soviet Union's huge and growing fleet of submarines – many equipped to fire strategic missiles – was obvious, yet the US Navy's only seagoing ASW aircraft was the S-2 Tracker. This was a piston-engined aircraft first flown in 1952, and to fuel it the Navy carriers had to contain large tanks of high-octane gas. Not before time, the Navy issued a concept for a VSX (fixed-wing ASW experimental) in 1964, followed with a Specific Operational Requirement in 1966. It received submissions from Lockheed-California and General Dynamics, and eventually announced Lockheed as winner on 4 August 1969. The first of eight YS-3As made its maiden flight at Palmdale on 21 January 1972.

The S-3A Viking was an amazing exercise in packaging a lot into a small space. This task was carried out by a team which included General Electric (9,275lb/4,207kg-thrust TF34-2 turbofan engines), LTV

(who designed and made the folding high-mounted wing, folding tail, engine pods and landing gears based on those of the F-8 Crusader) and, not least, Univac Federal Systems who integrated the mass of ASW sensors, navaids, flight control and weapon systems.

The wings taper on the leading edge, which from the nacelle pylons to the tips have electrically driven droop flaps. On the trailing edge are hydraulically driven Fowler flaps, ahead of which are spoilers above and below the wings to serve as speedbrakes and to augment the roll control from the small powered ailerons. The incidence of the tailplane

is varied electrically for trimming, the elevators and rudder are powered hydraulically.

Despite the small size of the engines they provide bleed air to de-ice the wings and tail. No reversers are fitted because an arrester hook is provided for carrier recovery. The steerable twin-wheel nose gear incorporates a towbar for the ship's catapult. Between the spars the fixed inboard wing serves as integral tankage for 1,582gal (1,900 US gal, 7,192 litres) of fuel, augmented by two 250gal (300 US gal, 1,136-litre) drop tanks. A long flight-refuelling probe can be extended horizontally ahead of the cockpit roof. In the nose is the Texas

An S-3A of VS-21 recovers aboard the USS John F. Kennedy (CV-67) on 27 February 1975. A lot of instrumentation in a relatively small package.

Instruments APS-116 radar, and the same company supplies the OR-89 FLIR (forward-looking infra-red) mounted in a turret which can be extended down behind the nose gear. The pilot and copilot climb in through the raised canopy with heavily tinted transparencies and settle in Escapac "zero/zero" seats. Behind them the Senso (sensor operator) and Tacco (tactical co-ordinator) also enter from above and sit on Escapacs. Behind them are the weapon bays for 2,000lb (907kg) of a very wide range of stores. Next come large bays occupied by avionics and then the bulky environmental control system, under which are the diagonal chutes for 60 sonobuoys, with dispensers for chaff and flares on each side. From the tail end can be extended a long tube carrying the ASQ-81 MAD (magnetic-anomaly detector). ESMs use passive receiver antennas grouped in boxes on the wingtips.

Deliveries began to VS-41 at North Island in February 1974. VS-21 took the Viking to sea aboard the carrier JFK in July 1975. Altogether Lockheed delivered 187 Vikings, the last in mid-1978. Four were

modified as six-passenger US-3A COD (Carrier On-board Delivery) transports, and one was tested as the KS-3A tanker (replaced by equipping Vikings for "buddy" refuelling).

From 1984 Lockheed completed upgrading 119 Vikings to S-3B standard, with new sensors and processors, enhanced ESM, a new APU (auxiliary power unit) and provision to fire Harpoon cruise missiles from the wing pylons. The Navy has 17 S-3As stored, and a further 16 have been converted into ES-3A electronic-reconnaissance aircraft. To replace the E-2 Hawkeye an AWACS-type rebuild has been studied, with an electronically scanned radar in a giant fixed triangular antenna carried above the aircraft. It is unlikely that this will be produced.

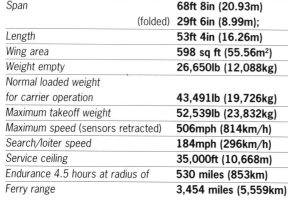

DATA FOR S-3 VIKING:		
Span		**68ft 8in (20.93m)**
	(folded)	**29ft 6in (8.99m);**
Length		**53ft 4in (16.26m)**
Wing area		**598 sq ft (55.56m²)**
Weight empty		**26,650lb (12,088kg)**
Normal loaded weight		
for carrier operation		**43,491lb (19,726kg)**
Maximum takeoff weight		**52,539lb (23,832kg)**
Maximum speed (sensors retracted)		**506mph (814km/h)**
Search/loiter speed		**184mph (296km/h)**
Service ceiling		**35,000ft (10,668m)**
Endurance 4.5 hours at radius of		**530 miles (853km)**
Ferry range		**3,454 miles (5,559km)**

S-3B Viking
1 Glass-fibre radome, open position
2 Radar scanner glass-fibre housing
3 Texas Instruments AN/APS-137(V) 1 radar scanner
4 Articulated scanner mounting
5 Radome hinge point
6 Retractable flight refuelling probe
7 Windscreen de-icing fluid tank and filler
8 Forward identification light
9 Radar mountings
10 Sloping front pressure bulkhead
11 Nose undercarriage pivot mounting
12 Catapult tow bar
13 Hinged axle beam
14 Twin nosewheels, aft retracting
15 Deck approach lights
16 Landing/taxiing light
17 Cabin air conditioning and pressurization outflow valves, port and starboard
18 Pitot head
19 Canopy external release panel
20 Rudder pedals
21 Instrument panel
22 Control column
23 Windscreen wipers
24 Instrument panel shroud
25 Electrically heated windscreen panels
26 Overhead switch panel
27 Second Pilot's seat
28 Tactical Co-ordinator's (TACCO's) instrument console
29 Pilot's McDonnell Douglas Escapac 1-E ejection seat
30 Seat arming/safety lever
31 Seat mounting, ejection rails
32 Jettisonable side window hatch
33 Electro-luminescent formation lighting strip
34 Engine throttle levers
35 Close pitched fuselage frames
36 OR-89/AA infra-red equipment bay, radar avionics on starboard side
37 Retractable Forward-Looking Infra-Red (FLIR) turret
38 FLIR turret doors
39 Auxiliary Power Unit (APU) bay, entry hatch on starboard side
40 APU exhaust
41 Port weapons bay door, open
42 Cabin conditioning air duct
43 Sloping seat mounting bulkhead
44 Side window with rotating polaroid blind
45 Sensor Operator's (SENSO's) seat
46 SENSO's instrument console
47 TACCO's seat
48 Circuit breaker panel
49 Rear crew compartment ejection/escape roof hatch
50 UHF L-band comm/IFF antenna
51 VHF antenna
52 Wing front spar centre section carry-through
53 Starboard wing integral fuel tank bay, total internal capacity 1,582 Imp gal (7,192 lit)
54 Engine fire extinguisher bottles
55 Starboard engine pylon
56 250 Imp gal (1,136 lit) external fuel tank
57 Starboard stores pylon
58 Leading edge stall strips
59 Starboard wing fold hinge
60 Leading edge torque shaft and actuating links
61 Starboard drooped leading edge
62 Forward and forward oblique ESM antennas
63 Starboard navigation light
64 Starboard Electronic Support Measures (ESM) wing tip pod
65 Aft and aft oblique ESM antennas
66 Starboard aileron
67 Aileron hinge control linkage
68 Outboard spoiler/airbrake panels, open
69 Ventral airbrake panel
70 Flap guide rails
71 Starboard single-slotted flap extended
72 Inboard spoiler panel
73 Flap actuating links
74 ADF antenna
75 Wing panel centreline rib
76 Avionics equipment racks port and starboard
77 Front spar/fuselage main frame attachment joint
78 Equipment bay centre aisle
79 Internal weapons bays, port and starboard
80 Weapons carriers/release units
81 Univac main computer
82 iCold plate avionics cooling air ducts

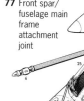

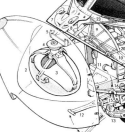

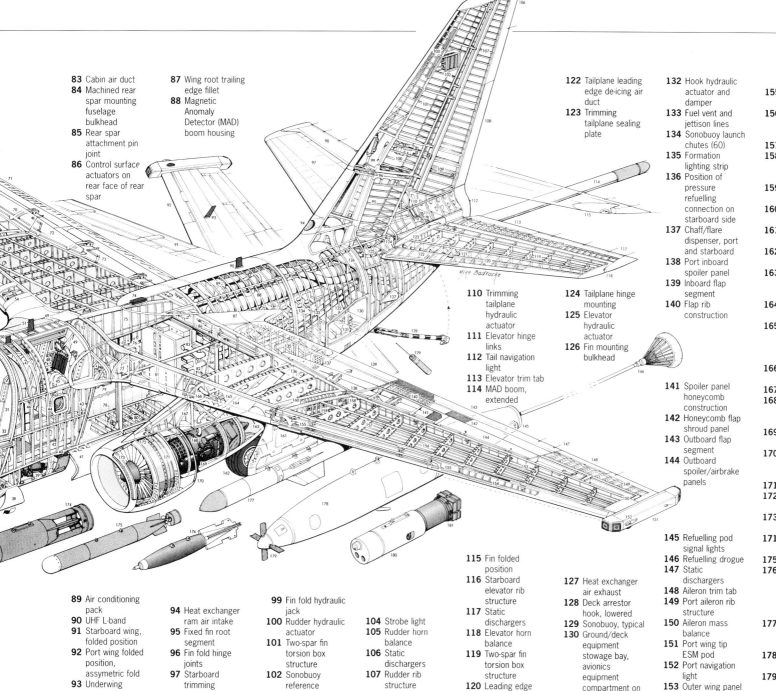

83 Cabin air duct
84 Machined rear spar mounting fuselage bulkhead
85 Rear spar attachment pin joint
86 Control surface actuators on rear face of rear spar

87 Wing root trailing edge fillet
88 Magnetic Anomaly Detector (MAD) boom housing

110 Trimming tailplane hydraulic actuator
111 Elevator hinge links
112 Tail navigation light
113 Elevator trim tab
114 MAD boom, extended

122 Tailplane leading edge de-icing air duct
123 Trimming tailplane sealing plate

124 Tailplane hinge mounting
125 Elevator hydraulic actuator
126 Fin mounting bulkhead

132 Hook hydraulic actuator and damper
133 Fuel vent and jettison lines
134 Sonobuoy launch chutes (60)
135 Formation lighting strip
136 Position of pressure refuelling connection on starboard side
137 Chaff/flare dispenser, port and starboard
138 Port inboard spoiler panel
139 Inboard flap segment
140 Flap rib construction

141 Spoiler panel honeycomb construction
142 Honeycomb flap shroud panel
143 Outboard flap segment
144 Outboard spoiler/airbrake panels

145 Refuelling pod signal lights
146 Refuelling drogue
147 Static dischargers
148 Aileron trim tab
149 Port aileron rib structure
150 Aileron mass balance
151 Port wing tip ESM pod
152 Port navigation light
153 Outer wing panel two-spar torsion box structure
154 Drooping leading

edge ribs
155 Leading edge de-icing air duct
156 Machined lower wing skin striger panel
157 Wing ribs
158 Control rod hinge and cross-over linkages
159 Wing fold rotary actuator
160 Port wing folding hinge joint
161 Port wing stores pylon
162 Port mainwheel, aft retracting
163 Core engine (hot stream) exhaust duct
164 Engine bleed air ducting
165 Main undercarriage leg and hydraulic retraction jack mountings
166 Engine pylon attachment joint
167 Port engine pylon
168 General Electric TF34-GE-2 turbofan engine
169 Engine accessory equipment
170 Fan air (cold stream) exhaust duct
171 Engine fan casing
172 Forward engine mounting
173 Intake lip de-icing air duct

171 Mk 54 depth charge
175 Mk 44 torpedo
176 Mk 36 destructor (Mk 82, 500 lb HE bomb with extended depth sensitive fuse)
177 AGM-84 Harpoon air-to-surface anti-shipping missile
178 D-704 îBuddyî refuelling pod
179 Refuelling pod power turbine
180 Mk 52 mine
181 Mine parachute pack

89 Air conditioning pack
90 UHF L-band
91 Starboard wing, folded position
92 Port wing folded position, assymetric fold
93 Underwing sonobuoy reference antennae

94 Heat exchanger ram air intake
95 Fixed fin root segment
96 Fin fold hinge joints
97 Starboard trimming tailplane
98 Starboard elevator

99 Fin fold hydraulic jack
100 Rudder hydraulic actuator
101 Two-spar fin torsion box structure
102 Sonobuoy reference antenna
103 Formation lighting strips

104 Strobe light
105 Rudder horn balance
106 Static dischargers
107 Rudder rib structure
108 Rudder tab
109 Trim tab linkage

115 Fin folded position
116 Starboard elevator rib structure
117 Static dischargers
118 Elevator horn balance
119 Two-spar fin torsion box structure
120 Leading edge ribs
121 Ventral fuel jettison

127 Heat exchanger air exhaust
128 Deck arrestor hook, lowered
129 Sonobuoy, typical
130 Ground/deck equipment stowage bay, avionics equipment compartment on starboard side
131 Tailhook hinge mounting

UPGRADE TO FIRST CLASS

Engagements over Vietnam proved that there was still a need for small agile aircraft able to win in a traditional dogfight. In January 1972 the USAF issued a request for LWF (Light Weight Fighter) proposals, selecting the General Dynamics YF-16 and Northrop YF-17 for a flyoff competition. This was won in January 1975 by the YF-16, first flown on 2 February 1974.

By then four European air forces saw it as a replacement for the F-104. Suddenly aware of huge global export potential, and equally conscious of the sheer merit of the basic aircraft, the USAF announced it would buy the F-16 for the inventory. The initial plan was to set the total at 650, but by 1997 this had been increased to 2,220, while sales to other customers have taken the total to just over 4,000.

The production aircraft, the first of which flew on 7 August 1978, are larger and heavier than the prototypes. Features include a wing tapered on the leading edge with variable camber from powered hinged

Lockheed Martin F-16C Fighting Falcon, Block 50
1 Pitot head/air data probe
2 Glass-fibre radome
3 Lightning conducting strips
4 Planar radar scanner
5 Radome hinge point, opens to starboard
6 Scanner tracking mechanism
7 ILS glideslope antenna
8 Radar mounting bulkhead
9 Incidence vane, port and starboard
10 IFF antenna
11 GBU-12B laser guided bomb
12 AN/APG-68 digital pulse-doppler, multi-mode radar equipment bay
13 Forward oblique radar warning antennas, port and starboard
14 Front pressure bulkhead
15 Static ports
16 Fuselage forebody strake fairing
17 Forward avionics equipment bay
18 Canopy jettison charge
19 Instrument panel shroud
20 Instrument panel, multi-function CRT head-down-displays
21 Side stick controller, fly-by-wire control system
22 Video recorder
23 GEC wide angle head-up-display
24 CBU-52/58/71 sub-munition dispenser
25 LAU-3A 19-round rocket launcher
26 2.75-in [70-mm] FFAR
27 CBU-87/89 Gator submunition dispenser
28 Intake flank [No 5R] stores pylon adaptor
29 LANTIRN [FLIR] targeting pod
30 One-piece frameless cockpit canopy
31 Ejection seat headrest
32 McDonnell-Douglas ACES II "zero-zero" ejection seat
33 Side console panel
34 Canopy frame fairing
35 Canopy external emergency release
36 Engine throttle lever incorporating HOTAS [hands-on-throttle-and-stick] radar controls
37 Canopy jettison handle
38 Cockpit section frame structure
39 Boundary layer splitter
40 Fixed geometry engine air intake
41 Nosewheel, aft retracting
42 LANTIRN [FLIR/TFR] navigation pod
43 Port intake flank [No 5L] stores pylon adaptor
44 Port position light
45 Intake duct framing
46 Intake ducting
47 Gun gas suppression muzzle aperture
48 Aft avionics equipment bay
49 Cockpit rear pressure bulkhead
50 Canopy hinge point
51 Ejection seat launch rails
52 Canopy rotary actuator
53 Conditioned air delivery duct
54 Canopy sealing frame
55 Canopy aft glazing
56 500 gal [600 Imp gal, 2271 litre] external fuel tank
57 Garrett hydrazine turbine emergency power unit [EPU]
58 Hydrazine fuel tank
59 Fuel tank bay access panel
60 Forward fuselage bag-type fuel tank, total internal capacty 6972 lb [3162 Kg]
61 Fuselage upper longeron
62 Conditioned air ducting
63 Cannon barrels
64 Forebody frame construction
65 Air system ground connection
66 Ventral air conditioning system equipment bay
67 Centreline 250 gal [600 US gal, 1136 litre] fuel tank
68 Mainwheel door hydraulic actuator
69 Mainwheel door
70 Hydraulic system ground connectors
71 Gun bay ventral gas vent
72 GE M 61A1 20-mm rotary cannon
73 Ammunition feed chute
74 Hydraulic gun drive motor
75 Port hydraulic reservoir
76 Centre fuselage integral fuel tank
77 Leading-edge flap drive hydraulic motor
78 Ammunition drum 511 rounds
79 Upper position light/refuelling floodlight
80 TACAN antenna
81 Hydraulic accumulator
82 Starboard hydraulic reservoir
83 Leading edge flap drive shaft
84 Inboard, No 6 stores station, 4,500 lb [2,041 Kg] capacity
85 Pylon attachment hardpoint
86 Leading edge flap drive shaft and rotary actuators
87 No 7 stores hard point, capacity 3,500lb [1,588Kg]
88 Starboard forward radar warning antenna
89 Missile launch rails
90 AIM-120 Advanced Medium Range Air-to-Air Missiles [AMRAAM]
91 Loading pod, carriage of essential ground equipment and personal effects for off-base deployment
92 Starboard leading edge manoeuvre flap, down position
93 Outboard, No 8 stores station, capacity 700lb [318Kg]
94 Wing tip, No 9 stores station, capacity 425lb [193Kg]
95 Wing tip AMRAAM
96 Starboard navigation light
97 Fixed portion of trailing edge
98 Static dischargers
99 Starboard flaperon
100 Starboard wing integral fuel tank
101 Fuel system piping
102 Fuel pump
103 Starboard wing root attachment fishplates
104 Fuel tank access panels
105 Universal air refuelling receptacle [UARSSI], open
106 Engine intake centrebody fairing
107 Airframe mounted accessory equipment gearbox
108 Jet fuel starter
109 Machined wing attachment bulk heads
110 Engine fuel management equipment
111 Pressure refuelling receptacle ventral adaptor
112 Pratt & Whitney F100-PW-200 afterburning turbofan engine
113 VHF/IFF antenna
114 Starboard flaperon hydraulic actuator
115 Fuel tank tail fins
116 Sidebody fairing integral fuel tank
117 Position light
118 Cooling air ram air intake
119 Fin root fairing
120 Forward engine support link
121 Rear fuselage integral fuel tank
122 Thermally insulated tank inner skin
123 Tank access panels
124 Radar warning system power amplifier
125 Fin root attachment fittings
126 Flight control system hydraulic accumulators
127 Multi-spar fin torsion box structure
128 Starboard all-moving tailplane [tailplane panels interchangeable]
129 General Electric F110-GE-100 alternative power plant
130 Fin leading edge honeycomb core
131 Dynamic pressure probe
132 Carbon-fibre fin skin panelling
133 VHF comm. antenna [AM/FM]
134 Fin tip antenna fairing
135 Anti-collision light
136 Threat warning antennas
137 Static dischargers
138 Rudder honeycomb core structure
139 Rudder hydraulic actuator
140 ECM antenna fairing
141 Tail navigation light
142 Variable area after burner nozzle
143 Afterburner nozzle flaps
144 Nozzle sealing fairing
145 Afterburner nozzle fueldraulic actuators [5]
146 Port split trailing edge airbrake panel, open, upper and lower surfaces
147 Airbrake actuating linkage
148 Port all-moving tailplane
149 Static dischargers
150 Graphite-epoxy tailplane skin panels
151 Leading edge honeycomb construction
152 Corrugated aluminium sub-structure
153 Tailplane pivot mounting
154 Tailplane hydraulic actuator
155 Fuel jettison chamber, port and starboard
156 Afterburner ducting
157 Rear fuselage machined bulk heads
158 Port navigation light
159 AN/ALE-40[VO-4] chaff/flare launcher, port and starboard
160 Main engine thrust mounting, port and starboard
161 Sidebody fairing frame structure
162 Runway arrester hook
163 Composite ventral fin, port and starboard
164 Port flaperon hydraulic actuator
165 Flaperon hinges
166 Port flaperon, lowered
167 External fuel tank tail fairing
168 Flaperon honeycomb core structure
169 Fixed portion of trailing edge

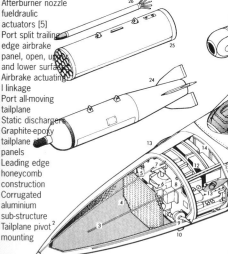

170 Static dischargers
171 Port navigation light
172 Wing tip, No 1 stores station, capacity 425lb [193Kg]
173 Port wing tip AMRAAM
174 AGM-88 HARM [High-speed Anti-Radiation Missile]
175 Mk 84 low-drag 2000lb [907Kg] HE bomb
176 Mk 83 Snakeye retarded bomb

177 AIM-9L Sidewinder air-to-air missile
178 Missile launch rails
179 No 2 stores station, capacity 700lb [318Kg]
180 No 3 stores station, capacity 3,500lb [1,588Kg]
181 Port forward radar warning antenna
182 Mk 82 500lb [227Kg] HE bombs

183 Triple ejector rack
184 Intermediate wing pylon
185 Leading-edge manoeuvre flap honeycomb core structure
186 Flap drive shaft and rotary actuators

187 Multi-spar wing torsion box structure
188 Port wing integral fuel tankage
189 No 4 stores station hardpoint, capacity 4,500lb [2,041Kg]
190 Wing panel root attachment fish-plates
191 Undercarriage leg mounted landing light
192 Articulated retraction/drag link
193 Main undercarriage leg strut

194 Shock absorber strut
195 Port leading edge manoeuvre flap, down position
196 Inboard wing pylon
197 Port mainwheel, forward retracting
198 Fuel filler caps
199 Port 308 gal [370 US gal, 1400 litre] external tank

200 Centreline, Bno 5 stores pylon, capacity 2,200lb [998Kg]
201 AN/ALQ-184[V]-2 [short] ECM pod
202 AGM-65 Maverick air-to-surface missiles
203 Triple missile carrier/launcher

Mike Badrocke

leading and trailing edges, slab horizontal tails driven like other surfaces by a fly-by-wire system which overcomes the almost unstable basic design to give exceptional manoeuvrability, and a single afterburning turbofan engine fed by a plain non-variable ventral inlet. The pilot is almost lying on his back under a frameless canopy giving unrivalled view with his right hand on a force-sensing sidestick with which he can make a sustained turn at 9g.

The original engine was the Pratt & Whitney F100-220, rated at 23,840lb. In the nose was a specially designed compact multimode radar, and armament comprised a 20mm gun, Sidewinder missiles on the wingtips and seven additional hardpoints on which could be hung up to 11,950lb (5,420kg) of stores for 9g combat, or up to 20,450lb (9,276kg) at reduced load factor. Predictably, the F-16 soon saw action, Israeli aircraft demonstrating outstanding accuracy with "iron bombs", as well as total mastery over all opposing aircraft.

Since first delivery in January 1979 the F-16 has been the subject of more upgrades, add-ons, new production blocks, modifications and even gross redesign than any previous aircraft. The gross redesign was represented by the two F-16XL prototypes, of tailless delta configuration, which were rejected in favour of the F-15E even though they carried double the weapon load of the F-16A (on 17 pylons) 45 per cent further. Basic production versions have been the F-16A and F-16C single-seaters and the F-16B and F-16D two-seaters, with the rear cockpit replacing fuel. Apart from briefly testing the F-16/79 (J79 engine) for possible export, the engines have been successive upgrades of the original F100, rated at up to 29,100lb, competing against the General Electric F110, rated at 29,588lb.

Major upgrades have included addition of LANTIRN (Low-Altitude Navigation and Targeting, Infra-Red, Night) packaged in two external pods, and the AMRAAM (Advanced Medium-Range Air-to-Air Missile). The former gives good all-weather attack capability against ground targets, and the new missile gives supposed BVR (Beyond Visual Range) air-to-air capability.

Other upgrades have concerned the radar, the navigation systems, the cockpit HUD (Head-Up Display) and addition of NVG (Night-Vision Goggle) compatibility and an HMS (Helmet-Mounted Sight), improved IFF (Identification Friend or Foe) and new communications and data links. There have been numerous special test aircraft, including aircraft modified in the CCV (Control-Configured Vehicle) and AFTI (Advanced Fighter Technology Integration) programmes. The US Navy uses the F-16N as its supersonic adversary, numerous variants have been developed for the reconnaissance role, and the Mitsubishi F-2 is a derivative.

In March 1993 General Dynamics became part of Lockheed and development of the F-16 has if anything accelerated, despite the need to devote large resources to the F-22 and X-35 JSF. One project involves converting numerous redundant F-16As into UCAVs (Uninhabited Combat Air Vehicles), with fuel and avionics or weapons replacing the cockpit. A dramatically upgraded version, which could be delivered 3½ years from go-ahead, is the Falcon 2000, with a large delta wing similar to that of the F-16XL, 20 store hardpoints and twice the normal internal fuel capacity. For service beyond 2010 the F-16X would have a wing derived from that of the F-22 (but smaller), a fuselage stretch, improved weapons and avionics and 80% more internal fuel.

DATA FOR F–16 WITH F100–129 ENGINE:	
Span (excluding missiles)	31ft 0in (9.45m)
Length	49ft 4in (15.03m)
Wing area	300.0 sq ft (27.87m²)
Weight empty	18,591lb (8,433kg)
Maximum takeoff weight	42,300lb (19,187kg)
Maximum speed	1,350mph (2,173km/h,
(tip AAMs only)	Mach 2.05)
	at 40,000ft (12,192m)
Radius of action	997 miles (1,604km)
(four AAMs and drop tanks)	

HAWK RIDES THE STORM

F-117A NIGHTHAWK

Even though both aircraft were lost, the Have Blue programme (see page 135) clearly indicated to the Air Force that stealth (Very Low Observables) was the way to go. Defense Under-Secretary Bill Perry was determined to exploit the new technology rapidly, and at the Air Force R&D headquarters five majors under Gen Al Slay wrote the specific range and pay-load requirement for a VLO fighter/attack air-craft. In order of priority, the broad requirements stressed security, perfor-mance, cost and timing.

On 16 November 1978, in a highly classified programme called Senior Trend, the Skunk Works received a contract for five FSD (full-scale develop-ment) aircraft (USAF 79-10780/4) with a guaranteed performance, radar cross-section and weapon accuracy. In December 1979 the first pro-duction contract was signed, for 15 aircraft. The vital flight-control laws and software were checked in Calspan's Lockheed NT-33, at the time the oldest aircraft in the USAF inventory.

The first FSD aircraft was flown by Hal Farley on 18 June 1981. The first production air-craft never received a USAF ser-ial; it was destroyed on its first takeoff, on 20 April 1982, because the flight-control mul-ticore cables were all plugged in incorrectly! Thus, the first production delivery was made on 23 August 1982 with the No 4 aircraft, 80-0787. After

Black programme, black jet. The secrecy surrounding the stealth programme was total: F-117As finally saw daylight in 1988.

producing 17 Senior Trend aircraft Lockheed took a fixed price for the remaining 42. Thus, the total cost of the 59 amounted to $2.5 billion, or a unit flyaway cost of $42.6 million including all government-furnished equipment. Aircraft 59 (87-0843) was delivered on 12 July 1990, two months ahead of schedule.

Major operating units comprised the 410th Flight Test Sqn, 4450th Tactical Group, 37th Tactical Fighter Wing, 49th Fighter Wing and 57th Fighter Weapons Wing. The carefully selected pilots and ground crew had many names for the Senior Trend aircraft, but when it came to filling in their logbooks and other documentation they wrote the meaningless number "117". Thus, when the existence of the aircraft was disclosed on 10 November 1988 it was described as the "F-117", which bears no relationship to any US numbering system.

Compared with XST Have Blue the F-117A is about 60 per cent larger in linear terms, and its ruddervators are inclined outward. The engines are 10,800lb General Electric F404-F1D2 low-bypass turbofans,

discharging through flat "platypus" slot jetpipes of high-nickel alloy. The inlets are covered with a fine-mesh grille tailored to the wavelengths of hostile radars. All three single-strut landing gears retract backwards. In the pointed nose are four air-data probes and forward- and downward-looking infra-red sensors.

The standard weapons are 2,000lb (907kg) JDAMs (joint direct attack munitions) or laser-guided bombs, such as the GBU-24 or GBU-27 families, ejected on powered trapeze arms from side-by-side internal bays with low-reflectivity doors. Instead of attack weapons, various air-to-air missiles can be carried in either bay, and provision is made for up to four external weapons or drop tanks under the wings. Many of the avionics antennas are normally retracted inside the fuselage.

Near the highest point of the aircraft, behind the cockpit, is a flight-refuelling boom receptacle. A braking parachute is housed in the top of the fuselage just ahead of the fixed lower fins.

Made like the Have Blue almost entirely of aluminium

alloys, the F-117 has over the years been progressively modified, not only in systems and equipment but also in the replacement of metal airframe sections (such as the ruddervators) by thermoplastic graphite composites. Of course, the exterior is made up of flat facets, and is almost entirely covered with radar-absorbent material. Originally the exterior was grey, but all operational aircraft have been matt black.

The F-117's combat debut was on 21 December 1989, when two aircraft uncharacteristically missed their Panama target by wide margins. It was a different story in Desert Storm, from 2.51 am on 17 January 1991, when 45 aircraft flew 2.5 per cent of the mis-

sions over Iraq yet hit over 31 per cent of the targets. In over 6,900 combat hours the mission-capable rate was 85.8 per cent, the average miss-distance a matter of inches, and not a single bullet hit any of the aircraft.

Since then Lockheed has never ceased to upgrade the avionics, engine installations and other parts. The only untoward incident was the structural failure of an F-117 during a gentle manoeuvre at an airshow in September 1997. Lockheed appears to have failed to sell any of at least four projected upgrades or derived aircraft, but who knows what the Skunk Works is really doing? (See pp 133-134 for cutaway.)

DATA FOR F-117A:	
Span	**43ft 4in (13.21m)**
Length (excluding sensors)	**65ft 11in (20.09m)**
Wing area	**1,140 sq ft (105.9m²)**
Weight empty	**29,000lb (13,154kg)**
Maximum takeoff (normal)	**52,000lb (23,814kg)**
Maximum speed	**646mph (1,040km/h)**
Cruising speed	**at 30,000ft, 562mph (904km/h)**
Combat radius	**535 miles (861km)**
	(4,000lb/1,814kg bombload and
	allowances, transits at 30,000ft

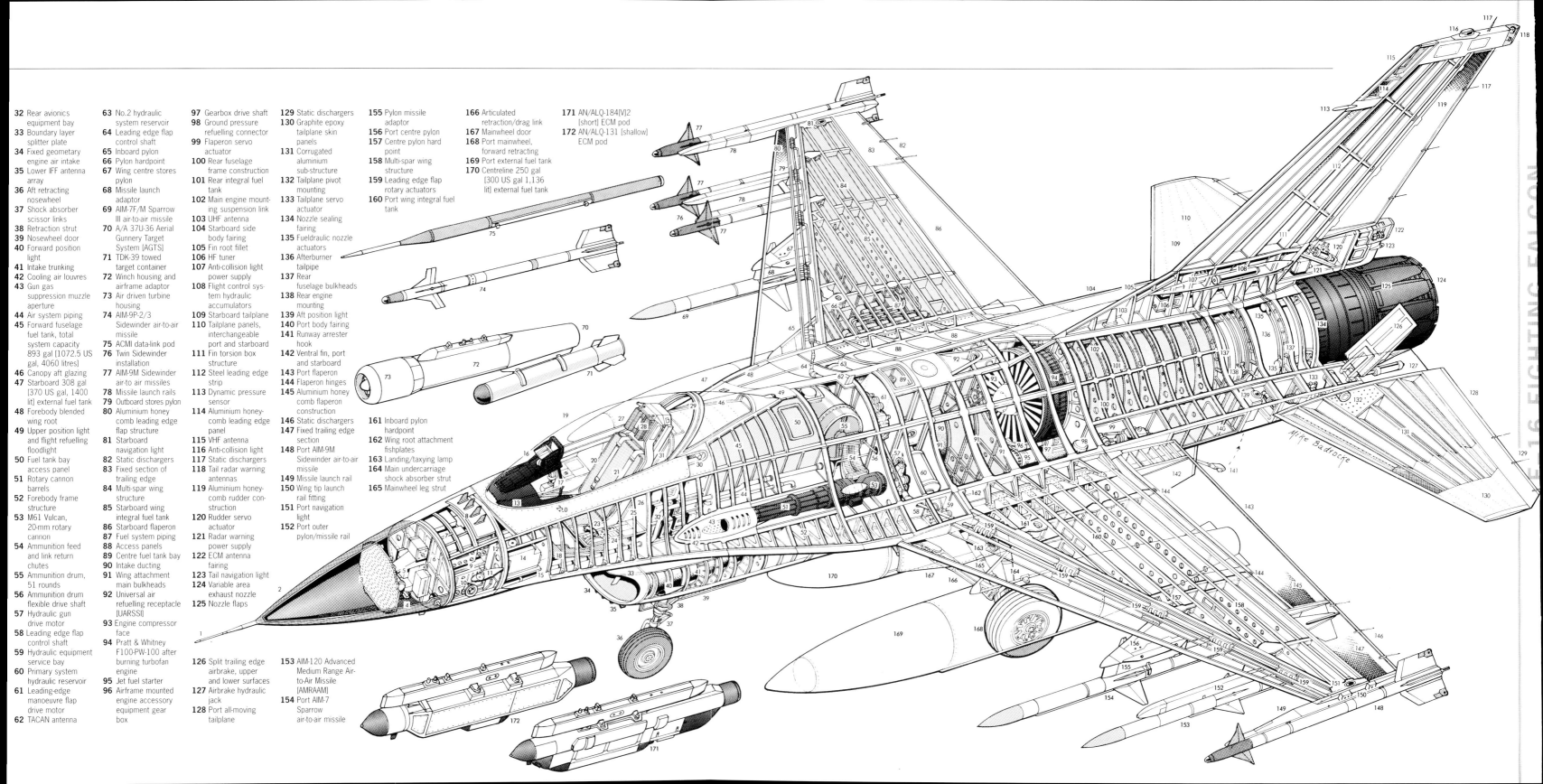

32 Rear avionics equipment bay
33 Boundary layer splitter plate
34 Fixed geometry engine air intake
35 Lower IFF antenna array
36 Aft retracting nosewheel
37 Shock absorber scissor links
38 Retraction strut
39 Nosewheel door
40 Forward position light
41 Intake trunking
42 Cooling air louvres
43 Gun gas suppression muzzle aperture
44 Air system piping
45 Forward fuselage fuel tank, total system capacity 893 gal [1072.5 US gal, 4060 litres]
46 Canopy aft glazing
47 Starboard 308 gal [370 US gal, 1400 lit] external fuel tank
48 Forebody blended wing root
49 Upper position light and flight refuelling floodlight
50 Fuel tank bay access panel
51 Rotary cannon barrels
52 Forebody frame structure
53 M61 Vulcan, 20-mm rotary cannon
54 Ammunition feed and link return chutes
55 Ammunition drum, 51 rounds
56 Ammunition drum flexible drive shaft
57 Hydraulic gun drive motor
58 Leading edge flap control shaft
59 Hydraulic equipment service bay
60 Primary system hydraulic reservoir
61 Leading-edge manoeuvre flap drive motor
62 TACAN antenna

63 No.2 hydraulic system reservoir
64 Leading edge flap control shaft
65 Inboard pylon
66 Pylon hardpoint
67 Wing centre stores pylon
68 Missile launch adaptor
69 AIM-7F/M Sparrow III air-to-air missile
70 A/A 37U-36 Aerial Gunnery Target System [AGTS]
71 TDK-39 towed target container
72 Winch housing and airframe adaptor
73 Air driven turbine housing
74 AIM-9P-2/3 Sidewinder air-to-air missile
75 ACMI data-link pod
76 Twin Sidewinder installation
77 AIM-9M Sidewinder air-to air missiles
78 Missile launch rails
79 Outboard stores pylon
80 Aluminium honey comb leading edge flap structure
81 Starboard navigation light
82 Static dischargers
83 Fixed section of trailing edge
84 Multi-spar wing structure
85 Starboard wing integral fuel tank
86 Starboard flaperon
87 Fuel system piping
88 Access panels
89 Centre fuel tank bay
90 Intake ducting
91 Wing attachment main bulkheads
92 Universal air refuelling receptacle [UARSSI]
93 Engine compressor face
94 Pratt & Whitney F100-PW-100 after burning turbofan engine
95 Jet fuel starter
96 Airframe mounted engine accessory equipment gear box

97 Gearbox drive shaft
98 Ground pressure refuelling connector
99 Flaperon servo actuator
100 Rear fuselage frame construction
101 Rear integral fuel tank
102 Main engine mount-ing suspension link
103 UHF antenna
104 Starboard side body fairing
105 Fin root fillet
106 HF tuner
107 Anti-collision light power supply
108 Flight control sys-tem hydraulic accumulators
109 Starboard tailplane
110 Tailplane panels, interchangeable port and starboard
111 Fin torsion box structure
112 Steel leading edge strip
113 Dynamic pressure sensor
114 Aluminium honey-comb leading edge panel
115 VHF antenna
116 Anti-collision light
117 Static dischargers
118 Tail radar warning antennas
119 Aluminium honey-comb rudder con-struction
120 Rudder servo actuator
121 Radar warning power supply
122 ECM antenna fairing
123 Tail navigation light
124 Variable area exhaust nozzle
125 Nozzle flaps

126 Split trailing edge airbrake, upper and lower surfaces
127 Airbrake hydraulic jack
128 Port all-moving tailplane

129 Static dischargers
130 Graphite epoxy tailplane skin panels
131 Corrugated aluminium sub-structure
132 Tailplane pivot mounting
133 Tailplane servo actuator
134 Nozzle sealing fairing
135 Fueldraulic nozzle actuators
136 Afterburner tailpipe
137 Rear fuselage bulkheads
138 Rear engine mounting
139 Aft position light
140 Port body fairing
141 Runway arrester hook
142 Ventral fin, port and starboard
143 Port flaperon
144 Flaperon hinges
145 Aluminium honey comb flaperon construction
146 Static dischargers
147 Fixed trailing edge section
148 Port AIM-9M Sidewinder air-to-air missile
149 Missile launch rail
150 Wing tip launch rail fitting
151 Port navigation light
152 Port outer pylon/missile rail

153 AIM-120 Advanced Medium Range Air-to-Air Missile [AMRAAM]
154 Port AIM-7 Sparrow air-to-air missile

155 Pylon missile adaptor
156 Port centre pylon
157 Centre pylon hard point
158 Multi-spar wing structure
159 Leading edge flap rotary actuators
160 Port wing integral fuel tank

161 Inboard pylon hardpoint
162 Wing root attachment fishplates
163 Landing/taxiing lamp
164 Main undercarriage shock absorber strut
165 Mainwheel leg strut

166 Articulated retraction/drag link
167 Mainwheel door
168 Port mainwheel, forward retracting
169 Port external fuel tank
170 Centreline 250 gal [300 US gal 1,136 lit] external fuel tank

171 AN/ALQ-184[V]2 [short] ECM pod
172 AN/ALQ-131 [shallow] ECM pod

F-117A of the 37th Tactical Fighter Wing, Tonopah Test Range airfield; aluminium and thermoplastic graphite.

F-117 Nighthawk

1 Omni-directional air data sensing probes
2 Nose avionics equipment bay
3 Air-data computer
4 Downward-Looking Infra-Red [DLIR] sighting and targetting unit, offset to starboard
5 Screened sensor aperture
6 Forward-Looking Infra-Red [FLIR] sighting and targetting unit
7 Cockpit front pressure bulkhead
8 Rudder pedals
9 Nosewheel bay
10 Forward retracting steering nose undercarriage
11 Taxying light
12 Hydraulic retraction jack
13 Cockpit pressure enclosure
14 Port side console panel
15 Engine throttle levers
16 Control column, digital fly-by-wire flight control system
17 Instrument panel
18 Multi-function CRT displays
19 Pilotis head-up-display [HUD]
20 Gold film coated windscreen panels
21 Canopy apex fairing with rear position light
22 Starboard engine air intake
23 One-piece, upward hingeing cockpit canopy
24 McDonnell-Douglas ACES II 'zero-zero' ejection seat
25 Hydraulic canopy actuator [2]
26 Close-pitched skin support frames
27 Avionics equipment bay, port and starboard, accessed via nosewheel bay
28 Forward position light and night vision goggles compatible covert lighting
29 Canopy emergency release
30 Intake de-icing air duct
31 Port engine air intake
32 Intake grille
33 Ventral weapons bay doors, open
34 Weapons bay retractable spoilers
35 Spoiler actuator and linkage
36 Retractable ILS antennas
37 Avionics equipment bay
38 Canopy hinge point
39 Flush ADF antenna panels
40 Starboard intake suction relief door
41 Rotating flight refuelling receptacle, illuminated
42 Forward fuselage fuel tank
43 Fuselage longitudinal beam structure
44 Port intake suction relief door
45 Port ventral weapons bay
46 Airframe mounted accessory equipment gearbox
47 Engine to gearbox drive shaft
48 Compressor intake
49 Engine fuel control equipment
50 Full-authority digital engine controller [FADEC]
51 General Electric F404-GE-F1D2, non-augmented turbofan engine
52 Forward engine mounting trunnion
53 Engine bleed-air heat exchanger exhaust
54 Detachable anti-collision beacon, above and below
55 Retractable communications antennas, port and starboard
56 Fuselage centre keel unit
57 Weapons launch trapeze mechanism, hydraulically actuated
58 Dorsal fuel tank
59 Starboard engine bleed air exhaust
60 Engine bay venting air grilles
61 Starboard wing integral fuel tank
62 Outboard elevon actuator
63 Outer wing panel dry bay
64 Starboard navigation light
65 Starboard outboard elevon
66 'Cats-eye' control surface interface
67 Inboard elevon
68 Starboard 'Platypus' exhaust duct
69 Fixed stub fin
70 Ruddervator torque shaft
71 Starboard all-moving ruddervator
72 Honeycomb composite leading and trailing edge panels
73 All-composite ruddervator structure
74 Ruddervator tip antenna fairing
75 Port ruddervator
76 Port engine "Platypus" exhaust
77 Exhaust lip heat shielding tiles
78 Slotted exhaust lip
79 Ruddervator hydraulic actuator
80 Brake parachute housing
81 Parachute bay doors
82 Auxiliary Power Unit [APU]
83 Exhaust bay venting air grille
84 Tapered and flattened engine exhaust duct with nickel alloy honeycomb reinforcement
85 Exhaust internal support post fittings
86 Port inboard elevon hydraulic actuator
87 Wing rear spar
88 Elevon light alloy rib structure
89 Honeycomb trailing edge panels
90 Port inboard elevon
91 Outboard elevon
92 Faceted wing tip fairing
93 Port navigation light
94 Wing bottom skin/stringer panel
95 Outboard elevon hydraulic actuator
96 Wing rib structure
97 Port wing integral fuel tank
98 Composite leading edge panel
99 Fuel feed and vent piping
100 Main spar
101 Fuel contents units
102 Bolted wing root attachment fittings
103 Close-pitched fuselage frame structure
104 Detachable radar reflector
105 Main under-carriage leg hinge mounting
106 Mainwheel bay
107 Hydraulic retraction jack
108 Mainwheel leg strut
109 Landing light
110 Torque scissor links
111 Mainwheel leg door
112 Forward retracting mainwheel
113 Wing front spar
114 Wing root rib
115 Front spar/fuselage bolted joint
116 GBU-10 2,000-lb laser guided bomb

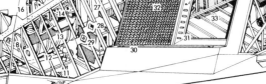
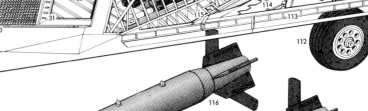

(R)EJECTED

Lockheed chose to follow the difficult technique of faceting in creating the first fully "stealth" type aircraft. It was obvious that this would result in an aircraft so severely compromised aerodynamically as to make it difficult or dangerous to fly. In August 1975 Lockheed began work against a study contract placed by the Defense Advanced Projects Research Agency for an experimental aircraft to explore the practicality of matching the faceting stealth technique with acceptable flying qualities. This programme would have some bearing on the F-117A; (see p 129).

The flight articles of the Have Blue programme were XST-1 and XST-2 (experimental survivable testbed). Alternative designations were HB-1001 and HB-1002. Each was a single-seat aircraft with a low-mounted wing with leading-edge sweepback of 72.5°. Above each wing root, blended into the strange humped fuselage, was an air duct feeding a General Electric J85-4A turbo-

jet (taken from a T-2B Buckeye trainer), of 2,950lb thrust. Each inlet was a parallelogram covered by a deep sharp-edged grille, coated with RAM (radar-absorbent material) and radar-absorbent paint. Each engine jetpipe was flattened into a "platypus" nozzle forming a 17:1 slot swept sharply forward, with the slots from the left and right engines meeting on the centreline. Above these nozzles were the ruddervators (fins with all-moving pivoted upper portions) swept sharply back and also canted inward so that their tips almost met on the aircraft centreline. The landing gears were cannibalised from a Northrop F-5 fighter, and the complete flight-control hardware, including the Lear-Siegler fly-by-wire system and cockpit

interfaces, came from an F-16. In side view the aluminium airframe looked like a flattened pyramid, the top being the upward-hinged canopy with four flat glass panes. A one-third model was tested at Grey Butte microwave test site in December 1975, and after much refinement the first XST-1 (HB-1001) was flown by Bill Park at Groom Lake on 1 December 1977. It proved to be even more difficult to fly than predicted, and on the 36th flight Park was forced to

> "The only thing it doesn't do [wrong] is tip back on its tail when parked." (Official report.)

eject. XST-2 (HB-1002) was first flown by Lt-Col Norman Dyson on 20 July 1978. This did succeed in completing the Low-Observables part of the programme when, on Flight 52 in July 1979, it suffered an inflight fire, Dyson ejecting. By this time the Senior Trend programme was in full swing, leading to the   F-117A.

DATA FOR XST HAVE BLUE:

Span	**22ft 6in (6.858m)**
Length (no boom)	**47ft 3in (14.40m)**
Wing area	**386 sq ft (35.86m²)**
Empty weight	**not disclosed**
Maximum takeoff weight	**12,500lb (5,670kg)**
Performance	**not disclosed but similar to F-117A**

BIRD OF PREY

F-22 RAPTOR

Spurred by outstanding fighters developed in the Soviet Union, in 1981 the USAF issued a Request for Information on an Advanced Tactical Fighter which could eventually replace the F-15. Key design features were to incorporate the new LO (Low Observables, or "stealth") technology and to achieve supercruise (cruising at supersonic speed without using afterburning or augmentation in the propulsion system). To support the objective two new engines were commissioned, the Pratt & Whitney YF119 and General Electric YF120. Both are high-compression augmented turbofans in the 35,000lb thrust class.

One of the two YF-22 prototypes wheels above the Mojave Desert during an early test flight in December 1990. Production Raptors are intended to be able to kill anything with wings.

Six companies submitted proposals, from which the Lockheed YF-22 and Northrop YF-23 were selected. Two prototypes of each were ordered, one powered by each type of engine. The first YF-22, fitted with YF120 engines, first flew on 29 September 1990. On 23 April 1991 the winning combination was announced as the F-22 powered by the Pratt & Whitney engine, largely on the grounds of supposed lower risk. Lockheed teamed with General Dynamics (Fort Worth) and Boeing Military Airplanes. The EMD (Engineering and Manufacturing Development) contract called for 11 (later reduced to nine) aircraft, plus static and fatigue airframes.

Two of the EMD aircraft were to have been two-seat F-22Bs, but this version was later cancelled. Like the F-15, the F-22 began as an uncompromised air-to-air fighter and later (in 1993) was required also to fly precision attack missions against surface targets. First flight was planned for June 1996, with low-rate production beginning in January 1997. Funding cuts and design changes delayed the first flight until 7 September 1997. The second aircraft (4002) is not due until mid-1998, with the first production delivery now postponed to November 2001.

The EMD aircraft are designated F-22A and named not Lightning II (as expected) but Raptor ("a ravisher or bird of prey"). They are very close to final production standard, and differ markedly from the YF-22 prototypes. The final configuration is driven by aerodynamics (for flight efficiency and the greatest possible dogfight manoevrability), by propulsion efficiency over the full range of flight Mach numbers, by structure (for minimum weight whilst sustaining a design load factor of 9 at maximum weight) and not least by LO "stealth" requirements.

Great attention has also been paid to reliability, ease of maintenance and the achievement of quick turnround for high sortie-generation rates.

Features include a conventional central fuselage with a propulsion duct on each side, with the variable inlet having a trapezoidal form alongside

The Raptor's 2D nozzles provide reverse thrust on landing, eliminating the need for a braking parachute.

Lockheed-Martin F-22A Raptor

1 Composite radome
2 Northrop-Grumman/Texas Instruments AN/APG-77 multi-mode radar scanner
3 Canted radar mounting bulkhead
4 Pitot head
5 Air-data sensor system receivers, four positions
6 Radar equipment bay
7 Missile launch detector windows
8 Cockpit front pressure bulkhead
9 Forward fuselage machined alluminium alloy sidewall panel
10 Underfloor avionics equipment bays
11 Avionics equipment modules, downward hingeing for access
12 Electro-luminescent formation lighting strip
13 Composite fuselage chine skin panelling
14 Rudder pedals
15 Instrument console housing six multi function full-colour LCD displays
16 GEC-Marconi Avionics head-up-Display
17 Upward hingeing cockpit canopy
18 McDonnell-Douglas ACES II [modified], ejection seat

19 Starboard side console panel with sidestick controller for digital fly-by–wire flight control system
20 Port side control panel with engine throttles
21 Off-base boarding ladder stowage
22 Cockpit sloping rear pressure bulkhead
23 Electrical power equipment bay
24 Battery bay
25 Nosewheel doors
26 Landing and taxying lights
27 Forward retracting nosewheel
28 Torque scissor links
29 Port engine air intake
30 Titanium intake frame
31 Intake bleed-air spill duct
32 Inlet bleed-air door/spoiler panel
33 Bleed-air door hydraulic actuator
34 Data-link support antenna, microwave landing system [MLS] antenna beneath intake
35 Air-cooled flight critical equipment cooling air intake in boundary layer diverter duct, blower for ground operations
36 Boundary layer diverter spill duct
37 On-board oxygen generating system [OBOGS]
38 No.1 fuselage fuel tank

39 Canopy hinge point
40 Canopy actuator, electrically powered
41 Starboard engine air intake
42 Intake spill and boundary layer bleed air ducts
43 Lateral avionics equipment bay
44 Missile launch detector window
45 Data-link antenna
46 ACFC cooling air exhaust ducts
47 Forward fuselage production joint
48 Composite intake dut
49 Canopy emergency jettison control
50 Lateral missile bay doors
51 Missile launch rail
52 Launch rail trapeze arm
53 Hydraulic rail actuator
54 Environmental control system equipment bay
55 Fuselage main longeron
56 Ventral missile bay
57 L-bank antenna
58 No. 2 integral fuselage fuel tank
59 Machined fuselage main frame, typical
60 Illuminated flight refuelling receptacle, open
61 Airframe-mounted auxiliary equipment gearbox, shaft-driven from engines

62 Intake overpressure spill doors
63 Global positioning system [GPS] antenna
64 Ammunition feed chute, 480-round ventral fuselage transverse magazine
65 M61AZ six-barrel lightweight rotary cannon
66 Cannon barrels
67 Cannon muzzle aperture beneath flip-up door
68 Wing root EW antenna
69 Comm'cation/ Navigation/ Identification [CNI] UHF antenna
70 CNI band 2 antenna
71 500 gal (600 US gal, 2,271 lit) external tanks
72 Starboard leading edge flap, lowered
73 Flap drive shaft and rotary actuators
74 ILS localiser antenna
75 Carbon-fibre composite wing skin panel
76 Starboard navigation light, above and below
77 Wing tip EW antenna
78 Starboard aileron

79 Formation lightning strip
80 Aileron hydraulic actuator
81 Starboard flaperon, down position
82 Starboard wing integral fuel tank
83 Power system inverter, port and starboard
84 Starboard mainwheel, stowed position
85 Fuselage sede-body integral fuel tank
86 Hyraulic equipment bay
87 Fuel/air and fuel/oil heat exchangers
88 Fuel transfer piping
89 No. 3 Fuselage integral fuel tank with on-board inert gas generating system [OBIGS]
90 Engine bleed-air primary heat exchanger
91 Engine compresor intake
92 Port hydraulic reservoir

93 Hydraulic accumulator
94 Port side-body integral fuel tankage
95 Pratt & Whitney F119-PW-100 afterburning turbofan engine
96 Engine bay machined frames
97 Central fireproof keel unit
98 Stored energy system [SES] reservoirs, engine relighting
99 Engine bay thermal lining
100 Fin root attachment joints

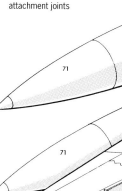
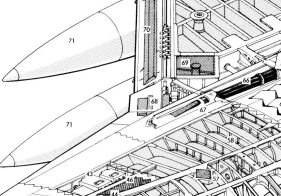
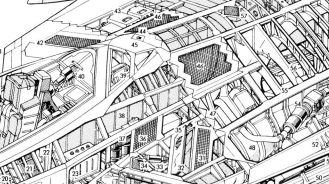
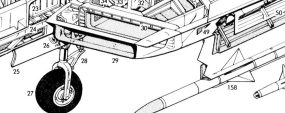

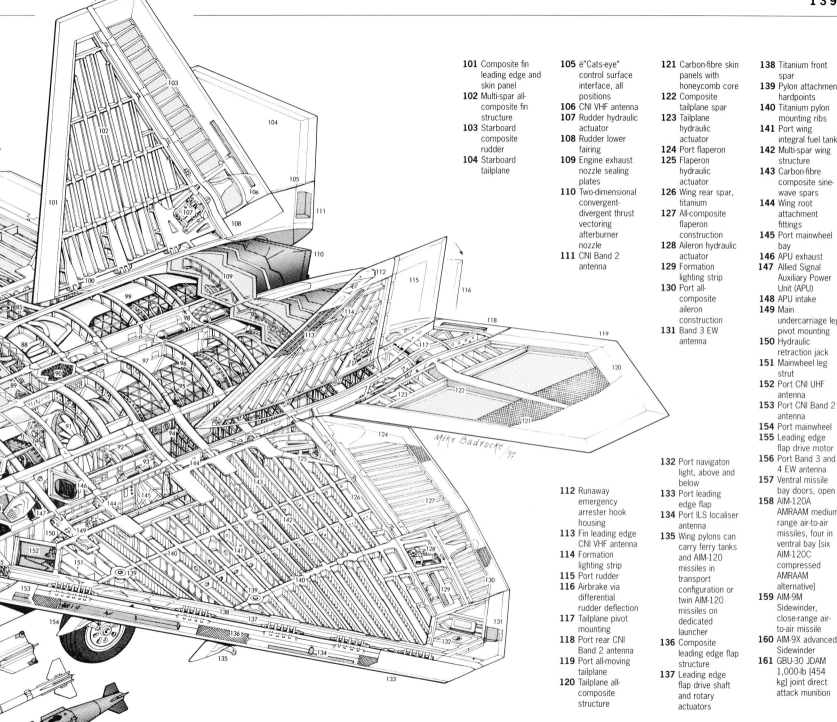

101 Composite fin leading edge and skin panel
102 Multi-spar all-composite fin structure
103 Starboard composite rudder
104 Starboard tailplane

105 ë"Cats-eye" control surface interface, all positions
106 CNI VHF antenna
107 Rudder hydraulic actuator
108 Rudder lower fairing
109 Engine exhaust nozzle sealing plates
110 Two-dimensional convergent-divergent thrust vectoring afterburner nozzle
111 CNI Band 2 antenna

112 Runaway emergency arrester hook housing
113 Fin leading edge CNI VHF antenna
114 Formation lighting strip
115 Port rudder
116 Airbrake via differential rudder deflection
117 Tailplane pivot mounting
118 Port rear CNI Band 2 antenna
119 Port all-moving tailplane
120 Tailplane all-composite structure

121 Carbon-fibre skin panels with honeycomb core
122 Composite tailplane spar
123 Tailplane hydraulic actuator
124 Port flaperon
125 Flaperon hydraulic actuator
126 Wing rear spar, titanium
127 All-composite flaperon construction
128 Aileron hydraulic actuator
129 Formation lighting strip
130 Port all-composite aileron construction
131 Band 3 EW antenna

132 Port navigaton light, above and below
133 Port leading edge flap
134 Port ILS localiser antenna
135 Wing pylons can carry ferry tanks and AIM-120 missiles in transport configuration or twin AIM-120 missiles on dedicated launcher
136 Composite leading edge flap structure
137 Leading edge flap drive shaft and rotary actuators

138 Titanium front spar
139 Pylon attachment hardpoints
140 Titanium pylon mounting ribs
141 Port wing integral fuel tank
142 Multi-spar wing structure
143 Carbon-fibre composite sine-wave spars
144 Wing root attachment fittings
145 Port mainwheel bay
146 APU exhaust
147 Allied Signal Auxiliary Power Unit (APU)
148 APU intake
149 Main undercarriage leg pivot mounting
150 Hydraulic retraction jack
151 Mainwheel leg strut
152 Port CNI UHF antenna
153 Port CNI Band 2 antenna
154 Port mainwheel
155 Leading edge flap drive motor
156 Port Band 3 and 4 EW antenna
157 Ventral missile bay doors, open
158 AIM-120A AMRAAM medium range air-to-air missiles, four in ventral bay [six AIM-120C compressed AMRAAM alternative]
159 AIM-9M Sidewinder, close-range air-to-air missile
160 AIM-9X advanced Sidewinder
161 GBU-30 JDAM 1,000-lb [454 kg] joint direct attack munition

Mike Badrocke /97

F-22 RAPTOR

the sloping side of the lozenge (diamond) section forward fuselage. This blends into the mid/high-mounted wing, of sharply tapered form (42° on the leading edge) with full-span leading-edge flaps and trailing-edge ailerons and flaperons. These movable surfaces are all driven by the digital triplex flight-control system, which also commands the swept tailplanes, the twin rudders in enormous tapered fins inclined outwards at 28° from the vertical, and the two-dimensional engine nozzles which vector ±20° in both the vertical and horizontal planes. Airbrakes are replaced by differential use of the rudders and flaperons. All units of the landing gear have single wheels with high-pressure tyres, and the flight-refuelling receptacle is in the centre of the top of the fuselage, between inlet bleed exits.

No attempt has been made to operate away from conventional airfields with paved runways, but the high thrust/weight ratio (typically 1.2 at takeoff weight) and vectored nozzles result in a very short run. The nozzles also enhance inflight manoeuvra-bility, reverse thrust on landing and enable aural and spectral signature to be to some degree controlled to enhance stealth. To an unprecedented degree propulsion is integrated with the unique VMS (Vehicle Management System), which is itself integrated with the Integrated Vehicle Subsystem Control and the Stores Management System which selects and launches weapons.

Basic armament comprises a long-barrel 20mm gun just inboard of the left wing, with 480 rounds and a hinged muzzle cover to increase stealth, and one Sidewinder (probably the advanced version called AIM-9X temporarily) in each internal bay in the side of the fuselage outboard of the inlet duct. Between the ducts is the large main internal bay, accommodating six AIM-120C or four AIM-120A AMRAAM beyond visible range missiles. In the attack mission the internal bay can accommodate six GBU-30 or -31 Joint Direct Attack Munitions, or many other stores, all ejected from hydraulic weapons racks. In addition there are two hard-points for pylons under each wing able to carry 5,000lb

(2,268kg) stores, including many bombs, Paveway 3 precision weapons, HARM anti-radar missiles, BLU-109 Penetrator bombs or the LOCAAS (Low-Cost Autonomous Attack System) for dispensing submunitions. Of course, the F-22 has comprehensive defensive avionics and countermeasures dispensers. The main radar is the Northrop Grumman/Texas Instruments APG-77 with electronic scanning.

The production programme has been repeatedly restructured, mainly to reduce cost (although the main result has been to reduce the numbers involved, whilst having little impact on cost.

Originally the basic USAF requirement was for 750 aircraft, including two-seaters. By 1998 this had been reduced to 438, all single-seaters. The prototypes were built in California and assembled at Palmdale. The production programme was to have been moved to Fort Worth, but it will now remain at the planned location at Marietta.

To help defray the escalating unit cost – estimated at $92.6 million in 1996 but now much higher – the Pentagon is expected to permit the F-22 to be exported to selected friendly nations (starting with South Korea) much earlier than had originally been planned. A naval version to replace the F-14 has been abandoned, but Lockheed Martin has numerous other planned derivatives.

DATA FOR F-22A:	
Span	**44ft 6in (13.56m)**
Length	**62ft 1in (18.92m)**
Wing area	**840.0 sq ft (78.04m²)**
Weight empty	**31,670lb (14,366kg)**
	(target not yet achieved)
Maximum takeoff weight	**60,000lb (27,216kg)**
	(target)
Maximum speed	**1,153mph (1,855km/h, Mach 1.7)**
	at 30,000ft (9,144m)
Supercruise Mach number	**1.58**
Range	**not stated**

STEALTH IN MINIATURE

The challenging Tier III strategic reconnaissance vehicle has been replaced by two "SR-71 replacement" contenders, one of which is the joint effort of a team led by Lockheed Martin and Boeing.

Called Tier III Minus, and named DarkStar, this UAV (unmanned air vehicle) flies at modest speeds and heights, and has none of the normal features of stealthy low-observable aircraft, such as faceted outer skin or acute sweepback.

Tier III Minus was designed for the DARO (Defense Airborne Reconnaissance Office) for future use by the USAF and Advanced Research Projects Agency. Remarkably, it is intended to be produced for a unit price not higher than $10 million. It has an airframe made largely of graphite-fibre composites, and comprises a central flattened-eggshape body blended into an unswept wing with an aspect ratio (14.8) previously seen only in sailplanes. Thus, virtually all the RCS (radar cross-section) is concentrated into a sharp spike projecting ahead and another reflected to the rear. The vehi-

cle would be manoeuvred to prevent either spike from pointing at enemy defences. It has been said that RCS has been miminised over the frequency bands of early-warning radars (140-180MHz) and fighters (8-12Ghz).

The engine is a tiny Williams Rolls F129 (FJ44-1D) turbofan rated at 1,900lb thrust. The principal flight-control surfaces are wingtip drag rudders, specially designed so that their use has minimal effect on RCS or sensor-pointing accuracy. It is intended that DarkStar will be operated in partnership with the U-2S and a second and larger UAV, the Teledyne Ryan Tier II Plus. This will carry a synthetic-aperture radar

and an electro-optical (EO) sensor, the DarkStar will carry either one or the other, but not simultaneously. Production may be authorised in 1999.

DarkStar is an ultra-stealthy UAV which could be the USAF's next-generation strategic reconnaissance platform.

DATA FOR DARKSTAR:		
Span		**69ft 0in (21.03m)**
Length		**15ft 1in (4.6m)**
Wing area		**322sq ft (29.9m²)**
Weight empty	(EO)	**5,440lb (2,468kg)**
	(radar)	**5,640lb (2,558kg)**
Maximum takeoff weight		**8,600lb (3,900kg)**
Operating speed		**"over 288mph (463.5km/h)"**
Endurance with 1,000lb (454kg) sensor payload		**eight hours**
	at	**45,000ft (13,716m)**
	at radius of	**575 miles (925km)** from base

X-35 JSF

UTILITY PLAYER

In the late 1980s the Advanced Research Projects Agency and other organizations studied various possible future tactical aircraft. These included SSF, A/F-X, ATA, JSSA, JAF and CALF. In 1993 these were all replaced by an all-embracing programme called JAST (Joint Advanced Strike Technology). In turn, this was renamed JSF (Joint Strike Fighter) in October 1995, reflecting equal emphasis on air-to-air and surface attack. The resulting aircraft is intended to replace the F-16, AV-8B and F/A-18, though development of all these is being continued (to some degree as insurance against delay with JSF).

The programme was, in early 1998, still far from firm, but the latest (January 1997) plan was for the USAF to procure 2,216 to replace the F-16, for the Navy to buy 300 to replace the A-6 and F-14, for the Marine Corps to take 642 to replace the F/A-18 and AV-8B and for the Royal Navy to receive 60 to replace the Sea

Harrier. At this time the RAF still had the notion that it could somehow go it alone with an FOA (Future Offensive Aircraft) to replace the Tornado, Jaguar and Harrier, but common sense suggests that these aircraft also will be replaced by one or more versions of the JSF.

Three teams competed, and in November 1966 the McDonnell Douglas-Northrop Grumman-British Aerospace team was eliminated. This left Boeing and Lockheed Martin, and while McDonnell Douglas was purchased by Boeing, the other two losing partners (NG and BAe) teamed with Lockheed Martin. The latter's final proposal to the Department of Defense was submitted on 13 June 1996, a $718.8 million contract being awarded five months later to cover the design, development and initial flight test of two X-35 prototype aircraft. These are now

In May 1995, the Skunk Works revealed the X-35 (complete with lift fan behind the cockpit), Lockheed Martin's proposed JAST fighter.

being built at the Palmdale Skunk Works.

One is to be the prototype X-35 Configuration 220A, for a CTOL (conventional takeoff and landing) version for operation from land airfields. This will replace the F-16 in the USAF. It will be powered by a Pratt & Whitney SE611 augmented turbofan in the 40,000lb class, derived from the F119, fitted with an axisymmetric vectoring nozzle. This prototype is expected to fly in 1999. After flight test and development it is expected to be returned to Palmdale to be torn apart and reconfigured as the 220C, the Navy version. This will be fitted with broader (increased-chord) wings, tailplanes and vertical tails, the wing having enhanced high-lift devices, folding outer panels and enlarged control surfaces. Other modifications will include a modified flight-control system, strengthened landing gears with a catapult tow-bar on the nose unit, an arrester hook and a retractable probe on the right (starboard) side instead of the original inflight-refuelling receptacle on the dorsal centreline.

The second X-35 will be to Configuration 220B, for a STOVL (short takeoff, vertical landing) version for the Marine Corps and Royal Navy. This will have the same aerodynamic surfaces as the 220A (though for the Royal Navy the wing will fold), but the forward fuselage tanks will be replaced by an Allison lift fan behind the cockpit (which will have a shorter canopy) driven by a shaft from the main engine, which itself will have a three-bearing swivelling nozzle so that, together with the fan, the aircraft can make short takeoffs (STO) and vertical landings (VL).

All versions have an aerodynamic configuration very similar to that of the F-22, though smaller and with unswept tailplanes. A detail is that the engine will be fed by trapezoidal inlets which have fixed (non-variable) geometry and in plan view are swept forward. Another detail is that, though they likewise retract forwards and inwards, the main legs are longer and are hinged at the top of the fuselage side under the wing.

Like the F-22, the X-35 will have a 20mm gun inside the fuselage immediately inboard of the port wing, above the left inlet duct. Most weapons will be carried in internal bays with zig-zag-edged doors for stealth reasons. The preferred USAF load comprises two AIM-120 AMRAAM missiles and two 1,000lb GBU-30 or -32 Joint Direct Attack Munitions. The Navy baseline load comprises two 2,000lb JDAMs. A very wide range of other weapons will be provided for, as well as special external pods for reconnaissance, night/all-weather attack, electronic warfare and other missions. The aircraft will be designed so that the alternative engine, the GE YF120, will be a "bolt-on" replacement. This engine is potentially even more powerful than the SE611. Should Lockheed Martin prove to be the final winner in the JSF competition the production aircraft would be built at Fort Worth. Of course, the world-wide export prospects for the winning (or even losing) JSF aircraft are huge.

Many countries, including Australia, Sweden and most of Western Europe and southeast Asia, have informally expressed interest. Tentative flyaway unit costs have been estimated at $28 million for the 220A, $30.4 million for 220B and $32.5 million for 220C. These figures, incredibly modest by current standards, reflect the benefits of a long production run of broadly similar aircraft.

DATA FOR X-35 JSF:		
Span		**33ft 0in (10.06m)**
Length		**50ft 9in (15.469m)**
Wing area	220A and B	**450 sq ft (41.8m²)**
	220C	**540 sq ft (50.17m²)**
Weight for STO about		**41,000lb (18,600kg)**
Weight for VL about		**36,000lb (16,330kg)**
Maximum speed (supercruise)		
	in the region of	**Mach 1.4**
		(about 950mph, 1,530km/h
	at	**30,000ft, 12,192m)**
Radius with 2,000lb (907kg)		
	internal weapons about	**690 miles (1,110km)**

WHAT NEXT?

CURRENT PROJECTS

In 1998 Lockheed Martin ranks as the No 2 defence contractor in the USA (and thus in the world), with annual turnover (revenues) in the bracket $37-38 billion, about $10 billion behind Boeing. Its huge resources are constantly being called upon to plan far ahead to make sure it does not slip from this position. Almost all its major projects are military or for the US government, and the following is a selection.

X-33 VentureStar

In July 1996 the Skunk Works was selected to build this sub-scale technology demonstrator for NASA's future RLV (Reusable Launch Vehicle), which is intended to replace the Space Shuttle launch system. Due to fly in March 1999, the X-33 will be an SSTO (single stage to orbit) system, taking off vertically and landing conventionally on a runway. Features will include a delta-shaped lifting-body configuration, and within the atmosphere it will use hypersonic air-breathing propulsion. Rocketdyne and Rohr are partners. The X-33 will have a span of about 68ft (about 21m), length of 67ft (20m) and launch weight of 273,275lb (123,958kg). The eventual RLV is expected to have span and length both close to 127ft (39m) and liftoff weight of 2,186,000lb (991,570kg).

NSA

The New Strategic Airlifter is intended to capture the huge future worldwide market, not only among air forces, for a multirole airlift transport. Powered by two turbofans in the 100,000lb (45,360kg) class, it is being studied with various configurations, including an unconventional diamond shape with sweptback front wings joined at the tips to sweptforward rear wings. The cargo hold would have a less-constricted cross-section than the C-130/C-141, but would be rather smaller than the C-5. Missions would include air refuelling, and the launch market is expected to be provided by the need to replace the USAF KC-135 from 2007. Strategic surveillance is one of several alternative missions. Lockheed Martin has for some time been talking to foreign potential partners.

CSA

The Common Support Aircraft is being intensively studied as a replacement in the Navy for the C-2A Greyhound carrier on-board delivery transport, the E-2C Hawkeye airborne early-warning platform and all versions of the S-3 Viking anti-submarine and ES-3 electronic platform. As all these aircraft were made and are supported by what are now Lockheed Martin companies, there is a fair chance their replacement might be also.

UNSA

The Unmanned Naval Strike Aircraft is an ambitious project for a VLO (stealth) aircraft which, without a human pilot, could fly challenging strike missions against surface ships and land targets. In the first half of 1998 Lockheed Martin was working on a Naval Air Systems Command study which would define a STOVL (short takeoff, vertical landing) version and a VATOL (vertical-attitude takeoff and landing) form, one version of which would unfold in flight after being fired from a submarine's Trident missile-launch tube.

SST

Though not enjoying a high priority, and not a member of NASA's HSR (high-speed research) team, Lockheed Martin continues to study supersonic commercial transports. Any return to the field of commercial jets would be in partnership with at least one company, and discussions on subsonic aircraft have been held with Airbus.

It must be added of course, that these are the projects about which we have some inkling, the projects that Lockheed Martin may wish to "advertise", however obliquely. The skunk only leaves a strong scent when it wishes to do so.

HIGH FLYERS:
SOME OF THE PILOTS
AND ENGINEERS WHO HELPED
BUILD LOCKHEED

Below **Pilot Sammy Mason with the F-94.** One of the many thousands of designers, engineers, flyers and planners who have played a part in the Lockheed story.

"KELLY" JOHNSON

Clarence L. Johnson (right) was nicknamed "Kelly" because as a boy he was something of a fighter. He graduated from the University of Michigan as an aeronautical engineer. His first post was as a consultant to the Studebaker car company, but after being invited to join Lockheed his rise was meteoric. By 1938 he was Chief Research Engineer, and he was given the coveted job of Chief Engineer in 1952. Not the least of his enormous achievements was his creation and management of the ADP (Advanced Development Projects) "Skunk Works". He died aged 80 in 1990.

EDDIE BELLANDE

Edward A. Bellande (below) was a test pilot for Curtiss at the age of 18, in 1915.

During World War 1 Eddie was a flight instructor for the Navy, and for nine years afterwards he was a barnstormer, crop duster, skywriter and freelance test pilot. In 1927-29 he worked for Lockheed, having been hired to make the first flight of the Vega. Subsequently he was awarded the Air Mail Medal of Honor flying for Maddox Airlines (later TWA) and he also became a director of Northrop before eventually exchanging the cockpit for the luxurious boardroom of the Garrett Corporation on LA's Sepulveda Boulevard.

MARSHALL HEADLE

Marshall Headle (below) was another of the great breed of freelance test pilots

available for hire in the inter-war years. Both the original and the reborn Lockheed companies made use of his services, and among much other work he performed the initial test flying of the Sirius, Altair and Orion. His fame as a Lockheed pilot was ensured by his masterly one-wheel landing of the prototype Model 10 Electra. Had it been written off, it would probably have spelled the end of the company. He carried out initial testing of the Models 14 and 18, and on 17 September 1940 made the first flight of the YP-38.

JOE TOWLE

Joe C. Towle (left) was one of the team of pilots who tested Lockheed aircraft at Bur-

bank in World War 2. His first major assignment was the YP-49, the derivative of the P-38 powered by the immature Continental XIV-1430 engines, first flown on 14 November 1942. This prepared him well for the even more demanding XP-58, which he was at last able to fly – four years after its design – on D-Day, 6 June 1944. The next big assignment was relaxing by comparison: on 17 May 1945 Joe headed the test crew on the Navy XP2V-1 Neptune. Staying with Navy aircraft, he then headed the test crew on the huge Constitution, from 9 November 1946.

HERMAN SALMON

Herman "Fish" Salmon (previous page, bottom right) was qualified on, according to an unbiased observer, "everything from helicopters to jets". He was the obvious choice to try to tame the strange and obviously dangerous vagaries of the XFV-1 "Pogo Stick." As the man with his neck on the line he played a central role in the management of its flight test programme, choosing to begin with conventional aeroplane flight. He made a very brief liftoff on 23 December 1953, followed by the start of proper flying on 16 June 1954. Salmon managed transitions to brief hovers, but never did achieve VTOL. In contrast, his next major assignment, the

Electra turboprop, could hardly have been safer or more comfortable.

TONY LeVIER

Anthony W. LeVier (below) could well take the laurels as the greatest Lockheed pilot of all. Tony LeVier was born in 1913 and from the early 1930s was a noted barnstormer and racing pilot. He flew with Mid-Continent Airlines in 1940, was test pilot for General Motors Research Labora-

tories, and in 1945 succeeded Burcham as Lockheed's Chief Enginering Test Pilot. His record of first flights is impressive (note that the following ignores sub-variants): XP-80A, 20 March 1945; Saturn, 17 June 1946; TP-80C (T-33), 22 March 1948; YF-94, 16 April 1949; XF-90, 3 June 1949; XF-104, 28 February 1954 (a probably fairly nervous hop), 4 March 1954 (flight); U-2, 1 August 1955; TriStar automatic test, 25 May 1972.

MILO BURCHAM

Milo Burcham (overleaf, top) was Lockheed's Chief Engineering Test Pilot during much of World War 2. As such he was the senior Lockheed pilot on the first flight of the the C-69 Constellation on 9 January 1943, though captain of the aircraft was Eddie Allen, borrowed from Boeing because of his experience with big R-3350-powered aircraft. Just a year later, on 8 January 1944, Burcham opened the flight test programme of the XP-80 Shooting Star. To say he put on a breathtaking show for the crowd at Muroc is an understatement, though many pilots would say it was foolhardy to take so many chances with a vital prototype. But Milo had been a barnstormer and circus display pilot, and he just got carried away by the performance capabilities of the brilliant new jet. Sadly, he was

killed on the first flight of the third of the the 13 service-test YP-80As in 1945. (Milo loved horses, and would often ride to work.) He was succeeded by LeVier.

BEN RICH

Ben R. Rich (below left) had since the 1950s been groomed by Kelly Johnson to succeed him as President of the Advanced Development Projects "Skunk Works". In 1984 this began to be restructured, moving to what had become the Kelly Johnson R&D Center at Rye Canyon, where it became a unit in the new Lockheed Advanced Aeronautics Co. This continued work on both "black" and "white" (unclassified) programmes, including not only the stealth programmes but also the Advanced Tactical Fighter. The latter was later moved to Lockheed Aeronautical Systems Co, while the Skunk works was shaken up yet again as the LADC (Lockheed Advanced Development Co). In July 1990, just before his retirement, Rich pointed out publicly how everything the Skunk Works had stood for – quick, quiet, low cost work – was being eroded by massive bureacracy. He urged: "Don't stifle this national asset."

INDEX